Improvement of the Mind

Isaac Watts, Jacob S. Denman

PART II.

THE

IMPROVEMENT OF THE MIND.

PART I.

DIRECTIONS FOR THE ATTAINMENT OF USEFUL KNOWLEDGE.

INTRODUCTION.

No man is obliged to learn and know every thing; this can neither be sought nor required, for it is utterly impossible; yet all persons are under some obligation to improve their own understanding; otherwise it will be a barren desert, or a forest overgrown with weeds and brambles. Universal ignorance or infinite errors will overspread the mind which is utterly neglected, and lies without any cultivation.

Skill in the sciences is indeed the business and profession but of a small part of mankind; but there are many others placed in such an exalted rank in the world, as allows them much leisure and large opportunities to cultivate their reason, and to beautify and enrich their minds with various knowledge. Even the lower orders of men have particular callings in life, wherein they ought to acquire a just degree of skill; and this is not to be done well, without thinking and reasoning about them.

The common duties and benefits of society, which belong to every man living, as we are social creatures, and even our native and necessary relations to a family, a neighbourhood or government, oblige all persons whatsoever to use their reasoning powers upon a thousand occasions; every hour of life calls for some regular exercise of our judgment, as to time and things, persons and actions: without a prudent and discreet determination in matters before us, we shall be plunged into perpetual errors in our conduct. Now that which should always be practised must at some time be learned.

Besides, every son and daughter of Adam has a most important concern in the affairs of the life to come, and therefore it is a matter of the highest moment, for every one to understand, to judge, and to reason right about the things of religion. It is vain for any to say, we have no leisure time for it. The daily intervals of time, and vacancies from necessary labour, together with the one day in seven in the Christian world, allows sufficient time for this, if men would but apply themselves to it with half so much zeal and diligence as they do to the trifles and amusements of this life, and it would turn to infinitely better account.

Thus it appears to be the necessary duty and the interest of every person living, to improve his understanding, to inform his judgment, to treasure up useful knowledge, and to acquire the skill of good reasoning, as far as his station, capacity, and circumstances furnish him with proper means for it. Our mistakes in judgment may plunge us into much folly and guilt in practice. By acting without thought or reason, we dishonour the God that made us reasonable creatures, we often become injurious to our neighbours, kindred, or friends, and we bring sin and misery upon ourselves; for we are accountable to God, our judge, for every part of our irregular and mistaken conduct, where he hath given us sufficient advantages to guard against those mistakes.

CHAPTER I.

GENERAL RULES FOR THE IMPROVEMENT OF KNOWLEDGE.*

RULE I.—DEEPLY possess your mind with the vast importance of a good judgment, and the rich and inestimable advantage of right reasoning. Review the instances of your own misconduct in life; think seriously with yourselves how many follies and sorrows you had escaped, and how much guilt and misery you had prevented, if from your early years you had but taken due pains to judge aright concerning persons, times, and things. This will awaken you with lively vigour to address yourselves to the work of improving your reasoning powers, and seizing every opportunity and advantage for that end.

II. Consider the weaknesses, frailties, and mistakes of human nature in general, which arise from the very constitution of a soul united to an animal body, and subjected to many inconveniences thereby. Consider the many additional weaknesses, mistakes, and frailties, which are derived from our original apostasy and fall from a state of innocence: how much our powers of understanding are yet more darkened, enfeebled, and imposed upon by our senses, our fancies, our unruly passions, &c. Consider the depth and difficulty of many truths, and the flattering appearances of falsehood, whence arises an infinite variety of dangers to which we are exposed in our judgment of things. Read with greediness those authors that treat of the doctrine of prejudices, prepossessions, and springs of error, on purpose to make your soul watchful on all sides, that it suffer itself, as far as possible, to be imposed upon, by none of them.

III. A slight view of things so momentous is not sufficient. You should therefore contrive and practise some

* Though the most of these following Rules are chiefly addressed to those whom their fortune or their station require to addict themselves to the peculiar improvement of their minds in greater degrees of knowledge, yet every one who has leisure and opportunity to be acquainted with such writings as these, may find something among them for their own use.

proper methods to acquaint yourself with your own ignorance, and to impress your mind with a deep and painful sense of the low and imperfect degrees of your present knowledge, that you may be incited with labour and activity to pursue after greater measures. Among others, you may find some such methods as these successful.

1. Take a wide survey now and then of the vast and unlimited regions of learning. Let your meditations run over the names of all the sciences, with their numerous branchings, and innumerable particular themes of knowledge; and then reflect how few of them you are acquainted with in any tolerable degree. The most learned of mortals will never find occasion to act over again what is fabled of Alexander the Great, that when he had conquered what was called the eastern world, he wept for want of more worlds to conquer. The worlds of science are immense and endless.

2. Think what a numberless variety of questions and difficulties there are belonging even to that particular science in which you have made the greatest progress, and how few of them there are in which you have arrived at a final and undoubted certainty; excepting only those questions in the pure and simple mathematics, whose theorems are demonstrable, and leave scarce any doubt; and yet, even in the pursuit of some few of these, mankind have been strangely bewildered.

3. Spend a few thoughts sometimes on the puzzling inquiries concerning vacuums and atoms, the doctrine of infinites, indivisibles, and incommensurables in geometry, wherein there appear some insolvable difficulties: do this on purpose to give you a more sensible impression of the poverty of your understanding, and the imperfection of your knowledge. This will teach you what a vain thing it is to fancy that you know all things, and will instruct you to think modestly of your present attainments, when every dust of the earth, and every inch of empty space, surmounts your understanding, and triumphs over your presumption. Arithmo had been bred up to accounts all his life, and thought himself a complete master of numbers. But when he was pushed hard to give the square root of the number 2, he tried

at it, and laboured long in millesimal fractions, till he confessed there was no end of the inquiry; and yet he learned so much modesty by this perplexing question, that he was afraid to say it was an impossible thing. It is some good degree of improvement, when we are afraid to be positive.

4. Read the accounts of those vast treasures of knowledge which some of the dead have possessed, and some of the living do possess. Read and be astonished at the almost incredible advances which have been made in science. Acquaint yourself with some persons of great learning, that by converse among them, and comparing yourself with them, you may acquire a mean opinion of your own attainments, and may thereby be animated with new zeal, to equal them as far as possible, or to exceed: thus let your diligence be quickened by a generous and laudable emulation. If Vanillus had never met with Scitorio and Palydes, he had never imagined himself a mere novice in philosophy, nor ever set himself to study in good earnest.

Remember this, that if upon some few superficial acquirements you value, exalt, and swell yourself, as though you were a man of learning already, you are thereby building a most unpassable barrier against all improvement; you will lie down and indulge idleness, and rest yourself contented in the midst of deep and shameful ignorance. Multi ad scientiam pervenissent si se illuc pervenisse non putassent.

IV. Presume not too much upon a bright genius, a ready wit, and good parts; for this, without labour and study, will never make a man of knowledge and wisdom. This has been an unhappy temptation to persons of a vigorous and gay fancy, to despise learning and study. They have been acknowledged to shine in an assembly, and sparkle in a discourse on common topics, and thence they took it into their heads to abandon reading and labour, and grow old in ignorance; but when they had lost their vivacity of animal nature and youth, they became stupid and sottish even to contempt and ridicule. Lucidus and Scintillo are young men of this stamp; they shine in conversation; they spread their native riches before the ignorant; they pride themselves in their own lively images of fancy, and imagine themselves wise and learned; but they had best avoid the presence of the skilful, and the test of reasoning; and I would advise them once a day to think forward a little, what a contemptible figure they will make in age.

The witty men sometimes have sense enough to know their own foible; and therefore they craftily shun the attacks of argument, or boldly pretend to despise and renounce them, because they are conscious of their own ignorance, and inwardly confess their want of acquaintance with the skill of reasoning.

V. As you are not to fancy yourself a learned man because you are blessed with a ready wit; so neither must you imagine that large and laborious reading, and a strong memory, can denominate you truly wise.

What that excellent critic has determined when he decided the question, whether wit or study makes the best poet, may well be applied to every sort of learning:

> . . . . . . Ego nec studium sine divite vena,
> Nec rude quid prosit, video, ingenium: alterius sic
> Altera poscit opem res, et conjurat amice.
>
> *Hor. de Art. Poet.*

Thus made English:

> Concerning poets there has been contest,
> Whether they're made by art or nature best;
> But if I may presume in this affair,
> Among the rest my judgment to declare,
> No art without a genius will avail,
> And parts without the help of art will fail:
> But both ingredients jointly must unite,
> Or verse will never shine with a transcendent light.
>
> *Oldham.*

It is meditation and studious thought, it is the exercise of your own reason and judgment upon all you read, that gives good sense even to the best genius, and affords your understanding the truest improvement. A boy of a strong memory may repeat a whole book of Euclid, yet be no geometrician; for he may not be able perhaps to demonstrate one single theorem. Memorino has learned half the Bible by heart, and is become a living concordance, and a speaking index to theological folios, and yet he understands little of divinity.

A well furnished library, and a capacious memory, are indeed of singular use toward the improvement of the mind; but if all your learning be nothing else but a mere amassement of what others have written, without a due penetration into the meaning, and without a judicious choice and determination of your own sentiments, I do not see what title your head has to true learning above your shelves. Though you have read philosophy and theology, morals and metaphysics in abundance, and every other art and science, yet if your memory is the only faculty employed, with the neglect of your reasoning powers, you can justly claim no higher character but that of a good historian of the sciences.

Here note, many of the foregoing advices are more peculiarly proper for those who are conceited of their abilities, and are ready to entertain a high opinion of themselves. But a modest, humble youth, of a good genius, should not suffer himself to be discouraged by any of these considerations. They are designed only as a spur to diligence, and a guard against vanity and pride.

VI. Be not so weak as to imagine, that a life of learning is a life of laziness and ease; dare not give up yourself to any of the learned professions, unless you are resolved to labour hard at study, and can make it your delight, and the joy of your life, according to the motto of our late Lord Chancellor King:

. . . . *Labor ipse voluptas.*

It is no idle thing to be a scholar indeed. A man much addicted to luxury and pleasure, recreation and pastime, should never pretend to devote himself entirely to the sciences, unless his soul be so reformed and refined, that he can taste all these entertainments eminently in his closet, among his books and papers. Sobrino is a temperate man, and a philosopher, and he feeds upon partridge and pheasant, venison and ragouts, and every delicacy, in a growing understanding, and a serene and healthy soul, though he dines on a dish of sprouts or turnips. Languinos loved his ease, and therefore chose to be brought up a scholar; he had much indolence in his temper; and as he never cared for study, he falls under universal contempt in his profession, because he has nothing but the gown and the name.

VII. Let the hope of new discoveries, as well as the satisfaction and pleasure of known truths, animate your daily industry. Do not think learning in general is arrived at its perfection, or that the knowledge of any particular subject in any science cannot be improved, merely because it has lain five hundred or a thousand years without improvement. The present age, by the blessing of God on the ingenuity and diligence of men, has brought to light such truths in natural philosophy, and such discoveries in the heavens and the earth, as seemed to be beyond the reach of man. But may there not be Sir Isaac Newtons in every science? You should never despair therefore of finding out that which has never yet been found, unless you see something in the nature of it which renders it unsearchable, and above the reach of our faculties.

Nor should a student in divinity imagine that our age is arrived at a full understanding of every thing which can be known by the Scriptures. Every age since the Reformation hath thrown some further light on difficult texts and paragraphs of the Bible, which have been long obscured by the early rise of antichrist: and since there are at present many difficulties and darknesses hanging about certain truths of the Christian religion, and since several of these relate to important doctrines, such as the origin of sin, the fall of Adam, the person of Christ, the blessed Trinity, and decrees of God, &c. which do still embarrass the minds of honest and inquiring readers, and which make work for noisy controversy; it is certain there are several things in the Bible yet unknown, and not sufficiently explained; and it is certain that there is some way to solve these difficulties, and to reconcile these seeming contradictions. And why may not a sincere searcher of truth in the present age, by labour, diligence, study, and prayer, with the best use of his reasoning powers, find out the proper solution of those knots and perplexities which have hitherto been unsolved, and which have afforded matter for angry quarrelling? Happy is every man who shall be favoured of Heaven, to give a helping hand towards the introduction of the blessed age of light and love.

VIII. Do not hover always on the surface of things, nor take up suddenly with mere appearances; but penetrate into the depth of matters, as far as your time and circumstances allow, especially in those things which relate to your own profession. Do not indulge yourselves to judge of things by the first glimpse, or a short and superficial view of them; for this will fill the mind with errors and prejudices, and give it a wrong turn and ill habit of thinking, and make much work for retraction. Subito is carried away with title pages, so that he ventures to pronounce upon a large octavo at once, and to recommend it wonderfully when he has read half the preface. Another volume of controversies, of equal size, was discarded by him at once, because it pretended to treat of the Trinity, and yet he could neither find the word essence nor subsistencies in the twelve first pages; but Subito changes his opinions of men and books and things so often, that nobody regards him.

As for those sciences, or those parts of knowledge, which either your profession, your leisure, your inclination, or your incapacity, forbid you to pursue with much application, or to search far into them, you must be contented with an historical and superficial knowledge of them, and not pretend to form any judgment of your own on those subjects which you understand very imperfectly.

IX. Once a day, especially in the early years of life and study, call yourselves to an account what new ideas, what new proposition or truth you have gained, what further confirmation of known truths, and what advances you have made in any part of knowledge; and let no day, if possible, pass away without some intellectual gain: such a course, well pursued, must certainly advance us in useful knowledge. It is a wise proverb among the learned, borrowed from the lips and practice of a celebrated painter, Nulla dies sine linea, "Let no day pass without one line at least;" and it was a sacred rule among the Pythagoreans, That they should every evening thrice run over the actions and affairs of the day, and examine what their conduct had been, what they had done, or what they had neglected: and they assured their pupils, that by this method they would make a noble progress in the path of virtue.

> Μηδ᾽ υπνον μαλακοισιν επ᾽ ομμασι προσδεξασθαι
> Πριν των ημερινων εργων τρις εκαστον επελθειν.
> Πη παρεβην; τι δ᾽ ερεξα; τι μοι δεον ουκ᾽ ετελεσθη;
> Ταυτα σε της θειης αρετης εις ιχνια θησει.

> Nor let soft slumber close your eyes,
> Before you've recollected thrice
> The train of action through the day:
> Where have my feet chose out their way?
> What have I learn'd, where'er I've been,
> From all I've heard, from all I've seen?
> What know I more that's worth the knowing?
> What have I done that's worth the doing?
> What have I sought that I should shun?
> What duty have I left undone?
> Or into what new follies run?
> These self-inquiries are the road
> That leads to virtue, and to God.

I would be glad, among a nation of Christians, to find young men heartily engaged in the practice of what this heathen writer teaches.

X. Maintain a constant watch at all times against a dogmatical spirit: fix not your assent to any proposition in a firm and unalterable manner, till you have some firm and unalterable ground for it, and till you have arrived at some clear and sure evidence; till you have turned the proposition on all sides, and searched the matter through and through, so that you cannot be mistaken. And even where you may think you have full grounds of assurance, be not too early, nor too frequent, in expressing this assurance in too peremptory and positive a manner, remembering that human nature is always liable to mistake in this corrupt and feeble state. A dogmatical spirit has many inconveniences attending it: as

1. It stops the ear against all further reasoning upon that subject, and shuts up the mind from all further improvements of knowledge. If you have resolutely fixed your opinion, though it be upon too slight and insufficient grounds, yet you will stand determined to renounce the strongest reason brought for the contrary opinion,

and grow obstinate against the force of the clearest argument. Positivo is a man of this character; and has often pronounced his assurance of the Cartesian vortexes: last year some further light broke in upon his understanding, with uncontrollable force, by reading something of mathematical philosophy; yet having asserted his former opinions in a most confident manner, he is tempted now to wink a little against the truth, or to prevaricate in his discourse upon that subject, lest by admitting conviction, he should expose himself to the necessity of confessing his former folly and mistake: and he has not humility enough for that.

2. A dogmatical spirit naturally leads us to arrogance of mind, and gives a man some airs in conversation which are too haughty and assuming. Audens is a man of learning, and very good company; but his infallible assurance renders his carriage sometimes insupportable.

A dogmatical spirit inclines a man to be censorious of his neighbours. Every one of his own opinions appears to him written as it were with sunbeams; and he grows angry that his neighbour does not see it in the same light. He is tempted to disdain his correspondents, as men of a low and dark understanding, because they will not believe what he does. Furio goes further in this wild track; and charges those who refuse his notions with wilful obstinacy and vile hypocrisy; he tells them boldly, that they resist the truth, and sin against their consciences.

These are the men that, when they deal in controversy, delight in reproaches. They abound in tossing about absurdity and stupidity among their brethren; they cast the imputation of heresy and nonsense plentifully upon their antagonists: and in matters of sacred importance, they deal out their anathemas in abundance upon Christians better than themselves; they denounce damnation upon their neighbours, without either justice or mercy; and when they pronounce sentences of divine wrath against supposed heretics, they add their own human fire and indignation. A dogmatist in religion is not a great way off from a bigot, and is in high danger of growing up to be a bloody persecutor.

XI. Though caution and slow assent will guard you against frequent mistakes and retractions; yet you should get humility and courage enough to retract any mistake, and confess an error: frequent changes are tokens of levity in our first determinations; yet you should never be too proud to change your opinion, nor frightened at the name of changeling. Learn to scorn those vulgar bugbears, which confirm foolish man in his old mistakes, for fear of being charged with inconstancy. I confess it is better not to judge, than to judge falsely; it is wiser to withhold our assent till we see complete evidence; but if we have too suddenly given up our assent, as the wisest man does sometimes, if we have professed what we find afterwards to be false, we should never be ashamed nor afraid to renounce a mistake. That is a noble essay which is found among the occasional papers "to encourage the world to practise retractations;" and I would recommend it to the perusal of every scholar and every Christian.

XII. He that would raise his judgment above the vulgar rank of mankind, and learn to pass a just sentence on persons and things, must take heed of a fanciful temper of mind, and a humorous conduct in his affairs. Fancy and humour, early and constantly indulged, may expect an old age overrun with follies.

The notion of a humourist is one that is greatly pleased, or greatly displeased with little things; who sets his heart much upon matters of very small importance; who has his will determined every day by trifles, his actions seldom directed by the reason and nature of things, and his passions frequently raised by things of little moment. Where this practice is allowed, it will insensibly warp the judgment to pronounce little things great, and tempt you to lay a great weight upon them. In short, this temper will incline you to pass an unjust value on almost every thing that occurs; and every step you take in this path is just so far out of the way to wisdom.

XIII. For the same reason have a care of trifling with things important and momentous, or of sporting with things awful and sacred: do not indulge a spirit of ridicule, as some witty men do on all occasions and subjects.

This will as unhappily bias the judgment on the other side, and incline you to pass a low esteem on the most valuable objects. Whatsoever evil habit we indulge in practice, it will insensibly obtain a power over our understanding, and betray us into many errors. Jocander is ready with his jests to answer every thing that he hears; he reads books in the same jovial humour, and has gotten the art of turning every thought and sentence into merriment. How many awkward and irregular judgments does this man pass upon solemn subjects even when he designs to be grave and in earnest! His mirth and laughing humour is formed into habit and temper, and leads his understanding shamefully astray. You will see him wandering in pursuit of a gay flying feather, and he is drawn by a sort of ignis fatuus into bogs and mire almost every day of his life.

XIV. Ever maintain a virtuous and pious frame of spirit; for an indulgence of vicious inclinations debases the understanding and perverts the judgment. Whoredom and wine, and new wine, take away the heart and soul, and reason of a man. Sensuality ruins the better faculties of the mind; an indulgence to appetite and passion enfeebles the powers of reason; it makes the judgment weak and susceptible of every falsehood, and especially of such mistakes as have a tendency towards the gratification of the animal: and it warps the soul aside strangely from that steadfast honesty and integrity that necessarily belongs to the pursuit of truth. It is the virtuous man who is in a fair way to wisdom. "God gives to those that are good in his sight wisdom, and knowledge, and joy," Eccles. ii. 26.

Piety towards God, as well as sobriety and virtue, are necessary qualifications to make a truly wise and judicious man. He that abandons religion must act in such a contradiction to his own conscience and best judgment that he abuses and spoils the faculty itself. It is thus in the nature of things, and it is thus by the righteous judgment of God: even the pretended sages among the heathens, who did not like to retain God in their knowledge they were given up to a reprobate mind, εις νουν αδοκιμον an undistinguishing or injudicious mi[illegible] [illegible]at they judged inconsistently, and practised mere absurdities, τα μη καθηκοντα, Rom. i. 28.

And it is the character of the slaves of antichrist, 2 Thess. ii. 10, &c. that those "who receive not the love of the truth were exposed to the power of diabolical sleights and lying wonders." When divine revelation shines and blazes in the face of men with glorious evidence, and they wink their eyes against it, the god of this world is suffered to blind them, even in the most obvious, common, and sensible things. The great God of Heaven, for this cause, sends them strong delusions, that they should believe a lie; and the nonsense of transubstantiation, in the popish world, is a most glaring accomplishment of this prophecy, beyond even what could have been thought of or expected among creatures who pretend to reason.

XV. Watch against the pride of your own reason, and a vain conceit of your own intellectual powers, with the neglect of divine aid and blessing. Presume not upon great attainments in knowledge by your own self-sufficiency: those who trust to their own understandings entirely are pronounced fools in the word of God; and it is the wisest of men gives them this character. "He that trusteth in his own heart is a fool," Prov. xxviii. 26. And the same divine writer advises us to "trust in the Lord with all our heart, and not to lean to our understandings, nor to be wise in our own eyes," chap. iii. 5. 7.

Those who, with a neglect of religion and dependence on God, apply themselves to search out every article in the things of God by the mere dint of their own reason, have been suffered to run into wild excesses of foolery, and strange extravagance of opinions. Every one who pursues this vain course, and will not ask for the conduct of God in the study of religion, has just reason to fear he shall be left of God, and given up a prey to a thousand prejudices; that he shall be consigned over to the follies of his own heart, and pursue his own temporal and eternal ruin. And even in common studies we should, by humility and dependence, engage the God of truth on our side.

XVI. Offer up, therefore, your daily requests to God

the father of lights, that he would bless all your attempts and labours in reading, study, and conversation. Think with yourself how easily and how insensibly, by one turn of thought, he can lead you into a large scene of useful ideas: he can teach you to lay hold on a clue which may guide your thoughts with safety and ease through all the difficulties of an intricate subject. Think how easily the Author of your beings can direct your motions, by his providence, so that the glance of an eye, or a word striking the ear, or a sudden turn of the fancy, shall conduct you to a train of happy sentiments. By his secret and supreme method of government, he can draw you to read such a treatise, or converse with such a person, who may give you more light into some deep subject in an hour, than you could obtain by a month of your own solitary labour.

Think with yourself with how much ease the God of spirits can cast into your minds some useful suggestion, and give a happy turn to your own thoughts, or the thoughts of those with whom you converse, whence you may derive unspeakable light and satisfaction, in a matter that has long puzzled and entangled you: he can show you a path which the vulture's eye has not seen, and lead you by some unknown gate or portal, out of a wilderness and labyrinth of difficulties, wherein you have been long wandering.

Implore constantly his divine grace to point your inclination to proper studies, and to fix your heart there. He can keep off temptations on the right hand, and on the left, both by the course of his providence, and by the secret and insensible intimations of his Spirit. He can guard your understandings from every evil influence of error, and secure you from the danger of evil books and men, which might otherwise have a fatal effect, and lead you into pernicious mistakes.

Nor let this sort of advice fall under the censure of the godless and profane, as a mere piece of bigotry or enthusiasm, derived from faith and the Bible: for the reasons which I have given to support this pious practice, of invoking the blessing of God on our studies, are derived from the light of nature as well as revelation.

He that made our souls, and is the Father of spirits, shall he not be supposed to have a most friendly influence toward the instruction and government of them? The Author of our rational powers can involve them in darkness when he pleases, by a sudden distemper; or he can abandon them to wander into dark and foolish opinions, when they are filled with a vain conceit of their own light. He expects to be acknowledged in the common affairs of life; and he does as certainly expect it in the superior operations of the mind, and in the search of knowledge and truth. The very Greek heathens, by the light of reason, were taught to say, Ἐκ Διὸς ἀρχώμεσθα, and the Latins, A Jove Principium Musæ. In works of learning they thought it necessary to begin with God. Even the poets call upon the muse as a goddess to assist them in their compositions.

The first lines of Homer in his Iliad and his Odyssey, the first line of Museus in his song of Hero and Leander, the beginning of Hesiod in his poem of Works and Days, and several others, furnish us with sufficient examples of this kind; nor does Ovid leave out this piece of devotion, as he begins his stories of the Metamorphoses. Christianity so much the more obliges us, by the precepts of Scripture, to invoke the assistance of the true God in all our labours of the mind, for the improvement of ourselves and others. Bishop Saunderson says, that study without prayer is atheism, as well as that prayer without study is presumption. And we are still more abundantly encouraged by the testimony of those who have acknowledged, from their own experience, that sincere prayer was no hinderance to their studies: they have gotten more knowledge sometimes upon their knees, than by their labour in perusing a variety of authors; and they have left this observation for such as follow, Bene orasse est bene studuisse, "praying is the best studying."

To conclude, let industry and devotion join together, and you need not doubt the happy success. Prov. ii. 2: "Incline thine ear to wisdom; apply thine heart to understanding: cry after knowledge, and lift up thy voice: seek her as silver, and search for her as for hidden treasures; then shalt thou understand the fear of the Lord," &c. which "is the beginning of wisdom." It is "the Lord who gives wisdom even to the simple, and out of his mouth cometh knowledge and understanding."

CHAPTER II.

OBSERVATION, READING, INSTRUCTION BY LECTURES, CONVERSATION, AND STUDY, COMPARED.

THERE are five eminent means or methods whereby the mind is improved in the knowledge of things; and these are observation, reading, instruction by lectures, conversation, and meditation; which last, in a most peculiar manner, is called study.

Let us survey the general definitions or descriptions of them all.

I. Observation is the notice that we take of all occurrences in human life, whether they are sensible or intellectual, whether relating to persons or things, to ourselves or others. It is this that furnishes us, even from our infancy, with a rich variety of ideas and propositions, words and phrases: it is by this we know that fire will burn, that the sun gives light, that a horse eats grass, that an acorn produces an oak, that man is a being capable of reasoning and discourse, that our judgment is weak, that our mistakes are many, that our sorrows are great, that our bodies die and are carried to the grave, and that one generation succeeds another. All those things which we see, which we hear or feel, which we perceive by sense or consciousness, or which we know in a direct manner, with scarce any exercise of our reflecting faculties, or our reasoning powers, may be included under the general name of observation.

When this observation relates to any thing that immediately concerns ourselves, and of which we are conscious, it may be called experience. So I am said to know or experience that I have in myself a power of thinking, fearing, loving, &c. that I have appetites and passions working in me, and many personal occurrences have attended me in this life.

Observation therefore includes all that Mr. Locke means by sensation and reflection.

When we are searching out the nature or properties of any being by various methods of trial, or when we apply some active powers, or set some causes to work to observe what effects they would produce, this sort of observation is called experiment. So when I throw a bullet into water, I find it sinks; and when I throw the same bullet into quicksilver, I see it swims: but if I beat out this bullet into a thin hollow shape, like a dish, then it will swim in the water too. So when I strike two flints together, I find they produce fire; when I throw a seed in the earth, it grows up into a plant.

All these belong to the first method of knowledge; which I shall call observation.

II. Reading is that means or method of knowledge whereby we acquaint ourselves with what other men have written, or published to the world in their writings. These arts of reading and writing are of infinite advantage; for by them we are made partakers of the sentiments, observations, reasonings, and improvements of all the learned world, in the most remote nations, and in former ages almost from the beginning of mankind.

III. Public or private lectures are such verbal instructions as are given by a teacher while the learners attend in silence. This is the way of learning religion from the pulpit; or of philosophy or theology from the professor's chair; or of mathematics, by a teacher showing us various theorems or problems, *i. e.* speculations or practices, by demonstration and operation, with all the instruments of art necessary to those operations.

IV. Conversation is another method of improving our minds, wherein, by mutual discourse and inquiry, we learn the sentiments of others, as well as communicate our sentiments to others in the same manner. Sometimes, indeed, though both parties speak by turns, yet the advantage is only on one side, as when a teacher and a learner meet and discourse together: but frequently the profit is mutual. Under this head of conversation we may also rank disputes of various kinds.

V. Meditation or study includes all those exercises of

the mind, whereby we render all the former methods useful for our increase in true knowledge and wisdom. It is by meditation we come to confirm our memory of things that pass through our thoughts in the occurrences of life, in our own experiences, and in the observations we make. It is by meditation that we draw various inferences, and establish in our minds general principles of knowledge. It is by meditation that we compare the various ideas which we derive from our senses, or from the operations of our souls, and join them in propositions. It is by meditation that we fix in our memory whatsoever we learn, and form our judgment of the truth or falsehood, the strength or weakness, of what others speak or write. It is meditation or study that draws out long chains of argument, and searches and finds deep and difficult truths which before lay concealed in darkness.

It would be a needless thing to prove, that our own solitary meditations, together with the few observations that the most part of mankind are capable of making, are not sufficient, of themselves, to lead us into the attainment of any considerable proportion of knowledge, at least in an age so much improved as ours is, without the assistance of conversation and reading, and other proper instructions that are to be attained in our days. Yet each of these five methods have their peculiar advantages, whereby they assist each other; and their peculiar defects, which have need to be supplied by the other's assistance. Let us trace over some of the particular advantages of each.

I. One method of improving the mind is observation; and the advantages of it are these.—

1. It is owing to observation, that our mind is furnished with the first simple and complex ideas. It is this lays the ground-work and foundation of all knowledge, and makes us capable of using any of the other methods for improving the mind: for if we did not attain a variety of sensible and intellectual ideas by the sensations of outward objects, by the consciousness of our own appetites and passions, pleasures and pains, and by inward experience of the actings of our own spirits,

it would be impossible either for men or books to teach us any thing. It is observation that must give us our first ideas of things, as it includes in it sense and consciousness.

2. All our knowledge derived from observation, whether it be of single ideas or of propositions, is knowledge gotten at first hand. Hereby we see and know things as they are, or as they appear to us; we take the impressions of them on our minds from the original objects themselves, which give a clearer and stronger conception of things: these ideas are more lively, and the propositions (at least in many cases) are much more evident. Whereas, what knowledge we derive from lectures, reading, and conversation, is but the copy of other men's ideas, that is, the picture of a picture; and it is one remove further from the original.

3. Another advantage of observation is, that we may gain knowledge all the day long, and every moment of our lives; and every moment of our existence we may be adding something to our intellectual treasures thereby, except only while we are asleep, and even then the remembrance of our dreaming will teach us some truths, and lay a foundation for a better acquaintance with human nature, both in the powers and in the frailties of it.

II. The next way of improving the mind is by reading, and the advantages of it are such as these:

1. By reading we acquaint ourselves, in a very extensive manner, with the affairs, actions, and thoughts, of the living and the dead, in the most remote nations, and most distant ages, and that with as much ease as though they lived in our own age and nation. By reading of books we may learn something from all parts of mankind; whereas, by observation we learn all from ourselves, and only what comes within our own direct cognizance; by conversation we can only enjoy the assistance of a very few persons, viz. those who are near us, and live at the same time when we do, that is, our neighbours and contemporaries; but our knowledge is much more narrowed still, if we confine ourselves merely to our own solitary reasonings, without much observation

eyes. A living teacher, therefore, is a most necessary help in these studies.

I might add also, that even where the subject of discourse is moral, logical, or rhetorical, &c. and which does not directly come under the notice of our senses, a tutor may explain his ideas by such familiar examples, and plain or simple similitudes, as seldom find place in books and writings.

4. When an instructer in his lectures delivers any matter of difficulty, or expresses himself in such a manner as seems obscure, so that you do not take up his ideas, clearly or fully, you have opportunity, at least when the lecture is finished, or at other proper seasons, to inquire how such a sentence should be understood, or how such a difficulty may be explained and removed.

If there be permission given to free converse with the tutor, either in the midst of the lecture, or rather at the end of it, concerning any doubts or difficulties that occur to the hearer, this brings it very near to conversation or discourse.

IV. Conversation is the next method of improvement, and it is attended with the following advantages:

1. When we converse familiarly with a learned friend, we have his own help at hand to explain to us every word and sentiment that seems obscure in his discourse, and to inform us of his whole meaning: so that we are in much less danger of mistaking his sense: whereas in books, whatsoever is really obscure may also abide always obscure without remedy, since the author is not at hand, that we may inquire his sense.

If we mistake the meaning of our friend in conversation, we are quickly set right again; but in reading, we many times go on in the same mistake, and are not capable of recovering ourselves from it. Thence it comes to pass that we have so many contests in all ages about the meaning of ancient authors, and especially the sacred writers. Happy should we be could we but converse with Moses, Isaiah, and St. Paul, and consult the prophets and apostles, when we meet with a difficult text: but that glorious conversation is reserved for the ages of future blessedness.

2. When we are discoursing upon any theme with a friend, we may propose our doubts and objections against his sentiments, and have them solved and answered at once.—The difficulties that arise in our minds may be removed by one enlightening word of our correspondent: whereas in reading, if a difficulty or question arise in our thoughts, which the author has not happened to mention, we must be content without a present answer or solution of it. Books cannot speak.

3. Not only the doubts which arise in the mind upon any subject or discourse are easily proposed and solved in conversation, but the very difficulties we meet with in books, and in our private studies, may find a relief by friendly conferences. We may pore upon a knotty point in solitary meditation many months without a solution, because perhaps we have gotten into a wrong tract of thought; and our labour (while we are pursuing a false scent) is not only useless and unsuccessful, but it leads us perhaps into a long train of error for want of being corrected in the first step. But if we note down this difficulty when we read it, we may propose it to an ingenious correspondent when we see him; we may be relieved in a moment, and find the difficulty vanish: he beholds the object perhaps in a different view, sets it before us in quite another light, leads us at once into evidence and truth, and that with a delightful surprise.

4. Conversation calls out into light what has been lodged in all the recesses and secret chambers of the soul: by occasional hints and incidents it brings old useful notions into remembrance; it unfolds and displays the hidden treasures of knowledge with which reading, observation, and study, had before furnished the mind. By mutual discourse the soul is awakened and allured to bring forth its hoards of knowledge, and it learns how to render them most useful to mankind. A man of vast reading without conversation is like a miser, who lives only to himself.

5. In free and friendly conversation, our intellectual powers are more animated, and our spirits act with a superior vigour in the quest and pursuit of unknown truths. There is a sharpness and sagacity of thought

that attends conversation beyond what we find whilst we are shut up reading and musing in our retirements. Our souls may be serene in solitude, but not sparkling, though perhaps we are employed in reading the works of the brightest writers. Often has it happened in free discourse, that new thoughts are strangely struck out, and the seeds of truth sparkle and blaze through the company, which in calm and silent reading would never have been excited. By conversation you will both give and receive this benefit; as flints, when put into motion, and striking against each other, produce living fire on both sides, which would never have arisen from the same hard materials in a state of rest.

6. In generous conversation, amongst ingenious and learned men, we have a great advantage of proposing our private opinions, and of bringing our own sentiments to the test, and learning in a more compendious and safer way what the world will judge of them, how mankind will receive them, what objections may be raised against them, what defects there are in our scheme, and how to correct our own mistakes; which advantages are not so easy to be obtained by our own private meditations: for the pleasure we take in our own notions, and the passion of self-love, as well as the narrowness of our views, tempt us to pass too favourable an opinion on our own schemes; whereas the variety of genius in our several associates will give happy notices how our opinions will stand in the view of mankind.

7. It is also another considerable advantage of conversation, that it furnishes the student with the knowledge of men and the affairs of life, as reading furnishes him with book learning. A man who dwells all his days among books may have amassed together a vast heap of notions; but he may be a mere scholar, which is a contemptible sort of character in the world. A hermit, who has been shut up in his cell in a college, has contracted a sort of mould and rust upon his soul, and all his airs of behaviour have a certain awkwardness in them; but these awkward airs are worn away by degrees in company: the rust and the mould are filed and brushed off by polite conversation. The scholar now becomes

a citizen or a gentleman, a neighbour, and a friend; he learns how to dress his sentiments in the fairest colours, as well as to set them in the strongest light. Thus he brings out his notions with honour; he makes some use of them in the world, and improves the theory by the practice.

But before we proceed too far in finishing a bright character by conversation, we should consider that something else is necessary besides an acquaintance with men and books: and therefore I add,

V. Mere lectures, reading, and conversation, without thinking, are not sufficient to make a man of knowledge and wisdom. It is our own thought and reflection, study and meditation, must attend all the other methods of improvement, and perfect them. It carries these advantages with it:

1. Though observation and instruction, reading and conversation, may furnish us with many ideas of men and things, yet it is our own meditation, and the labour of our own thoughts, that must form our judgment of things. Our own thoughts should join or disjoin these ideas in a proposition for ourselves: it is our own mind that must judge for ourselves concerning the agreement or disagreement of ideas, and form propositions of truth out of them. Reading and conversation may acquaint us with many truths, and with many arguments to support them; but it is our own study and reasoning that must determine whether these propositions are true, and whether these arguments are just and solid.

It is confessed there are a thousand things which our eyes have not seen, and which would never come within the reach of our personal and immediate knowledge and observation, because of the distance of times and places: these must be known by consulting other persons; and that is done either in their writings or in their discourses. But after all, let this be a fixed point with us, that it is our own reflection and judgment must determine how far we should receive that which books or men inform us of, and how far they are worthy of our assent and credit.

2. It is meditation and study that transfers and con-

veys the notions and sentiments of others to ourselves, so as to make them properly our own. It is our own judgment upon them, as well as our memory of them, that makes them become our own property. It does as it were concoct our intellectual food, and turns it into a part of ourselves: just as a man may call his limbs and his flesh his own, whether he borrowed the materials from the ox or the sheep, from the lark or the lobster: whether he derived it from corn or milk, the fruits of the trees, or the herbs and roots of the earth; it is all now become one substance with himself, and he wields and manages those muscles and limbs for his own proper purposes, which once were the substance of other animals or vegetables; that very substance which last week was grazing in the field or swimming in the sea, waving in the milk-pail, or growing in the garden, is now become part of the man.

3. By study and meditation we improve the hints that we have acquired by observation, conversation, and reading: we take more time in thinking, and by the labour of the mind we penetrate deeper into the themes of knowledge, and carry our thoughts sometimes much farther on many subjects, than we ever met with, either in the books of the dead or discourses of the living. It is our own reasoning that draws out one truth from another, and forms a whole scheme or science from a few hints which we borrowed elsewhere.

By a survey of these things we may [illegible] that he who spends all his time in hea[illegible] or poring upon books, without observation, med[illegible], or converse, will have but a mere historical knowledge of learning, and be able only to tell what others have known or said on the subject: he that lets all his time flow away in conversation, without due observation, reading, or study, will gain but a slight and superficial knowledge, which will be in danger of vanishing with the voice of the speaker: and he that confines himself merely to his closet, and his own narrow observation of things, and is taught only by his own solitary thoughts, without instruction by lectures, reading, or free conversation, will be in danger of a narrow spirit, a vain conceit of himself, and an unreasonable contempt of others; and after all, he will obtain but a very limited and imperfect view and knowledge of things, and he will seldom learn how to make that knowledge useful.

These five methods of improvement should be pursued jointly, and go hand in hand, where our circumstances are so happy as to find opportunity and conveniency to enjoy them all; though I must give opinion that two of them, viz: reading and meditation, should employ much more of our time than public lectures, or conversation and discourse. As for observation, we may be always acquiring knowledge that way, whether we are alone or in company.

But it will be for our further improvement, if we go over all these five methods of obtaining knowledge more distinctly and more at large, and see what special advances in useful science we may draw from them all.

CHAPTER III.

RULES RELATING TO OBSERVATION.

THOUGH observation, in the strict sense of the word, and as it is distinguished from meditation and study, is the first [illegible] improvement, and in its strictest sense [illegible] in it any reasonings of the mind upon the thing[illegible] we observe, or inferences drawn from them; yet [illegible] motions of the mind are so exceedingly swift, that it is hardly possible for a thinking man to gain experiences or observations without making some secret and short reflections upon them, and therefore in giving a few directions concerning this method of improvement, I shall not so narrowly confine myself to the first mere impression of object on the mind by observation; but include also some hints which relate to the first, most easy, and obvious reflections or reasonings which arise from them.

1. Let the enlargement of your knowledge be one constant view and design in life; since there is no time

or place, no transactions, occurrences, or engagements in life, which exclude us from this method of improving the mind. When we are alone, even in darkness and silence, we may converse with our own hearts, observe the working of our own spirits, and reflect upon the inward motions of our own passions in some of the latest occurrences in life; we may acquaint ourselves with the powers and properties, the tendencies and inclinations both of body and spirit, and gain a more intimate knowledge of ourselves. When we are in company, we may discover something more of human nature, of human passions and follies, and of human affairs, vices, and virtues, by conversing with mankind, and observing their conduct. Nor is there any thing more valuable than the knowledge of ourselves, and the knowledge of men, except it be the knowledge of God who made us, and our relation to him as our Governor.

When we are in the house or the city, wheresoever we turn our eyes, we see the works of men; when we are abroad in the country, we behold more of the works of God. The skies above, and the ground beneath us, and the animal and vegetable world round about us, may entertain our observation with ten thousand varieties.

Endeavour therefore to derive some instruction or improvement of the mind from every thing which you see or hear, from every thing which occurs in human life, from every thing within you or without you.

Fetch down some knowledge from the clouds, the stars, the sun, the moon, and the revolutions of all the planets. Dig and draw up some valuable meditations from the depths of the earth, and search them through the vast oceans of water. Extract some intellectual improvements from the minerals and metals; from the wonders of nature among the vegetables, and herbs, trees, and flowers. Learn some lessons from the birds and the beasts, and the meanest insect. Read the wisdom of God, and his admirable contrivance in them all: read his almighty power, his rich and various goodness in all the works of his hands.

From the day and the night, the hours and the flying

minutes, learn a wise improvement of time, and be watchful to seize every opportunity to increase in knowledge.

From the vicissitudes and revolutions of nations and families, and from the various occurrences of the world, learn the instability of mortal affairs, the uncertainty of life, the certainty of death. From a coffin and a funeral, learn to meditate upon your departure.

From the vices and follies of others, observe what is hateful in them; consider how such a practice looks in another person, and remember that it looks as ill or worse in yourself. From the virtue of others, learn something worthy of your imitation.

From the deformity, the distress, or calamity of others, derive lessons of thankfulness to God, and hymns of grateful praise to your Creator, Governor, and Benefactor, who has formed you in a better mould, and guarded you from those evils. Learn also the sacred lesson of contentment in your own estate, and compassion to your neighbour under his miseries.

From your natural powers, sensations, judgment, memory, hands, feet, &c. make this inference, that they were not given you for nothing, but for some useful employment to the honour of your Maker, and for the good of your fellow creatures, as well as for your own best interest and final happiness.

From the sorrows, the pains, the sicknesses, and sufferings that attend you, learn the evil of sin, and the imperfection of your present state. From your own sins and follies, learn the patience of God toward you, and the practice of humility toward God and man.

Thus from every appearance in nature, and from every occurrence of life, you may derive natural, moral, and religious observations to entertain your minds, as well as rules of conduct in the affairs relating to this life and that which is to come.

II. In order to furnish the mind with a rich variety of ideas, the laudable curiosity of young people should be indulged and gratified, rather than discouraged. It is a very hopeful sign in young persons, to see them curious in observing, and inquisitive in searching into the greatest part of things that occur; nor should such an inquiring temper be frowned into silence, nor be rigorously restrained, but should rather be satisfied with proper answers given to all those queries.

For this reason also, where time and fortune allow it, young people should be led into company at proper seasons, should be carried abroad to see the fields, and the woods, and the rivers, the buildings, towns, and cities distant from their own dwelling; they should be entertained with the sight of strange birds, beasts, fishes, insects, vegetables, and productions both of nature and art of every kind, whether they are the products of their own or foreign nations: and in due time, where Providence gives opportunity, they may travel under a wise inspector or tutor to different parts of the world for the same end, that they may bring home treasures of useful knowledge.

III. Among all these observations write down what is most remarkable and uncommon: reserve these remarks in store for proper occasions, and at proper seasons take a review of them. Such a practice will give you a habit of useful thinking; this will secure the workings of your soul from running to waste; and by this means even your looser moments will turn to happy account both here and hereafter.

And whatever useful observations have been made, let them be at least some part of the subject of your conversation among your friends at next meeting.

Let the circumstances or situation in life be what or where they will, a man should never neglect this improvement which may be derived from observation. Let him travel into the East or West Indies, and fulfil the duties of the military or the mercantile life there; let him rove through the earth or the seas, for his own humour as a traveller, or pursue his diversions in what part of the world he pleases as a gentleman: let prosperous or adverse fortune call him to the most distant parts of the globe; still let him carry on his knowledge and the improvement of his soul by wise observations. In due time, by this means, he may render himself some way useful to the societies of mankind.

Theobaldino, in his younger years, visited the forests of Norway on the account of trade and timber, and besides his proper observations of the growth of trees on those northern mountains, he learned there was a sort of people called Fins, in those confines which border upon Sweden, whose habitation is in the woods; and he lived afterwards to give a good account of them and some of their customs to the Royal Society for the improvement of natural knowledge. Puteoli was taken captive into Turkey in his youth, and travelled with his master in their holy pilgrimage to Mecca, whereby he became more intelligent in the forms, ceremonies, and fooleries of the Mahometan worship, than perhaps any Briton knew before; and by his manuscripts we are more acquainted in this last century with the Turkish sacreds, than any one had ever informed us.

IV. Let us keep our minds as free as possible from passions and prejudices; for these will give a wrong turn to our observations both on persons and things. The eyes of a man in the jaundice make yellow observations on every thing; and the soul, tinctured with any passion or prejudice, diffuses a false colour over the real appearance of things, and disguises many of the common occurrences of life: it never beholds things in a true light, nor suffers them to appear as they are. Whensoever, therefore, you would make proper observations, let self, with all its influences, stand aside as far as possible; abstract your own interest and your own concern from them, and bid all friendships and enmities stand aloof and keep out of the way, in the observations that you make relating to persons and things.

If this rule were well obeyed, we should be much better guarded against those common pieces of misconduct in the observations of men, viz: the false judgments of pride and envy. How ready is envy to mingle with the notices which we take of other persons! How often is mankind prone to put an ill sense upon the action of their neighbours, to take a survey of them in an evil position and in an unhappy light! And by this means we form a worse opinion of our neighbours than they deserve; while at the same time pride and self-flattery tempt us to make unjust observations on ourselves in our own favour. In all the favourable judgments we pass concerning ourselves, we should allow a little abatement on this account.

V. In making your observations on persons, take care of indulging that busy curiosity which is ever inquiring into private and domestic affairs, with an endless itch of learning the secret history of families. It is but seldom that such a prying curiosity attains any valuable ends: it often begets suspicions, jealousies, and disturbances in households, and it is a frequent temptation to persons to defame their neighbours: some persons cannot help telling what they know: a busybody is most liable to become a tattler upon every occasion.

VI. Let your observation, even of persons and their conduct, be chiefly designed in order to lead you to a better acquaintance with things, particularly with human nature; and to inform you what to imitate and what to avoid, rather than to furnish out matter for the evil passions of the mind, or the impertinencies of discourse and reproaches of the tongue.

VII. Though it may be proper sometimes to make your observations concerning persons as well as things the subject of your discourse in learned or useful conversations, yet what remarks you make on particular persons, particularly to their disadvantage, should for the most part lie hid in your own breast, till some just and apparent occasion, some necessary call of Providence, leads you to speak to them.

If the character or conduct which you observe be greatly culpable, it should so much the less be published. You may treasure up such remarks of the follies, indecencies, or vices of your neighbours as may be a constant guard against your practice of the same, without exposing the reputation of your neighbour on that account. It is a good old rule, that our conversation should rather be laid out on things than on persons; and this rule should generally be observed, unless names be concealed, wheresoever the faults or follies of mankind are our present theme.

Our late Archbishop Tillotson has written a small but

excellent discourse on evil speaking, wherein he admirably explains, limits, and applies, that general apostolic precept, Speak evil of no man, Tit. iii. 2.

VIII. Be not too hasty to erect general theories from a few particular observations, appearances, or experiments. This is what the logicians call a false induction. When general observations are drawn from so many particulars as to become certain and indubitable, these are jewels of knowledge, comprehending great treasure in little room: but they are therefore to be made with the greater care and caution, lest errors become large and diffusive, if we should mistake in these general notions.

A hasty determination of some universal principles, without a due survey of all the particular cases which may be included in them, is the way to lay a trap for our own understandings, in their pursuit of any subject, and we shall often be taken captives into mistake and falsehood. Niveo in his youth observed, that on three Christmas Days together there fell a good quantity of snow, and now hath writ it down in his almanac, as a part of his wise remarks on the weather, that it will always snow at Christmas. Euron, a young lad, took notice ten times, that there was a sharp frost when the wind was in the north-east, therefore, in the middle of the last July, he almost expected it should freeze, because the weather-cocks showed him a north-east wind; and he was still more disappointed, when he found it a very sultry season. It is the same hasty judgment that hath thrown scandal on a whole nation for the sake of some culpable characters belonging to several particular natives of that country; whereas all the Frenchmen are not gay and airy; all the Italians are not jealous and revengeful; nor are all the English overrun with the spleen.

CHAPTER IV.

OF BOOKS AND READING.

I. The world is full of Books; but there are multitudes which are so ill written, they were never worth any man's reading; and there are thousands more which may be good in their kind, yet are worth nothing when the month or year, or occasion is past for which they were written. Others may be valuable in themselves for some special purpose, or in some peculiar science, but are not fit to be perused by any but those who are engaged in that particular science or business. To what use is it for a divine or physician, or a tradesman, to read over the huge volumes of reports of judged cases in the law? or for a lawyer to learn Hebrew, and read the Rabbins? It is of vast advantage for improvement of knowledge, and saving time, for a young man to have the most proper books for his reading recommended by a judicious friend.

II. Books of importance of any kind, and especially complete treatises on any subject, should be first read in a more general and cursory manner, to learn a little what the treatise promises, and what you may expect from the writer's manner and skill. And for this end I would advise always that the preface be read, and a survey taken of the table of contents, if there be one, before the survey of the book. By this means you will not only be better fitted to give the book the first reading, but you will be much assisted in your second perusal of it, which should be done with greater attention and deliberation, and you will learn with more ease and readiness what the author pretends to teach. In your reading, mark what is new or unknown to you before and review those chapters, pages, or paragraphs. Unless a reader has an uncommon and most retentive memory, I may venture to affirm, that there is scarce any book or chapter worth reading once, that is not worthy of a second perusal. At least to take a careful review of all the lines or paragraphs which you marked, and make a recollection of the sections which you thought truly valuable.

There is another reason also why I would choose to take a superficial and cursory survey of a book, before I sit down to read it, and dwell upon it with studious attention; and that is, that there may be several difficul ties in it which we cannot easily understand and conquer at the first reading, for want of a fuller comprehension of the author's whole scheme. And therefore in such treatises, we should not stay till we master every difficulty at the first perusal; for perhaps many of these would appear to be solved when we have proceeded further in that book, or would vanish of themselves upon a second reading.

III. If three or four persons agreed to read the same book, and each brings his own remarks upon it, at some set hours appointed for conversation, and they communicate mutually their sentiments on the subject, and debate about it in a friendly manner, this practice will render the reading any author more abundantly beneficial to any one of them.

IV. If several persons engaged in the same study, take into their hands distinct treatises on one subject, and appoint a season of communication once a week, they may inform each other in a brief manner concerning the sense, sentiments, and methods of those several authors, and thereby promote each other's improvement, either by recommending the perusal of the same book to their companions, or perhaps by satisfying their inquiries concerning it by conversation, without every one's perusing it.

V. Remember that your business in reading or in conversation, especially on subjects of natural, moral, or divine science, is not merely to know the opinion of the author or speaker, for this is but the mere knowledge of history; but your chief business is to consider whether their opinions are right or no, and to improve your own solid knowledge on that subject by meditation on the themes of their writing or discourse. Deal freely with every author you read, and yield up your assent only to evidence and just reasoning on the subject.

Here I would be understood to speak only of human authors, and not of the sacred and inspired writings. In these our business is only to find out the true sense, and understand the true meaning of the paragraph and page, and our assent then is bound to follow when we are before satisfied that the writing is divine. Yet I might add also, that even this is sufficient evidence to demand our assent.

But in the composures of men, remember you are a man as well as they; and it is not their reason but your own that is given to guide you when you arrive at years of discretion, of manly age and judgment.

VI. Let this therefore be your practice, especially after you have gone through one course of any science in your academical studies; if a writer on that subject maintains the same sentiments as you do, yet if he does not explain his ideas or prove his positions well, mark the faults or defects, and endeavour to do better, either in the margin of your book, or rather in some papers of your own, or at least let it be done in your private meditations. As for instance:—

Where the author is obscure, enlighten him: where he is imperfect, supply his deficiencies: where he is too brief and concise, amplify a little, and set his notions in a fairer view: where he is redundant, mark those paragraphs to be retrenched: when he trifles and grows impertinent, abandon those passages or pages: when he argues, observe whether his reasons be conclusive: if the conclusion be true, and yet the argument weak, endeavour to confirm it by better proofs: where he derives or infers any proposition darkly and doubtfully, make the justice of the inference appear, and make further inferences or corollaries, if such occur to your mind: where you suppose he is in a mistake, propose your objections and correct his sentiments: what he writes so well as to approve itself of your judgment, both as just and useful, treasure it up in your memory, and count it a part of your intellectual gains.

Note, Many of these same directions, which I have now given, may be practised with regard to conversation as well as reading, in order to render it useful in the most extensive and lasting manner.

VII. Other things also of the like nature may be usefully practised with regard to the authors which you read, viz. If the method of a book be irregular, reduce it into form, by a little analysis of your own, or by hints in the margin: If those things are heaped together, which should be separated, you may wisely distinguish and divide them: if several things relating to the same subject are scattered up and down separately through the treatise, you may bring them all to one view by references; or if the matter of a book be really valuable and deserving, you may throw it into a better method, reduce it to a more logical scheme, or abridge it into a lesser form: all these practices will have a tendency both to advance your skill in logic and method, to improve your judgment in general, and to give you a fuller survey of that subject in particular. When you have finished the treatise with all your observations upon it, recollect and determine what real improvements you have made by reading that author.

VIII. If a book has no index to it, or good table of contents, it is very useful to make one as you are reading it: not with that exactness as to include the sense of every page and paragraph, which should be done if you designed to print it; but it is sufficient in your index to take notice only of those parts of the book which are new to you, or which you think well written, and well worthy of your remembrance or review.

Shall I be so free as to assure my younger friends, from my own experience, that these methods of reading will cost some pains in the first year of your study, and especially in the first authors which you peruse in any science, or on any particular subject: but the profit will richly compensate the pains. And in the following years of life, after you have read a few valuable books on any special subject in this manner, it will be easy to read others of the same kind, because you will not usually find very much new matter in them which you have not already examined.

If the writer be remarkable for any peculiar excellencies or defects in his style or manner of writing, make just observations upon this also; and whatsoever ornaments you find there, or whatsoever blemishes occur in the language or manner of the writer, you may make just remarks upon them. And remember that one book read over in this manner, with all this laborious meditation, will tend more to enrich your understanding, than the skimming over the surface of twenty authors.

IX. By perusing books in the manner I have described, you will make all your reading subservient not only to the enlargement of your treasures of knowledge, but also to the improvement of your reasoning powers.

There are many who read with constancy and diligence, and yet make no advances in true knowledge by it. They are delighted with the notions which they read or hear, as they would be with stories that are told; but they do not weigh them in their minds as in a just balance, in order to determine their truth or falsehood; they make no observations upon them, or inferences from them. Perhaps their eye slides over the pages, or the words slide over their ears, and vanish like a rhapsody of evening tales, or the shadows of a cloud flying over a green field in a summer's day.

Or if they review them sufficiently to fix them in their remembrance, it is merely with a design to tell the tale over again, and show what men of learning they are. Thus they dream out their days in a course of reading, without real advantage. As a man may be eating all day, and, for want of digestion is never nourished; so those endless readers may cram themselves in vain with intellectual food, and without real improvement of their minds, for want of digesting it by proper reflections.

X. Be diligent therefore in observing these directions. Enter into the sense and arguments of the authors you read; examine all their proofs, and then judge of the truth or falsehood of their opinions; and thereby you shall not only gain a rich increase of your understanding, by those truths which the author teaches, when you see them well supported, but you shall acquire also by degrees a habit of judging justly, and of reasoning well, in imitation of the good writer whose works you peruse.

This is laborious indeed, and the mind is backward to undergo the fatigue of weighing every argument, and tracing every thing to its original. It is much less labour to take all things upon trust: believing is much easier than arguing. But when Studentio had once persuaded his mind to tie itself down to this method which I have prescribed, he sensibly gained an admirable facility to read, and judge of what he read by his daily practice of it, and the man made large advances in the pursuit of truth; while Plumbinus and Plumeo made less progress in knowledge, though they had read over more folios. Plumeo skimmed over the pages like a swallow over the flowery meads in May. Plumbinus read every line and syllable, but did not give himself the trouble of thinking and judging about them. They both could boast in company of their great reading, for they knew more titles and pages than Studentio, but were far less acquainted with science.

I confess those whose reading is designed only to fit them for much talk, and little knowledge, may content themselves to run over their authors in such a sudden and trifling way; they may devour libraries in this manner, yet be poor reasoners at last; and have no solid wisdom or true learning. The traveller who walks on fair and softly in a course that points right, and examines every turning before he ventures upon it, will come sooner and safer to his journey's end, than he who runs through every lane he meets, though he gallops full speed all the day. The man of much reading, and a large retentive memory, but without meditation, may become, in the sense of the world, a knowing man; and if he converse much with the ancients, he may attain the fame of learning too; but he spends his days afar off from wisdom and true judgment, and possesses very little of the substantial riches of the mind.

XI. Never apply yourselves to read any human author with a determination beforehand either for or against him, or with a settled resolution to believe or disbelieve, to confirm or to oppose, whatsoever he saith; but always read with a design to lay your mind open to truth, and to embrace it wheresoever you find it, as well as to reject every falsehood, though it appear under ever so fair a disguise. How unhappy are those men who seldom take an author into their hands but they have determined before they begin whether they will like or dislike him! They have got some notion of his name, his character, his party, or his principles, by general conversation, or perhaps by some slight view of a few pages; and having all their own opinions adjusted beforehand, they read all that he writes with a prepossession either for or against him. Unhappy those who hunt and purvey for a party, and scrape together out of every author all those things, and those only, which favour their own tenets, while they despise and neglect all the rest!

XII. Yet take this caution. I would not be understood here, as though I persuaded a person to live without any settled principles at all, by which to judge of men, and books, and things: or that I would keep a man always doubting about his foundations. The chief things that I design in this advice, are these three:

1. That after our most necessary and important principles of science, prudence, and religion, are settled upon good grounds, with regard to our present conduct and our future hopes, we should read with a just freedom of thought all those books which treat of such subjects as may admit of doubt and reasonable dispute. Nor should any of our opinions be so resolved upon, especially in younger years, as never to hear or to bear an opposition to them.

2. When we peruse those authors who defend our own settled sentiments, we should not take all their arguments for just and solid; but we should make a wise distinction between the corn and the chaff, between solid reasoning and the mere superficial colours of it; nor should we readily swallow down all their lesser opinions because we agree with them in the greater.

3 That when we read those authors which oppose our most certain and established principles, we should be ready to receive any informations from them in other points, and not abandon at once every thing they say, though we are well fixed in our opposition to their main point of arguing.

.... Fas est ab hoste doceri. *Virg.*

Seize upon truth where'er 'tis found,
Amongst your friends, amongst your foes,
On Christian or on heathen ground;
The flower's divine where'er it grows:
Neglect the prickles and assume the rose.

XIII. What I have said hitherto on this subject, relating to books and reading, must be chiefly understood of that sort of books, and those hours of our reading and study, whereby we design to improve the intellectual powers of the mind with natural, moral, or divine knowledge. As for those treatises which are written to direct or to enforce and persuade our practice, there is one thing further necessary; and that is, that when our consciences are convinced that these rules of prudence or duty belong to us, and require our conformity to them, we should then call ourselves to account, and inquire seriously whether we have put them in practice or no; we should dwell upon the arguments, and impress the motives and methods of persuasion upon our own hearts, till we feel the force and power of them inclining us to the practice of the things which are there recommended.

If folly or vice be represented in its open colours, or its secret disguises, let us search our hearts, and review our lives, and inquire how far we are criminal; nor should we ever think we have done with the treatise while we feel ourselves in sorrow for our past misconduct, and aspiring after a victory over those vices, or till we find a cure of those follies begun to be wrought upon our souls.

In all our studies and pursuits of knowledge, let us remember that virtue and vice, sin and holiness, and the conformation of our hearts and lives to the duties of true religion and morality, are things of far more consequence than all the furniture of our understanding, and the richest treasures of more speculative knowledge; and that because they have a more immediate and effectual influence upon our eternal felicity or eternal sorrow.

XIV. There is yet another sort of books, of which it is proper I should say something, while I am treating on this subject; and these are history, poesy, travels; books of diversion or amusement: among which we may reckon also little common pamphlets, newspapers, or such like: for many of these I confess once reading may be sufficient, where there is a tolerable good memory.

Or when several persons are in company, and one reads to the rest such a sort of writing, once hearing may be sufficient, provided that every one be so attentive, and so free, as to make their occasional remarks on such lines or sentences, such periods or paragraphs, as in their opinion deserve it. Now all those paragraphs or sentiments deserve a remark, which are new and uncommon, are noble and excellent for the matter of them, are strong and convincing for the argument contained in them, are beautiful and elegant for the language or the manner, or any way worthy of a second rehearsal; and at the request of any of the company let those paragraphs be read over again.

Such parts also of these writings as may happen to be remarkably stupid or silly, false or mistaken, should become subjects of an occasional criticism, made by some of the company; and this may give occasion to the repetition of them, for the confirmation of the censure, for amusement or diversion.

Still let it be remembered, that where the historical narration is of considerable moment, where the poesy, oratory, &c. shine with some degrees of perfection and glory, a single reading is neither sufficient to satisfy a mind that has a true taste of this sort of writings; nor can we make the fullest and best improvement of them without proper reviews, and that in our retirement as well as in company. Who is there that has any *gout* for polite writings that would be sufficiently satisfied with hearing the beautiful pages of Steele or Addison, the admirable descriptions of Virgil or Milton, or some of the finest poems of Pope, Young, or Dryden, once read over to them, and then lay them by for ever?

XV. Among these writings of the latter kind we may justly reckon short miscellaneous essays on all manner of subjects; such as the Occasional Papers, the Tatlers, the Spectators, and some other books that have been compiled out of the weekly or daily products of the press, wherein are contained a great number of bright thoughts, ingenious remarks, and admirable observations, which have had a considerable share in furnishing the present age with knowledge and politeness.

I wish every paper among these writings could have been recommended both as innocent and useful. I wish every unseemly idea and wanton expression had been banished from amongst them, and every trifling page had been excluded from the company of the rest when they had been bound up in volumes: but it is not to be expected, in so imperfect a state, that every page or piece of such mixed public papers should be entirely blameless and laudable. Yet in the main it must be confessed, there is so much virtue, prudence, ingenuity, and goodness in them, especially in eight volumes of Spectators, there is such a reverence for things sacred, so many valuable remarks for our conduct in life, that they are not improper to lie in parlours, or summer-houses, or places of usual residence, to entertain our thoughts in any moments of leisure or vacant hours that occur. There is such a discovery of the follies, iniquities, and fashionable vices of mankind contained in them, that we may learn much of the humours and madnesses of the age and the public world, in our own solitary retirement, without the danger of frequenting vicious company, or receiving the mortal infection.

XVI. Among other books which are proper and requisite, in order to improve our knowledge in general, or our acquaintance with any particular science, it is necessary that we should be furnished with Vocabularies and Dictionaries of several sorts, viz. of common words, idioms and phrases, in order to explain their sense; of technical words or the terms of art, to show their use in arts and sciences; of names of men, countries, towns, rivers, &c. which are called historical and geographical dictionaries, &c. These are to be consulted and used upon every occasion; and never let an unknown word pass in your reading without seeking for its sense and meaning in some of these writers.

If such books are not at hand, you must supply the want of them as well as you can, by consulting such as can inform you: and it is useful to note down the matters of doubt and inquiry in some pocket-book, and take the first opportunity to get them resolved, either by persons or books, when we meet with them.

XVII. Be not satisfied with a mere knowledge of the best authors that treat of any subject, instead of acquainting ourselves thoroughly with the subject itself.

There is many a young student that is fond of enlarging his knowledge of books, and he contents himself with the notice he has of their title-page, which is the attainment of a bookseller rather than a scholar. Such persons are under a great temptation to practise these two follies. (1.) To heap up a great number of books at a greater expense than most of them can bear, and to furnish their libraries infinitely better than their understanding. And. (2) when they have gotten such rich treasures of knowledge upon their shelves, they imagine themselves men of learning, and take a pride in talking of the names of famous authors, and the subjects of which they treat, without any real improvement of their own minds in true science or wisdom. At best their learning reaches no further than the indexes and table of contents, while they know not how to judge or reason concerning the matters contained in those authors.

And indeed how many volumes of learning soever a man possesses, he is still deplorably poor in his understanding, till he has made those several parts of learning his own property by reading and reasoning, by judging for himself, and remembering what he has read.

CHAPTER V.

JUDGMENT OF BOOKS.

I. If we would form a judgment of a book which we have not seen before, the first thing that offers is the title-page, and we may sometimes guess a little at the import and design of a book thereby; though it must be confessed that titles are often deceitful, and promise more than the book performs. The author's name, if it be known in the world, may help us to conjecture at the performance a little more, and lead us to guess in what manner it is done. A perusal of the preface or introduction (which I before recommended) may further assist our judgment; and if there be an index of the contents, it will give us still some advancing light.

If we have not leisure or inclination to read over the

book itself regularly, then by the titles of chapters we may be directed to peruse several particular chapters or sections, and observe whether there be any thing valuable or important in them. We shall find hereby whether the author explains his ideas clearly, whether he reasons strongly, whether he methodizes well, whether his thought and sense be manly, and his manner polite; or, on the other hand, whether he be obscure, weak, trifling, and confused; or, finally, whether the matter may not be solid and substantial, though the style and manner be rude and disagreeable.

II. By having run through several chapters and sections in this manner, we may generally judge whether the treatise be worth a complete perusal or no. But if by such an occasional survey of some chapters our expectation be utterly discouraged, we may well lay aside that book; for there is great probability he can be but an indifferent writer on that subject, if he affords but one prize to divers blanks, and it may be some downright blots too. The piece can hardly be valuable if in seven or eight chapters which we peruse there be but little truth, evidence, force of reasoning, beauty, ingenuity of thought, &c. mingled with much error, ignorance, impertinence, dulness, mean and common thoughts, inaccuracy, sophistry, railing, &c. Life is too short, and time is too precious, to read every new book quite over, in order to find that it is not worth the reading.

III. There are some general mistakes which persons are frequently guilty of in passing a judgment on the books which they read.

One is this; when a treatise is written but tolerably well, we are ready to pass a favourable judgment of it, and sometimes to exalt its character far beyond its merit, if it agree with our own principles, and support the opinions of our party. On the other hand, if the author be of different sentiments, and espouse contrary principles, we can find neither wit nor reason, good sense, nor good language in it; whereas, alas! if our opinions of things were certain and infallible truth, yet a silly author may draw his pen in the defence of them, and he may attack even gross errors with feeble and ridiculous arguments. Truth in this world is not always attended and supported by the wisest and safest methods; and error, though it can never be maintained by just reasoning, yet may be artfully covered and defended. An ingenious writer may put excellent colours upon his own mistakes. Some Socinians who deny the Atonement of Christ, have written well, and with much appearance of argument for their own unscriptural sentiments; and some writers for the Trinity and Satisfaction of Christ, have exposed themselves and the sacred doctrine by their feeble and foolish manner of handling it. Books are never to be judged of merely by their subject, or the opinion they represent, but by the justness of their sentiment, the beauty of their manner, the force of their expression, or the strength of reason, and the weight of just and proper argument which appears in them.

But this folly and weakness of trifling, instead of arguing, does not happen to fall only to the share of Christian writers; there are some who have taken the pen in hand to support the Deistical or Antichristian scheme of our days, who make big pretences to reason upon all occasions, but seem to have left it all behind them when they are jesting with the Bible, and grinning at the books which we call sacred.

Some of these performances would scarce have been thought tolerable, if they had not assaulted the Christian faith, though they have now grown up to a place amongst the admired pens. I much-question whether several of the rhapsodies called the Characteristics, would ever have survived the first edition, if they had not discovered so strong a tincture of infidelity, and now and then cast out a profane sneer at our holy religion. I have sometimes indeed been ready to wonder how a book, in the main so loosely written, should ever obtain so many readers among men of sense. Surely they must be conscious in the perusal, that sometimes a patrician may write as idly as a man of plebeian rank, and trifle as much as an old school-man, though it is in another form. I am forced to say, there are few books that ever I read, which made any pretences to a great genius, from which I derived so little valuable knowledge as from these treatises. There is indeed amongst them a lively pertness, a parade of literature, and much of what some folks nowadays call politeness; but it is hard that we should be bound to admire all the reveries of this author under the penalty of being unfashionable.

IV. Another mistake which some persons fall into is this: when they read a treatise on a subject with which they have but little acquaintance, they find almost every thing new and strange to them: their understandings are greatly entertained and improved by the occurrence of many things which were unknown to them before; they admire the treatise, and commend the author at once; whereas if they had but attained a good degree of skill in that science, perhaps they would find that the author had written very poorly, that neither his sense nor his method was just and proper, and that he had nothing in him but what was very common or trivial in his discourses on that subject.

Hence it comes to pass that Cario and Faber, who were both bred up to labour, and unacquainted with the sciences, shall admire one of the weekly papers, or a little pamphlet that talks pertly on some critical or learned theme, because the matter is all strange and new to them, and they join to extol the writer to the skies; and for the same reason a young academic shall dwell upon a Journal or an Observator that treats of trade and politics in a dictatorial style, and shall be lavish in the praise of the author: while at the same time persons well skilled in those different subjects, hear the impertinent tattle with a just contempt: for they know how weak and awkward many of those little diminutive discourses are; and that those very papers of science, politics, or trade, which were so much admired by the ignorant, are perhaps but very mean performances; though it must also be confessed there are some excellent essays in those papers, and that upon science as well as trade.

V. But there is a danger of mistake in our judgment of books, on the other hand also: for when we have made ourselves masters of any particular theme of knowledge, and surveyed it long on all sides, there is perhaps scarce any writer on that subject who much entertains and pleases us afterwards, because we find little or nothing new in him; and yet, in a true judgment, perhaps his sentiments are most proper and just, his explication clear, and his reasoning strong, and all the parts of the discourse are well connected and set in a happy light; but we know most of those things before, and therefore they strike us not, and we are in danger of discommending them.

Thus the learned and the unlearned have their several distinct dangers and prejudices ready to attend them in their judgment of the writings of men. These which I have mentioned are a specimen of them, and indeed but a mere specimen; for the prejudices that warp our judgment aside from truth are almost infinite and endless.

VI. Yet I cannot forbear to point out two or three more of these follies, that I may attempt something towards the correction of them, or at least to guard others against them.

There are some persons of a forward and lively temper, and who are fond to intermeddle with all appearances of knowledge, will give their judgment on a book as soon as the title of it is mentioned, for they would not willingly seem ignorant of any thing that others know. And especially if they happen to have any superior character or possessions of this world, they fancy they have a right to talk freely upon every thing that stirs or appears, though they have no other pretence to this freedom. Divito is worth forty thousand pounds. Politulus is a fine young gentleman, who sparkles in all the shining things of dress and equipage. Aulinus is a small attendant on a minister of state, and is at court almost every day. These three happened to meet on a visit where an excellent book of warm and refined devotions lay in the window. What dull stuff is here! said Divito; I never read so much nonsense in one page in my life; nor would I give a shilling for a thousand such treatises. Aulinus, though a courtier, had not used to speak roughly, yet would not allow there was a line of good sense in the book, and pronounced him a madman that wrote it in his secret retirement, and declared him a fool that published it after his death. Politulus had more manners than to differ from men of such rank and character, and therefore he sneered at the devout expressions as he heard them read, and made the divine treatise a matter of scorn and ridicule; and yet it was well known, that neither this fine gentleman, nor the courtier, nor the man of wealth, had a grain of devotion in them beyond their horses that waited at the door with their gilded chariots. But this is the way of the world; blind men will talk of the beauty of colours, and of the harmony or disproportion of figures in painting; the deaf will prate of discords in music; and those who have nothing to do with religion will arraign the best treatise on divine subjects, though they do not understand the very language of the scripture, nor the common terms or phrases used in Christianity.

VII. I might here name another sort of judges, who will set themselves up to decide in favour of an author, or will pronounce him a mere blunderer, according to the company they have kept, and the judgment they have heard passed upon a book by others of their own stamp or size, though they have no knowledge or taste of the subject themselves. These, with a fluent and voluble tongue, become mere echoes of the praises or censures of other men. Sonillus happened to be in the room where the three gentlemen just mentioned gave out their thoughts so freely upon an admirable book of devotion: and two days afterwards he met with some friends of his, where this book was the subject of conversation and praise. Sonillus wondered at their dulness, and repeated the jests which he had heard cast upon the weakness of the author. His knowledge of the book, and his decision upon it, was all from hearsay, for he had never seen it; and if he had read it through, he had no manner of right to judge about the things of religion, having no more knowledge or taste of any thing of inward piety than a hedgehog or a bear has of politeness.

When I had written these remarks, Probus, who knew all the four gentlemen, wished they might have an opportunity to read their own character as it is represented here. Alas! Probus, I fear it would do them very little good, though it may guard others against their folly: for there is never a one of them would find their own name in these characters if they read them; though all their acquaintance would acknowledge the features immediately, and see the persons almost alive in the picture.

VIII. There is yet another mischievous principle which prevails among some persons in passing a judgment on the writings of others, and that is, when from the secret stimulations of vanity, pride, or envy, they despise a valuable book, and throw contempt upon it by wholesale: and if you ask them the reason of their severe censure, they will tell you, perhaps, they have found a mistake or two in it, or there are a few sentiments or expressions not suited to their tooth and humour. Bavius cries down an admirable treatise of philosophy, and says there is atheism in it, because there are a few sentences that seem to suppose brutes to be mere machines. Under the same influence, Momus will not allow Paradise Lost to be a good poem, because he has read some flat and heavy lines in it; and he thought Milton had too much honour done him. It is a paltry humour that inclines a man to rail at any human performance, because it is not absolutely perfect. Horace would give us a better example:—

> Sunt delicta tamen quibus ignovisse velimus,
> Nam neque chorda sonum reddit quem vult manus et mens,
> Nec semper feriet quodcunque minabitur arcus:
> Verum ubi plura nitent in carmine, non ego paucis
> Offendar maculis, quas aut incuria fudit,
> Aut humana parum cavit natura.
>
> *Hor. de Art. Poet.*

Thus Englished:—

> Be not two rigidly censorious:
> A string may jar in the best master's hand,
> And the most skilful archer miss his aim:
> So in a poem elegantly writ,
> I will not quarrel with a small mistake,
> Such as our nature's frailty may excuse.
>
> *Roscommon.*

This noble translator of Horace, whom I here cite, has a very honourable opinion of Homer in the main;

yet he allows him to be justly censured for some grosser spots and blemishes in him:—

> For who without aversion ever looked
> On holy garbage, though by Homer cooked;
> Whose railing heroes, and whose wounded gods,
> Make some suspect he snores as well as nods.

Such wise and just distinctions ought to be made when we pass a judgment on mortal things; but Envy condemns by wholesale. Envy is a cursed plant; some fibres of it are rooted almost in every man's nature, and it works in a sly and imperceptible manner, and that even in some persons who in the main are men of wisdom and piety. They know not how to bear the praises that are given to an ingenious author, especially if he be living, and of their profession; and therefore they will, if possible, find some blemish in his writings, that they may nibble and bark at it. They will endeavour to diminish the honour of the best treatise that has been written on any subject, and to render it useless by their censures, rather than suffer their envy to lie asleep, and the little mistakes of that author to pass unexposed. Perhaps they will commend the work in general with a pretended air of candour; but pass so many sly and invidious remarks upon it afterwards, as shall effectually destroy all their cold and formal praises.*

IX. When a person feels any thing of this invidious humour working in him, he may by the following consideration attempt the correction of it. Let him think with himself how many are the beauties of such an author whom he censures, in comparison of his blemishes, and remember that it is a much more honourable and good-natured thing to find out peculiar beauties than faults; true and undisguised candour is a much more amiable and divine talent than accusation. Let

* I grant when Wisdom itself censures a weak and foolish performance, it will pass its severe sentence, and yet with an air of candour, if the author has any thing valuable in him: but Envy will sometimes imitate the same favourable airs, in order to make its false cavils appear more just and credible, when it has a mind to snarl at some of the brightest performances of a human writer.

him reflect again, what an easy matter it is to find a mistake in all human authors, who are necessarily fallible and imperfect.

I confess, where an author sets up himself to ridicule divine writers, and things sacred, and yet assumes an air of sovereignty and dictatorship, to exalt and almost deify all the pagan ancients, and cast his scorn upon all the moderns, especially if they do but savour of miracles and the gospel; it is fit the admirers of this author should know, that nature and these ancients are not the same, though some writers always unite them. Reason and nature never made these ancient heathens their standard, either of art or genius, of writing or heroism. Sir Richard Steele, in his little essay, called the Christian Hero, has shown our Saviour and St. Paul in a more glorious and transcendent light than a Virgil or Homer could do for their Achilles, Ulysses, or Æneas: and I am persuaded, if Moses and David had not been inspired writers, these very men would have ranked them at least with Herodotus and Horace, if not given them the superior place.

But where an author has many beauties consistent with virtue, piety, and truth, let not little critics exalt themselves, and shower down their ill nature upon him without bounds or measure; but rather stretch their own powers of soul till they write a treatise superior to that which they condemn. This is the noblest and surest manner of suppressing what they censure.

A little wit, or a little learning, with a good degree of vanity and ill nature, will teach a man to pour out whole pages of remark and reproach upon one real or fancied mistake of a great and good author: and this may be dressed up by the same talents, and made entertaining enough to the world, which loves reproach and scandal: but if the remarker would but once make this attempt, and try to outshine the author by writing a better book on the same subject, he would soon be convinced of his own insufficiency, and perhaps might learn to judge more justly and favourably of the performance of other men. A cobbler or a shoemaker may find some little fault with the latchet of a shoe that an Apelles had painted, and perhaps with justice too, when the whole figure and portraiture is such as none but Apelles could paint. Every poor low genius may cavil at what the richest and the noblest hath performed; but it is a sign of envy and malice, added to the littleness and poverty of genius, when such a cavil becomes a sufficient reason to pronounce at once against a bright author, and a whole valuable treatise.

X. Another, and that a very frequent fault, in passing a judgment upon books, is this, that persons spread the same praises or the same reproaches over a whole treatise, and all the chapters in it, which are due only to some of them. They judge as it were by wholesale, without making a due distinction between the several parts or sections of the performance; and this is ready to lead those who hear them talk into a dangerous mistake. Florus is a great and just admirer of the late Archbishop of Cambray, and mightily commends every thing he has written, and will allow no blemish in him; whereas the writings of that excellent man are not all of a piece; nor are those very books of his, which have a good number of beautiful and valuable sentiments in them, to be recommended throughout, or all at once without distinction. There is his demonstration of the Existence and Attributes of God, which has justly gained a universal esteem, for bringing down some new and noble thoughts of the wisdom of the creation to the understanding of the unlearned, and they are such as well deserve the perusal of the man of science, perhaps as far as the 50th section; but there are many of the following sections which are very weakly written, and some of them built upon an enthusiastical and mistaken scheme, akin to the peculiar opinions of Father Malebranche; such as sect 51, 53, "That we know the finite only by the ideas of the infinite." Sect. 55, 60, "That the superior reason in man is God himself acting in him." Sect. 61, 62, "That the idea of unity cannot be taken from creatures, but from God only:" and several of his sections, from 65 to 68, upon the doctrine of liberty, seem to be inconsistent. Again, toward the end of his book, he spends more time and pains than are needful in refuting the Epicurian fancy of atoms moving eternally through infinite changes, which might be done effectually in a much shorter and better way.

So in his posthumous essays, and his letters, there are many admirable thoughts in practical and experimental religion, and very beautiful and divine sentiments in devotion; but sometimes in large paragraphs, or in whole chapters together, you find him in the clouds of mystic divinity, and he never descends within the reach of common ideas or common sense.

But remember this also, that there are but few such authors as this great man, who talks so very weakly sometimes, and yet in other places is so much superior to the greatest part of writers.

There are other instances of this kind, where men of good sense in the main set up for judges, but they carry too many of their passions about them, and then, like lovers, they are in rapture at the name of their fair idol: they lavish out all their incense upon that shrine, and cannot bear the thought of admitting a blemish in them.

You shall hear Altisono not only admire Casimire of Poland in his lyrics, as the utmost purity and perfection of Latin poesy; but he will allow nothing in him to be extravagant or faulty, and will vindicate every line: nor can I much wonder at it, when I have heard him pronounce Lucan the best of the ancient Latins, and idolize his very weaknesses and mistakes. I will readily acknowledge the Odes of Casimire to have more spirit and force, more magnificence and fire in them, and in twenty places arise to more dignity and beauty than I could ever meet with in any of our modern poets: yet I am afraid to say that "Palla sutilis e luce" has dignity enough in it for a robe made for the Almighty: Lib. iv. Od. 7, l. 37, or that the man of virtue in Od. 3, l. 44, "under the ruins of heaven and earth, will bear up the fragments of the falling world with a comely wound on his shoulders."

. . . . Late ruenti
Subjiciens sua colla cælo
Mundum decoro vulnere fulciet;
Interque cæli fragmina.

Yet I must needs confess also, that it is hardly possible a man should rise to so exalted and sublime a vein of poesy as Casimire, who is not in danger now and then of such extravagances; but still they should not be admired or defended, if we pretend to pass a just judgment on the writings of the greatest men.

Milton is a noble genius, and the world agrees to confess it: his poem of Paradise Lost is a glorious performance, and rivals the most famous pieces of antiquity; but that reader must be deeply prejudiced in favour of the poet, who can imagine him equal to himself through all that work. Neither the sublime sentiments, nor dignity of numbers, nor force or beauty of expression, are equally maintained, even in all those parts which require grandeur or beauty, force or harmony. I cannot but consent to Mr. Dryden's opinion, though I will not use his words, that for some scores of lines together there is a coldness and flatness, and almost a perfect absence of that spirit of poesy which breathes, and lives, and flames in other pages.

XI. When you hear any person pretending to give his judgment of a book, consider with yourself whether he be a capable judge, or whether he may not lie under some unhappy bias or prejudice, for or against it, or whether he has made a sufficient inquiry to form his justest sentiments upon it.

Though he be a man of good sense, yet he is incapable of passing a true judgment of a particular book, if he be not well acquainted with the subject of which it treats, and the manner in which it is written, be it verse or prose: or if he hath not had an opportunity or leisure to look sufficiently into the writing itself.

Again, though he be ever so capable of judging on all other accounts, by the knowledge of the subject, and of the book itself, yet you are to consider also whether there be any thing in the author, in his manner, in his language, in his opinions, and his particular party, which may warp the sentiments of him that judgeth, to think well or ill of the treatise, and to pass too favourable or too severe a sentence concerning it.

If you find that he is either an unfit judge because of

his ignorance or because of his prejudices, his judgment of that book should go for nothing. Philographo is a good divine, a useful preacher, and an approved expositor of scripture; but he never had a taste for any of the polite learning of the age; he was fond of every thing that appeared in a devout dress; but all verse was alike to him: he told me last week there was a very fine book of poems published on the three Christian Graces, Faith, Hope, and Charity; and a most elegant piece of oratory on the four last things, Death, Judgment, Heaven, and Hell. Do you think I shall buy either of those books merely on Philographo's recommendation?

CHAPTER VI.

OF LIVING INSTRUCTIONS AND LECTURES, OF TEACHERS AND LEARNERS.

I. There are few persons of so penetrating a genius, and so just a judgment, as to be capable of learning the arts and sciences without the assistance of teachers. There is scarce any science so safely and so speedily learned, even by the noblest genius and the best books, without a tutor. His assistance is absolutely necessary for most persons, and it is very useful for all beginners. Books are a sort of dumb teachers; they point out the way to learning; but if we labour under any doubt or mistake, they cannot answer sudden questions, or explain present doubts and difficulties: this is properly the work of a living instructor.

II. There are very few tutors who are sufficiently furnished with such universal learning, as to sustain all the parts and provinces of instruction. The sciences are numerous, and many of them lie far wide of each other; and it is best to enjoy the instructions of two or three tutors at least, in order to run through the whole encyclopædia, or circle of sciences, where it may be obtained; then we may expect that each will teach the few parts of learning which are committed to his care in greater perfection. But where this advantage cannot be had with convenience, one great man must supply the place of two or three common instructors.

III. It is not sufficient that instructors be competently skilful in those sciences which they profess and teach; but they should have skill also in the art or method of teaching, and patience in the practice of it.

It is a great unhappiness indeed, when persons by a spirit of party, or faction, or interest, or by purchase, are set up for tutors, who have neither due knowledge of science, nor skill in the way of communication. And, alas! there are others who, with all their ignorance and insufficiency, have self-admiration and effrontery enough to set up themselves; and the poor pupils fare accordingly, and grow lean in their understandings.

And let it be observed also, there are some very learned men, who know much themselves, but have not the talent of communicating their own knowledge; or else they are lazy, and will take no pains at it. Either they have an obscure and perplexed way of talking, or they show their learning uselessly, and make a long periphrasis on every word of the book they explain, or they cannot condescend to young beginners, or they run presently into the elevated parts of the science, because it gives themselves greater pleasure, or they are soon angry and impatient, and cannot bear with a few impertinent questions of a young inquisitive and sprightly genius; or else they skim over a science in a very slight and superficial survey, and never lead their disciples into the depths of it.

IV. A good tutor should have characters and qualifications very different from all these. He is such a one as both can and will apply himself with diligence and concern, and indefatigable patience, to effect what he undertakes; to teach his disciples, and see that they learn; to adapt his way and method, as near as may be, to the various dispositions, as well as to the capacities of those whom he instructs, and to inquire often into their progress and improvement.

And he should take particular care of his own temper and conduct, that there be nothing in him or about him which may be of ill example; nothing that may savour of a haughty temper, or a mean and sordid spirit; nothing that may expose him to the aversion or to the contempt of his scholars, or create a prejudice in their minds against him and his instructions: but, if possible, he should have so much of a natural candour and sweetness mixed with all the improvements of learning, as might convey knowledge into the minds of his disciples with a sort of gentle insinuation and sovereign delight, and may tempt them into the highest improvements of their reason by a resistless and insensible force. But I shall have occasion to say more on this subject, when I come to speak more directly of the methods of the communication of knowledge.

V. The learner should attend with constancy and care on all the instructions of his tutor; and if he happens to be at any time unavoidably hindered, he must endeavour to retrieve the loss by double industry for time to come. He should always recollect and review his lectures, read over some other author or authors upon the same subject, confer upon it with his instructor, or with his associates, and write down the clearest result of his present thoughts, reasonings, and inquiries, which he may have recourse to hereafter, either to re-examine them and to apply them to proper use, or to improve them farther to his own advantage.

VI. A student should never satisfy himself with bare attendance on the lectures of his tutor, unless he clearly takes up his sense and meaning, and understands the things which he teaches. A young disciple should behave himself so well as to gain the affection and ear of his instructor, that upon every occasion he may, with the utmost freedom, ask questions, and talk over his own sentiments, his doubts, and difficulties with him, and in an humble and modest manner desire the solution of them.

VII. Let the learner endeavour to maintain an honorable opinion of his instructor, and heedfully listen to his instructions, as one willing to be led by a more experienced guide; and though he is not bound to fall in with every sentiment of his tutor, yet he should so far comply with him as to resolve upon a just consideration of the matter, and try and examine it thoroughly with an honest heart, before he presume to determine against him: and then it should be done with great modesty, with an humble jealousy of himself, and apparent unwillingness to differ from his tutor, if the force of argument and truth did not constrain him.

VIII. It is a frequent and growing folly in our age, that pert young disciples soon fancy themselves wiser than those who teach them: at the first view, or upon a very little thought, they can discern the insignificancy, weakness, and mistake of what their teacher asserts. The youth of our day, by an early petulancy, and pretended liberty of thinking for themselves, dare reject at once, and that with a sort of scorn, all those sentiments and doctrines which their teachers have determined, perhaps, after long and repeated consideration, after years of mature study, careful observation, and much prudent experience.

IX. It is true teachers and masters are not infallible, nor are they always in the right; and it must be acknowledged, it is a matter of some difficulty for younger minds to maintain a just and solemn veneration for the authority and advice of their parents and the instructions of their tutors, and yet at the same time to secure to themselves a just freedom in their own thoughts. We are sometimes too ready to imbibe all their sentiments without examination, if we reverence and love them; or, on the other hand, if we take all freedom to contest their opinions, we are sometimes tempted to cast off that love and reverence to their persons which God and nature dictate. Youth is ever in danger of these two extremes.

X. But I think I may safely conclude thus: Though the authority of a teacher must not absolutely determine the judgment of his pupil, yet young and raw and unexperienced learners should pay all proper deference that can be to the instructions of their parents and teachers, short of absolute submission to their dictates. Yet still we must maintain this, that they should never receive any opinion into their assent, whether it be conformable or contrary to the tutor's mind, without sufficient evidence of it first given to their own reasoning powers.

CHAPTER VII.

OF LEARNING A LANGUAGE.

The first thing required in reading an author, or in hearing lectures of a tutor, is, that you well understand the language in which they write or speak. Living languages, or such as are the native tongue of any nation in the present age, are more easily learned and taught by a few rules and much familiar converse, joined to the reading some proper authors. The dead languages are such as cease to be spoken in any nation; and even these are more easy to be taught (as far as may be) in that method wherein living languages are best learned, *i. e.* partly by rule, and partly by rote or custom. And it may not be improper in this place to mention a very few directions for that purpose.

I. Begin with the most necessary and most general observations and rules which belong to that language, compiled in the form of a grammar; and these are but few in most languages. The regular declensions and variations of nouns and verbs should be early and thoroughly learned by heart, together with twenty or thirty of the plainest and most necessary rules of syntax.

But let it be observed that, in almost all languages, some of the very commonest nouns and verbs have many irregularities in them; such are the common auxiliary verbs—to be, and to have—to do, and to be done, &c. The comparatives and superlatives of the words—good, bad, great, small, much, little, &c.; and these should be learned among the first rules and variations, because they continually occur.

But as to other words, which are less frequent, let but few of the anomalies or irregularities of the tongue be taught among the general rules to young beginners. These will come in afterwards to be learned by advanced scholars in a way of notes on the rules, as in the Latin Grammar, called the Oxford Grammar, or in Ruddiman's notes on his Rudiments, &c. Or they may be learned by examples alone, when they do occur; or by a larger and more complete system of grammar, which descends to the more particular forms of speech; so the heteroclite nouns of the Latin tongue, which are taught in the school-book called Quæ Genus, should not be touched in the first learning of the rudiments of the tongue.

II. As the grammar by which you learn any tongue should be very short at first, so it must be written in a tongue with which you are well acquainted, and which is very familiar to you. Therefore I much prefer even the common English accidence (as it is called) to any grammar whatsoever written in Latin for this end. The English accidence has, doubtless, many faults; but those editions of it which were printed since the year 1728, under the correction of a learned professor, are the best; or the English rudiments of the Latin tongue, by that learned North Briton, Mr. Ruddiman, which are perhaps the most useful books of this kind I am acquainted with; especially because I would not depart too far from the ancient and common forms of teaching, which several good grammarians have done, to the great detriment of such lads as have been removed to other schools.

The tiresome and unreasonable method of learning the Latin tongue by a grammar, with Latin rules, would appear, even to those masters who teach it so, in its proper colours of absurdity and ridicule, if those very masters would attempt to learn the Chinese or Arabic tongue, by a grammar written in the Chinese or Arabic language. Mr. Clarke, of Hull, has said enough in a few pages of the preface to his new grammar, 1723, to make that practice appear very irrational and improper; though he has said it in so warm and angry a manner, that it has kindled Mr. Ruddiman to write against him, and to say what can be said to vindicate a practice, which, I think, is utterly indefensible.

III. At the same time when you begin the rules, begin also the practice. As, for instance, when you decline musa, musæ, read and construe the same day some easy Latin author, by the help of a tutor, or with some English translation: choose such a book whose style is simple, and the subject of discourse is very plain, obvious, and not hard to be understood: many little books have been composed with this view, as Corderius's Colloquies, some of Erasmus's little writings, the sayings of the wise men of Greece, Cato's moral distiches, and the rest which are collected at the end of Mr. Ruddiman's English Grammar; or the Latin Testament, of Castellio's translation, which is accounted the purest Latin, &c. These are very proper upon this occasion, together with Æsop's and Phædrus's Fables, and little stories, and the common and daily affairs of domestic life, written in the Latin tongue. But let the higher poets, and orators, and historians, and other writers whose language is more laboured, and whose sense is more remote from common life, be rather kept out of sight till there be some proficiency made in the language.

It is strange that masters should teach children so early Tully's Epistles or Orations, or the poems of Ovid or Virgil, whose sense is often difficult to find because of the great transposition of the words; and when they have found the grammatical sense, they have very little use of it, because they have scarce any notion of the ideas and design of the writer, it being so remote from the knowledge of a child: whereas little common stories and colloquies, and the rules of a child's behaviour, and such obvious subjects, will much better assist the memory of the words by their acquaintance with the things.

IV. Here it may be useful also to appoint the learner to get by heart the more common and useful words, both nouns and adjectives, pronouns and verbs, out of some well formed and judicious vocabulary. This will furnish him with names for the most familiar ideas.

V. As soon as ever the learner is capable, let the tutor converse with him in the tongue which is to be learned, if it be a living language, or if it be Latin, which is the living language of the learned world: thus he will acquaint himself with it a little by rote, as well as by rule, and by living practice, as well as by reading the writings of the dead. For if a child of two years old by this method learns to speak his mother tongue, I am sure the same method will greatly assist and facilitate the learning of any other language to those who are older.

VI. Let the chief lessons, and the chief exercises of schools, v. c. where Latin is learned (at least for the first year or more,) be the nouns, verbs, and general rules of syntax, together with a mere translation out of some Latin author into English; and let scholars be employed and examined by their teacher daily in reducing the words to their original or theme, to the first case of nouns or first tense of verbs, and giving an account of their formations and changes, their syntax and dependencies, which is called parsing. This is a most useful exercise to lead boys into a complete and thorough knowledge of what they are doing.

The English translations, which the learner has made, should be well corrected by the master, and then they should be translated back again for the next day's exercise by the child into Latin, while the Latin author is withheld from him; but he should have the Latin words given him in their first case and tense; and should never be left to seek them himself from a dictionary; and the nearer he translates it to the words of the author whence he derives his English, the more should the child be commended. Thus he will gain skill in two languages at once. I think Mr. Clarke has done good service to the public by his translations of Latin books for this end.

But let the foolish custom of employing every silly boy to make themes or declamations and verses upon moral subjects, in a strange tongue, before he understands common sense, even in his own language, be abandoned and cashiered for ever.

VII. As the learner improves, let him acquaint himself with the anomalous words, the irregular declensions of nouns and verbs, the more uncommon connexions of words in syntax, and the exceptions to the general rules of grammar. But let them all be reduced, as far as possible, to those several original and general rules, which he has learned, as the proper rank and place to which they belong.

VIII. While he is doing this, it may be proper for him to converse with authors which are a little more difficult, with historians, orators, poets, &c.; but let his tutor inform him of the Roman or Greek customs which occur therein. Let the lad then translate some parts of them into his mother tongue, or into some other well known language, and thence back again into the original language of the author. But let the verse be translated into prose, for poesy does not belong to grammar.

IX. By this time he will be able to acquaint himself with some of the special emphases of speech, and the peculiar idioms of the tongue. He should be taught also the special beauties and ornaments of the language; and this may be done partly by the help of authors, who have collected such idioms and cast them into an easy method, and partly by the judicious remarks which his instructor may make upon the authors which he reads, wheresoever such peculiarities of speech or special elegancies occur.

X. Though the labour of learning all the lessons by heart that are borrowed from poetical authors which they construe, is an unjust and unnecessary imposition upon the learner, yet he must take the pains to commit to memory the most necessary, if not all the common rules of grammar, with an example or two under each of them: and some of the select and most useful periods or sentences in the Latin or Greek author which he reads may be learned by heart, together with some of the choicer lessons out of their poets; and sometimes whole episodes out of heroic poems, &c. as well as whole odes among the lyrics, may deserve this honour.

XI. Let this be always carefully observed, that the learners perfectly understand the sense as well as the language of all those rules, lessons, or paragraphs, which they attempt to commit to memory. Let the teacher possess them of their true meaning, and then the labour will become easy and pleasant: whereas, to impose on a child to get by heart a long scroll of unknown phrases or words, without any ideas under them, is a piece of useless tyranny, a cruel imposition, and a practice fitter for a jackdaw or a parrot, than for any thing that wears the shape of a man.

XII. And here, I think, I have a fair occasion given me to consider that question which has been often debated in conversation, viz. whether the teaching of a school full of boys to learn Latin by the heathen poets, as Ovid in his Epistles, and the silly fables of his Metamorphoses, Horace, Juvenal, and Martial, in their impure odes, satires, and epigrams, &c. is so proper and agreeable a practice in a Christian country.

XIII. (1.) I grant the language and style of those men, who wrote in their own native tongue, must be more pure and perfect, in some nice elegancies and peculiarities, than modern writers of other nations who have imitated them; and it is owned also, that the beauties of their poësy may much excel; but in either of these things boys cannot be supposed to be much improved or injured by one or the other.

XIV. (2.) It shall be confessed too that modern poets, in every living language, have brought into their work so many words, epithets, phrases, and metaphors, from the heathen fables and stories of their gods and heroes, that in order to understand these modern writers, it is necessary to know a little of those ancient follies: but it may be answered, that a good dictionary, or such a book as the Pantheon or history of those Gentile deities, may give sufficient information of those stories, so far as they are necessary and useful to school boys.

XV. (3.) I will grant yet further, that lads who are designed to make great scholars or divines, may, by reading these heathen poets, be taught better to understand the writings of the ancient fathers against the heathen religion; and they learn here what ridiculous fooleries the Gentile nations believed as the articles of their faith, what wretched and foul idolatries they indulged and practised as duties of religion, for want of the divine revelation. But this perhaps may be learned as well either by the Pantheon, or some other collection at school; or after they have left the school, they may read what their own inclinations lead them to, and whatsoever of this kind may be really useful for them.

XVI. But the great question is, whether all these advantages which have been mentioned will compensate for the long months and years that are wasted among their incredible and trifling romances, their false and shameful stories of their gods and goddesses and their amours, and the lewd heroes and vicious poets of the heathen world. Can these idle and ridiculous tales be of any real and solid advantage in human life? Do they not too often defile the mind with vain, mischievous, and impure ideas? Do they not stick long upon the fancy, and leave an unhappy influence upon youth? Do they not tincture the imagination with folly and vice very early, and pervert it from all that is good and holy?

XVII. Upon the whole survey of things it is my opinion that, for almost all boys who learn this tongue, it would be much safer to be taught Latin poesy (as soon and as far as they can need it) from those excellent translations of David's Psalms, which are given us by Buchanan in the various measures of Horace; and the lower classes had better read Dr. Johnston's translation of these psalms, another elegant writer of the Scots nation, instead of Ovid's Epistles; for he has turned the same psalms, perhaps with greater elegance, into elegiac verse, whereof the learned W. Benson, esq. has lately published a noble edition, and I hear that these psalms are honoured with an increasing use in the schools of Holland and Scotland. A stanza or a couplet of these writers would now and then stick upon the minds of youth, and would furnish them infinitely better with pious and moral thoughts, and do something towards making them good men and Christians.

XVIII. A little book collected from the psalms of both these translators Buchanan and Johnston, and a few other Christian poets, would be of excellent use for schools to begin their instructions in Latin poesy; and I am well assured this would be richly sufficient for all those in lower rank, who never design a learned profession, and yet custom has foolishly bound them to learn that language.

But lest it should be thought hard to cast Horace and Virgil, Ovid and Juvenal entirely out of the schools, I add, if here and there a few lyric odes, or pieces of satires, or some episodes of heroic verse, with here and there an epigram of Martial, all which shall be clear from the stains of vice and impiety, and which may inspire the mind with noble sentiments, fire the fancy with bright and warm ideas, or teach lessons of morality and prudence, were chosen out of those ancient Roman writers for the use of the schools, and were collected and printed in one moderate volume, or two at the most, it would be abundantly sufficient provision out of the Roman poets for the instruction of boys in all that is necessary in that age of life.

Surely Juvenal himself would not have the face to vindicate the masters who teach boys his sixth satire, and many paragraphs of several others, when he himself has charged us,

> Nil dictu fœdum, visuque, hæc limina tangat
> Intra quæ puer est. *Sat.* 14.
>
> Suffer no lewdness, nor indecent speech,
> Th' apartment of the tender youth to reach.
> *Dryden.*

Thus far in answer to the foregoing question.

But I retire; for Mr. Clarke, of Hull, in his treatise on education, and Mr. Philips, preceptor to the Duke of Cumberland, have given more excellent directions for learning Latin.

XIX. When a language is learned, if it be of any use at all, it is a pity it should be forgotten again. It is proper, therefore, to take all just opportunities to read something frequently in that language, when other necessary and important studies will give you leave. As in learning any tongue, dictionaries which contain words and phrases should always be at hand, so they should be ever kept within reach by persons who would remember a tongue which they have learned. Nor should we at any time content ourselves with a doubtful guess at the sense or meaning of any words which occur, but consult the dictionary, which may give us certain information, and thus secure us from mistake. It is mere sloth which makes us content ourselves with uncertain guesses; and indeed this is neither safe nor useful for persons who would learn any language or science, or have a desire to retain what they have acquired.

XX. When you have learned one or many languages ever so perfectly, take heed of priding yourself in these acquisitions: they are but mere treasures of words, or instruments of true and solid knowledge, and whose chief design is to lead us into an acquaintance with things, or to enable us the more easily to convey those ideas or that knowledge to others. An acquaintance with the various tongues is nothing else but a relief against the mischief which the building of Babel introduced: and were I master of as many languages as were spoken at Babel, I should make but a poor pretence to true learning or knowledge, if I had not clear and distinct ideas, and useful notions in my head under the words which my tongue could pronounce. Yet so unhappy a thing is human nature, that this sort of knowledge of sounds and syllables is ready to puff up the mind with vanity, more than the most valuable and solid improvements of it. The pride of a grammarian, or a critic, generally exceeds that of a philosopher.

CHAPTER VIII.

OF INQUIRING INTO THE SENSE AND MEANING OF ANY WRITER OR SPEAKER, AND ESPECIALLY THE SENSE OF THE SACRED WRITINGS.

It is a great unhappiness that there is such an ambiguity in words and forms of speech, that the same sentence may be drawn into different significations: whereby it comes to pass, that it is difficult sometimes for the reader exactly to hit upon the ideas which the writer or speaker had in his mind. Some of the best rules to direct us herein are such as these:

I. Be well acquainted with the tongue itself, or language, wherein the author's mind is expressed. Learn not only the true meaning of each word, but the sense which those words obtain when placed in such a particular situation and order. Acquaint yourself with the peculiar power and emphasis of the several modes of speech, and the various idioms of the tongue. The secondary ideas which custom has superadded to many words should also be known, as well as the particular and primary meaning of them, if we would understand any writer. See Logic, part I. cap. 4. § 3.

II. Consider the signification of those words and phrases, more especially in the same nation, or near the same age in which that writer lived, and in what sense they are used by authors of the same nation, opinion, sect, party, &c.

Upon this account we may learn to interpret several phrases of the New Testament, out of that version of the Hebrew Bible into Greek, which is called the Septuagint; for though that version be very imperfect and defective in many things, yet it seems to me evident that the holy writers of the New Testament made use of that version many times in their citation of texts out of the Bible.

III. Compare the words and phrases in one place of an author, with the same or kindred words and phrases used in other places of the same author, which are generally called parallel places; and as one expression explains another which is like it, so sometimes a contrary expression will explain its contrary.

Remember always that a writer best interprets himself; as we believe the Holy Spirit to be the supreme agent in the writings of the Old Testament and the New, he can best explain himself. Hence the theological rule arises, that scripture is the best interpreter of scripture; and therefore concordances, which show us parallel places, are of excellent use for interpretation.

IV. Consider the subject on which the author is treating, and by comparing other places where he treats of the same subject, you may learn his sense in the place which you are reading, though some of the terms which he uses in those two places may be very different.

And, on the other hand, if the author uses the same words where the subject of which he treats is not just the same, you cannot learn his sense by comparing those two places, though the mere words may seem to agree: for some authors, when they are treating of a quite different subject, may use perhaps the same words in a very different sense, as St. Paul does the words faith, and law, and righteousness.

V. Observe the scope and design of the writer; inquire into his aim and end in that book, or section, or paragraph, which will help to explain particular sentences: for we suppose a wise and judicious writer directs his expressions generally toward his designed end.

VI. When an author speaks of any subject occasionally, let his sense be explained by those places where he treats of it distinctly and professedly: where he speaks of any subject in mystical or metaphorical terms, explain them by other places where he treats of the same subject in terms that are plain and literal: where he speaks in an oratorical, affecting, or persuasive way, let this be explained by other places where he treats of the same theme in a doctrinal or instructive way: where the author speaks more strictly and particularly on any theme, it will explain the more loose and general expressions: where he treats more largely, it will explain the shorter hints and brief intimations; and wheresoever he writes more obscurely, search out some more perspicuous passages in the same writer, by which to determine the sense of that obscure language.

VII. Consider not only the person who is introduced speaking, but the persons to whom the speech is directed, the circumstances of time and place, the temper and spirit of the speaker, as well as the temper and spirit of the hearers: in order to interpret scripture well, there needs a good acquaintance with the Jewish customs, some knowledge of the ancient Roman and Greek times and manners, which sometimes strike a strange and surprising light upon passages which were before very obscure.

VIII. In particular propositions, the sense of an author may sometimes be known by the inferences which he draws from them; and all those senses may be excluded which will not allow of that inference.

Note. This rule indeed is not always certain, in reading and interpreting human authors, because they may mistake in drawing their inferences; but in explaining scripture it is a sure rule; for the sacred and inspired writers always make just inferences from their own propositions. Yet even in them, we must take heed we do not mistake an allusion for an inference, which is many times introduced almost in the same manner.

IX. If it be a matter of controversy, the true sense of the author is sometimes known by the objections that are brought against it. So we may be well assured, the apostle speaks against our "justification in the sight of God, by our own works of holiness," in the 3d, 4th, and 5th chapters of the epistle to the Romans, because of the objection brought against him in the beginning of the 6th chapter, viz. "What shall we say then? shall we continue in sin that grace may abound?" which objection could never have been raised, if he had been proving our justification by our own works of righteousness.

X. In matters of dispute, take heed of warping the sense of the writer to your own opinion, by any latent prejudices of self-love and party spirit. It is this reigning principle of prejudice and party, that has given such a variety of senses both to the sacred writers and others, which would never have come into the mind of the reader if he had not laboured under some such prepossessions.

XI. For the same reason take heed of the prejudices of passion, malice, envy, pride, or opposition to an author, whereby you may be easily tempted to put a false and invidious sense upon his words. Lay aside therefore a carping spirit, and read even an adversary with attention and diligence, with an honest design to find out his true meaning; do not snatch at little lapses and appearances of mistake, in opposition to his declared and avowed meaning; nor impute any sense or opinion to him which he denies to be his opinion, unless it be proved by the most plain and express language.

Lastly, remember that you treat every author, writer,

or speaker, just as you yourselves would be willing to be treated by others, who are searching out the meaning of what you write or speak; and maintain upon your spirit an awful sense of the presence of God, who is the judge of hearts, and will punish those who, by a base and dishonest turn of mind, wilfully pervert the meaning of the sacred writers, or even of common authors, under the influence of culpable prejudices. See more, Logic, part I. cap. 6, § 3, "Directions concerning the definitions of names."

CHAPTER IX.

RULES OF IMPROVEMENT BY CONVERSATION.

I. If we would improve our minds by conversation, it is a great happiness to be acquainted with persons wiser than ourselves. It is a piece of useful advice therefore to get the favour of their conversation frequently, as far as circumstances will allow: and if they happen to be a little reserved, use all obliging methods to draw out of them what may increase your own knowledge.

II. Whatsoever company you are in, waste not the time in trifle and impertinence. If you spend some hours amongst children, talk with them according to their capacity; mark the young buddings of infant reason; observe the different motions and distinct workings of the animal and the mind, as far as you can discern them; take notice by what degrees the little creature grows up to the use of his reasoning powers, and what early prejudices beset and endanger his understanding. By this means you will learn to address yourself to children for their benefit, and perhaps you may derive some useful philosophemes or theorems for your own entertainment.

III. If you happen to be in company with a merchant or a sailor, a farmer or a mechanic, a milk-maid or a spinster, lead them into a discourse of the matters of their own peculiar province or profession; for every one

7*

knows, or should know, their own business best. In this sense a common mechanic is wiser than the philosopher. By this means you may gain some improvement in knowledge from every one you meet.

IV. Confine not yourself always to one sort of company, or to persons of the same party or opinion, either in matters of learning, religion, or civil life, lest, if you should happen to be nursed up or educated in early mistake, you should be confirmed and established in the same mistake, by conversing only with persons of the same sentiments. A free and general conversation with men of very various countries and of different parties, opinions, and practices, so far as it may be done safely, is of excellent use to undeceive us in many wrong judgments which we may have framed, and to lead us into juster thoughts. It is said, when the king of Siam, near China, first conversed with some European merchants, who sought the favour of trading on his coast, he inquired of them some of the common appearances of summer and winter in their country; and when they told him of water growing so hard in their rivers, that men and horses and laden carriages passed over it, and that rain sometimes fell down as white and light as feathers, and sometimes almost as hard as stones, he would not believe a syllable they said; for ice, snow, and hail, were names and things utterly unknown to him and to his subjects in that hot climate: he renounced all traffic with such shameful liars, and would not suffer them to trade with his people. See here the natural effects of gross ignorance.

Conversation with foreigners on various occasions, has a happy influence to enlarge our minds, and to set them free from many errors and gross prejudices we are ready to imbibe concerning them. Domicillus has never travelled five miles from his mother's chimney, and he imagines all outlandish men are papishes, and worship nothing but a cross. Tityrus, the shepherd, was bred up all his life in the country, and never saw Rome; he fancied it to be only a huge village, and was therefore infinitely surprised to find such palaces, such streets, such glittering treasures and gay magnificence as his first journey to the city showed him, and with wonder he confesses his folly and mistake.

So Virgil introduces a poor shepherd,

Urbem quam dicunt Romam, Melibœc, putavi
Stultus ego huic nostræ similem, quo sæpe solemus
Pastores ovium teneros depellere fœtus, &c.

Thus Englished:—

Fool that I was! I thought imperial Rome
Like market-towns, where once a week we come,
And thither drive our tender lambs from home.

Conversation would have given Tityrus a better notion of Rome, though he had never happened to travel thither.

V. In mixed company, among acquaintance and strangers, endeavour to learn something from all. Be swift to hear; but be cautious of your tongue, lest you betray your ignorance, and perhaps offend some of those who are present too. The scripture severely censures those who speak evil of the things they know not. Acquaint yourself therefore sometimes with persons and parties which are far distant from your common life and customs: this is a way whereby you may form a wiser opinion of men and things. Prove all things, and hold fast that which is good, is a divine rule, and it comes from the Father of light and truth. But young persons should practise it indeed with due limitation, and under the eye of their elders.

VI. Be not frighted nor provoked at opinions different from your own. Some persons are so confident they are in the right, that they will not come within the hearing of any notions but their own: they canton out to themselves a little province in the intellectual world, where they fancy the light shines; and all the rest is in darkness. They never venture into the ocean of knowledge, nor survey the riches of other minds, which are as solid and as useful, and perhaps are finer gold than what they ever possessed. Let not men imagine there is no certain truth but in the sciences which they study, and amongst that party in which they were born and educated.

VII. Believe that it is possible to learn something

from persons much below yourself. We are all short-sighted creatures; our views are also narrow and limited; we often see but one side of a matter, and do not extend our sight far and wide enough to reach every thing that has a connexion with the thing we talk of; we see but in part, and know but in part; therefore it is no wonder we form not right conclusions; because we do not survey the whole of any subject or argument. Even the proudest admirer of his own parts might find it useful to consult with others, though of inferior capacity and penetration. We have a different prospect of the same thing (if I may so speak) according to the different position of our understandings towards it: a weaker man may sometimes light on notions which have escaped a wiser, and which the wiser man might make a happy use of, if he would condescend to take notice of them.

VIII. It is of considerable advantage, when we are pursuing any difficult point of knowledge, to have a society of ingenious correspondents at hand, to whom we may propose it: for every man has something of a different genius and a various turn of mind, whereby the subject proposed will be shown in all its lights, it will be represented in all its forms, and every side of it be turned to view, that a juster judgment may be framed.

IX. To make conversation more valuable and useful, whether it be in a designed or accidental visit, among persons of the same or of different sexes, after the necessary salutations are finished, and the stream of common talk begins to hesitate, or runs flat and low, let some one person take a book which may be agreeable to the whole company, and by common consent let him read in it ten lines, or a paragraph or two, or a few pages, till some word or sentence gives an occasion for any of the company to offer a thought or two relating to that subject: interruption of the reader should be no blame; for conversation is the business: whether it be to confirm what the author says, or to improve it, to enlarge upon or to correct it, to object against it, or to ask any question that is akin to it; and let every one that please add their opinion and promote the conversation.

When the discourse sinks again, or diverts to trifles, let him that reads pursue the page, and read on further paragraphs or pages, till some occasion is given by a word or sentence for a new discourse to be started, and that with the utmost ease and freedom. Such a method as this would prevent the hours of a visit from running all to waste; and by this means, even among scholars, they would seldom find occasion for that too just and bitter reflection, "I have lost my time in the company of the learned."

By such a practice as this, young ladies may very honourably and agreeably improve their hours; while one applies herself to reading, the others employ their attention, even among the various artifices of the needle; but let all of them make their occasional remarks or inquiries. This will guard a great deal of that precious time from modish trifling, impertinence, or scandal, which might otherwise afford matter for painful repentance.

Observe this rule in general, whensoever it lies in your power to lead the conversation, let it be directed to some profitable point of knowledge or practice, so far as may be done with decency; and let not the discourse and the hours be suffered to run loose without aim or design: and when a subject is started, pass not hastily to another, before you have brought the present theme of discourse to some tolerable issue, or a joint consent to drop it.

X. Attend with sincere diligence, while any one of the company is declaring his sense of the question proposed: hear the argument with patience, though it differ ever so much from your sentiments, for you yourself are very desirous to be heard with patience by others who differ from you. Let not your thoughts be active and busy all the while to find out something to contradict, and by what means to oppose the speaker, especially in matters which are not brought to an issue. This is a frequent and unhappy temper and practice. You should rather be intent and solicitous to take up the mind and meaning of the speaker, zealous to seize and approve all that is true in his discourse; nor yet should you want courage to oppose where it is necessary; but let your modesty and patience, and a friendly temper, be as conspicuous as your zeal.

XI. When a man speaks with much freedom and ease, and gives his opinion in the plainest language of common sense, do not presently imagine you shall gain nothing by his company. Sometimes you will find a person who, in his conversation or his writings, delivers his thoughts in so plain, so easy, so familiar, and perspicuous a manner, that you both understand and assent to every thing he saith, as fast as you read or hear it: hereupon some hearers have been ready to conclude in haste, Surely this man saith none but common things; I knew as much before, or I would have said all this myself. This is a frequent mistake. Pellucido was a very great genius; when he spoke in the senate, he was wont to convey his ideas in so simple and happy a manner as to instruct and convince every hearer, and to enforce the conviction through the whole illustrious assembly; and that with so much evidence, that you would have been ready to wonder, that every one who spoke had not said the same things: but Pellucido was the only man that could do it; the only speaker who had attained this art and honour. Such is the writer of whom Horace would say,

> . . . . Ut sibi quivis
> Speret idem; sudet multum, frustraque laboret
> Ausus idem. *De Art. Poet.*

> Smooth be your style, and plain and natural,
> To strike the sons of Wapping or Whitehall.
> While others think this easy to attain,
> Let them but try, and with their utmost pain,
> They'll sweat and strive to imitate in vain.

XII. If any thing seem dark in the discourse of your companion, so that you have not a clear idea of what is spoken, endeavour to obtain a clearer conception of it by a decent manner of inquiry. Do not charge the speaker with obscurity, either in his sense or his words, but entreat his favour to relieve your own want of penetration, or to add an enlightening word or two, that you may take up his whole meaning.

If difficulties arise in your mind, and constrain your

dissent to the things spoken, represent what objection some persons would be ready to make against the sentiments of the speaker, without telling him you oppose. This manner of address carries something more modest and obliging in it, than to appear to raise objections of your own by way of contradiction to him that spoke.

XIII. When you are forced to differ from him who delivers his sense on any point, yet agree as far as you can, and represent how far you agree; and if there be any room for it, explain the words of the speaker in such a sense to which you can in general assent, and so agree with him, or at least, by a small addition or alteration of his sentiments, show your own sense of things. It is the practice and delight of a candid hearer, to make it appear how unwilling he is to differ from him that speaks. Let the speaker know that it is nothing but truth constrains you to oppose him; and let that difference be always expressed in few, and civil, and chosen words, such as may give the least offence.

And be careful always to take Solomon's rule with you, and let your correspondent fairly finish his speech before you reply; "for he that answereth a matter before he heareth it, it is folly and shame unto him." Prov. xviii. 13.

A little watchfulness, care, and practice in younger life, will render all these things more easy, familiar, and natural to you, and will grow into habit.

XIV. As you should carry about with you a constant and sincere sense of your own ignorance, so you should not be afraid nor ashamed to confess this ignorance, by taking all proper opportunities to ask and inquire for farther information; whether it be the meaning of a word, the nature of a thing, the reason of a proposition, the custom of a nation, &c. never remain in ignorance for want of asking.

Many a person had arrived at some considerable degree of knowledge, if he had not been full of self-conceit, and imagined that he had known enough already, or else was ashamed to let others know that he was unacquainted with it. God and man are ready to teach the meek, the humble, and the ignorant; but he that fancies himself to know any particular subject well, or that will not venture to ask a question about it, such a one will not put himself into the way of improvement by inquiry and diligence. A fool may be "wiser in his own conceit than ten men who can render a reason;" and such a one is very likely to be an everlasting fool; and perhaps also it is a silly shame renders his folly incurable.

> Stultorum incurata pudor malus ulcera celat.
>
> *Hor. Epist.* 16. *Lib.* j.

In English thus:

> If fools have ulcers, and their pride conceal them,
> They must have ulcers still, for none can heal them.

XV. Be not too forward, especially in the younger part of life, to determine any question in company with an infallible and peremptory sentence, nor speak with assuming airs, and with a decisive tone of voice. A young man, in the presence of his elders, should rather hear and attend, and weigh the arguments which are brought for the proof or refutation of any doubtful proposition: and when it is your turn to speak, propose your thoughts rather in the way of inquiry. By this means your mind will be kept in a fitter temper to receive truth, and you will be more ready to correct and improve your own sentiments, where you have not been too positive in affirming them. But if you have magisterially decided the point, you will find a secret unwillingness to retract, though you should feel an inward conviction that you were in the wrong.

XVI. It is granted, indeed, that a season may happen, when some bold pretender to science may assume haughty and positive airs, to assert and vindicate a gross and dangerous error, or to renounce and vilify some very important truth: and if he has a popular talent of talking, and there be no remonstrance made against him, the company may be tempted too easily to give their assent to the imprudence and infallibility of the presumer. They may imagine a proposition so much vilified can never be true, and that a doctrine which is so boldly censured and renounced can never be defended.

Weak minds are too ready to persuade themselves, that a man would never talk with so much assurance unless he were certainly in the right, and could well maintain and prove what he said. By this means truth itself is in danger of being betrayed or lost, if there be no opposition made to such a pretending talker.

Now in such a case, even a wise and a modest man may assume airs too, and repel insolence with its own weapons. There is a time, as Solomon, the wisest of men, teaches us, "when a fool should be answered according to his folly, lest he be wise in his own conceit," and lest others too easily yield up their faith and reason to his imperious dictates. Courage and positivity are never more necessary than on such an occasion. But it is good to join some argument with them of real and convincing force, and let it be strongly pronounced too.

When such a resistance is made, you shall find some of those bold talkers will draw in their horns, when their fierce and feeble pushes against truth and reason are repelled with pushing and confidence. It is pity indeed that truth should ever need such sort of defences; but we know that a triumphant assurance hath sometimes supported gross falsehoods, and a whole company have been captivated to error by this means, till some man with equal assurance has rescued them. It is pity that any momentous point of doctrine should happen to fall under such reproaches, and require such a mode of vindication: though if I happen to hear it, I ought not to turn my back and to sneak off in silence, and leave the truth to lie baffled, bleeding, and slain. Yet I must confess, I should be glad to have no occasion ever given me to fight with any man at this sort of weapons, even though I should be so happy as to silence his insolence and to obtain an evident victory.

XVII. Be not fond of disputing every thing pro and con, nor indulge yourself to show your talent of attacking and defending. A logic which teaches nothing else is little worth. This temper and practice will lead you just so far out of the way of knowledge, and divert your honest inquiry after the truth which is debated or sought. In set disputes, every little straw is often laid hold on to support our own cause; every thing that can be drawn in any way to give colour to our argument is advanced, and that perhaps with vanity and ostentation. This puts the mind out of a proper posture to seek and receive the truth.

XVIII. Do not bring a warm party spirit into a free conversation which is designed for mutual improvement in the search of truth. Take heed of allowing yourself in those self-satisfied assurances which keep the doors of the understanding barred fast against the admission of any new sentiments. Let your soul be ever ready to hearken to farther discoveries, from a constant and ruling consciousness of our present fallible and imperfect state; and make it appear to your friends, that it is no hard task to you to learn and pronounce those little words, "I was mistaken," how hard soever it be for the bulk of mankind to pronounce them.

XIX. As you may sometimes raise inquiries for your own instruction and improvement, and draw out the learning, wisdom, and fine sentiments of your friends, who perhaps may be too reserved or modest; so, at other times, if you perceive a person unskilful in the matter of debate, you may, by questions aptly proposed in the Socratic method, lead him into a clearer knowledge of the subject: then you become his instructor, in such a manner as may not appear to make yourself his superior.

XX. Take heed of affecting always to shine in company above the rest, and to display the riches of your own understanding or your oratory, as though you would render yourself admirable to all that are present. This is seldom well taken in polite company; much less should you use such forms of speech as should insinuate the ignorance or dulness of those with whom you converse.

XXI. Though you should not affect to flourish in a copious harangue and a diffusive style in company, yet neither should you rudely interrupt and reproach him that happens to use it: but when he has done speaking, reduce his sentiments into a more contracted form; not with a show of correcting, but as one who is doubtful whether you hit upon his true sense or no. Thus matters may be brought more easily from a wild confusion into a single point, questions may be sooner determined, and difficulties more easily removed.

XXII. Be not so ready to charge ignorance, prejudice, and mistake upon others, as you are to suspect yourself of it: and in order to show how free you are from prejudices, learn to bear contradiction with patience; let it be easy to you to hear your own opinion strongly opposed, especially in matters which are doubtful and disputable, amongst men of sobriety and virtue. Give a patient hearing to arguments on all sides; otherwise, you give the company occasion to suspect that it is not the evidence of truth has led you into this opinion, but some lazy anticipation of judgment, some beloved presumption, some long and rash possession of a party scheme, in which you desire to rest undisturbed. If your assent has been established upon just and sufficient grounds, why should you be afraid to let the truth be put to the trial of argument?

XXIII. Banish utterly out of all conversation, and especially out of all learned and intellectual conference, every thing that tends to provoke passion or raise a fire in the blood. Let no sharp language, no noisy exclamations, no sarcasms, or biting jests be heard among you; no perverse or invidious consequences be drawn from each other's opinions, and imputed to the person: let there be no wilful perversion of another's meaning; no sudden seizure of a lapsed syllable to play upon it, nor any abused construction of an innocent mistake: suffer not your tongue to insult a modest opponent that beigns to yield; let there be no crowing and triumph, even where there is evident victory on your side. All these things are enemies to friendship, and the ruin of free conversation. The impartial search of truth requires all calmness and serenity, all temper and candour; mutual instructions can never be attained in the midst of passion, pride, and clamour, unless we suppose, in the midst of such a scene, there is a loud and penetrating lecture read by both sides, on the folly and shameful infirmities of human nature.

XXIV. Whensoever, therefore, any unhappy word shall arise in company, that might give you a reasonable disgust, quash the rising resentment, be it ever so just, and command your soul and your tongue into silence, lest you cancel the hopes of all improvement for that hour, and transform the learned conversation into the mean and vulgar form of reproaches and railing. The man who began to break the peace in such a society, will fall under the shame and conviction of such a silent reproof, if he has any thing ingenuous about him. If this should not be sufficient, let a grave admonition, or a soft and gentle turn of wit, with an air of pleasantry, give the warm disputer an occasion to stop the progress of his indecent fire, if not to retract the indecency and quench the flame.

XXV. Inure yourself to a candid and obliging manner in your conversation, and acquire the art of pleasing address, even when you teach, as well as when you learn; and when you oppose, as well as when you assert or prove. This degree of politeness is not to be attained without a diligent attention to such kind of directions as are here laid down, and a frequent exercise and practice of them.

XXVI. If you would know what sort of companions you should select for the cultivation and advantage of the mind, the general rule is, choose such as, by their brightness of parts, and their diligence in study, or by their superior advancement in learning, or peculiar excellency in any art, science, or accomplishment, divine or human, may be capable of administering to your improvement; and be sure to maintain and keep some due regard to their moral character always, lest while you wander in quest of intellectual gain, you fall into the contagion of irreligion and vice. No wise man can venture into a house infected with the plague, in order to see the finest collections of any virtuoso in Europe.

XXVII. Nor is it every sober person of your acquaintance, no, nor every man of bright parts, or rich in learning, that is fit to engage in free conversation for the inquiry after truth. Let a person have ever so illustrious talents, yet he is not a proper associate for such a purpose, if he lie under any of the following infirmities:

1. If he be exceedingly reserved, and hath either

no inclination to discourse, or no tolerable capacity of speech and language for the communication of his sentiments.

2. If he be haughty and proud of his knowledge, imperious in his airs, and is always fond of imposing his sentiments on all the company.

3. If he be positive and dogmatical in his own opinions, and will dispute to the end; if he will resist the brightest evidence of truth, rather than suffer himself to be overcome, or yield to the plainest and strongest reasonings.

4. If he be one who always affects to outshine all the company, and delights to hear himself talk and flourish upon a subject, and make long harangues, while the rest must be all silent and attentive.

5. If he be a person of whiffling and unsteady turn of mind, who cannot keep close to a point of controversy, but wanders from it perpetually, and is always solicitous to say something, whether it be pertinent to the question or no.

6. If he be fretful and peevish, and given to resentment upon all occasions: if he knows not how to bear contradiction, or is ready to take things in a wrong sense; if he is swift to feel a supposed offence, or to imagine himself affronted, and then break out into a sudden passion, or retain silent and sullen wrath.

7. If he affect wit on all occasions, and is full of his conceits and puns, quirks or quibbles, jests and repartees; these may agreeably entertain and animate an hour of mirth, but they have no place in the search after truth.

8. If he carry always about him a sort of craft, and cunning, and disguise, and act rather like a spy than a friend. Have a care of such a one as will make an ill use of freedom in conversation, and immediately charge heresy upon you, when you happen to differ from those sentiments which authority or custom has established.

In short, you should avoid the man, in such select conversation, who practises any thing that is unbecoming the character of a sincere, free, and open searcher after truth.

Now, though you may pay all the relative duties of

life to persons of these unhappy qualifications, and treat them with decency and love, so far as religion and humanity oblige you, yet take care of entering into a free debate on matters of truth or falsehood in their company, and especially about the principles of religion. I confess, if a person of such a temper happens to judge and talk well on such a subject, you may hear him with attention, and derive what profit you can from his discourse; but he is by no means to be chosen for a free conference in matters of learning and knowledge.

XXVIII. While I would persuade you to beware of such persons, and abstain from too much freedom of discourse amongst them, it is very natural to infer that you should watch against the working of these evil qualities in your own breast, if you happen to be tainted with any of them yourself. Men of learning and ingenuity will justly avoid your acquaintance, when they find such an unhappy and unsocial temper prevailing in you.

XXIX. To conclude, when you retire from company, then converse with yourself in solitude, and inquire what you have learned for the improvement of your understanding, or for the rectifying your inclinations, for the increase of your virtues, or the ameliorating your conduct and behaviour in any future parts of life. If you have seen some of your company candid, modest, humble in their manner, wise and sagacious, just and pious in their sentiments, polite and graceful, as well as clear and strong in their expression, and universally acceptable and lovely in their behaviour, endeavour to impress the idea of all these upon your memory, and treasure them up for your imitation.

XXX. If the laws of reason, decency, and civility, have not been well observed amongst your associates, take notice of those defects for your own improvement: and from every occurrence of this kind remark something to imitate or to avoid, in elegant, polite, and useful conversation. Perhaps you will find that some persons present have really displeased the company, by an excessive and too visible an affectation to please, *i. e.* by giving loose to servile flattery or promiscuous praise;

while others were as ready to oppose and contradict every thing that was said. Some have deserved just censure for a morose and affected taciturnity; and others have been anxious and careful lest their silence should be interpreted a want of sense, and therefore they have ventured to make speeches, though they had nothing to say which was worth hearing. Perhaps you will observe that one was ingenious in his thoughts, and bright in his language, but he was so topful of himself that he let it spill on all the company; that he spoke well indeed, but that he spoke too long, and did not allow equal liberty or time to his associates. You will remark that another was full charged, to let out his words before his friend had done speaking, or impatient of the least opposition to any thing he said. You will remember that some persons have talked at large, and with great confidence, of things which they understood not, and others counted every thing tedious and intolerable that was spoken upon subjects out of their sphere, and they would fain confine the conference entirely within the limits of their own narrow knowledge and study. The errors of conversation are almost infinite.

XXXI. By a review of such irregularities as these, you may learn to avoid those follies and pieces of ill conduct which spoil good conversation, or make it less agreeable and less useful; and by degrees you will acquire that delightful and easy manner of address and behaviour in all useful correspondencies, which may render your company every where desired and beloved; and at the same time, among the best of your companions, you may make the highest improvement, in your own intellectual acquisitions, that the discourse of mortal creatures will allow, under all our disadvantages in this sorry state of mortality. But there is a day coming when we shall be seized away from this lower class in the school of knowledge, where we labour under the many dangers and darknesses, the errors and the incumbrances of flesh and blood, and our conversation shall be with angels and more illuminated spirits, in the upper regions of the universe.

CHAPTER X.

OF DISPUTES IN GENERAL.

I. Under the general head of conversation for the improvement of the mind, we may rank the practice of disputing; that is, when two or more persons appear to maintain different sentiments, and defend their own or oppose the other's opinion, in alternate discourse, by some methods of argument.

II. As these disputes often arise in good earnest, where the two contenders do really believe the different propositions which they support; so sometimes they are appointed as mere trials of skill in academies or schools by the students; sometimes they are practised, and that with apparent fervour, in courts of judicature by lawyers, in order to gain the fees of their different clients, while both sides perhaps are really of the same sentiment with regard to the cause which is tried.

III. In common conversation, disputes are often managed without any forms of regularity or order, and they turn to good or evil purposes, chiefly according to the temper of the disputants. They may sometimes be successful to search out truth, sometimes effectual to maintain truth, and convince the mistaken; but at other times a dispute is a mere scene of battle in order to victory and vain triumph.

IV. There are some few general rules which should be observed in all debates whatsoever, if we would find out truth by them, or convince a friend of his error, even though they be not managed according to any settled forms of disputation; and as there are almost as many opinions and judgments of things as there are persons, so when several persons happen to meet and confer together upon any subject, they are ready to declare their different sentiments, and support them by such reasonings as they are capable of. This is called debating or disputing, as is above described.

V When persons begin a debate, they should always take care that they are agreed in some general principles or propositions, which either more nearly or remotely affect the question in hand; for otherwise they have no foundation or hope of convincing each other; they must have some common ground to stand upon, while they maintain the contest.

When they find they agree in some remote propositions, then let them search farther, and inquire how near they approach to each other's sentiments, and whatsoever propositions they agree in, let these lay a foundation for the mutual hope of conviction. Hereby you will be prevented from running at every turn to some original and remote propositions and axioms, which practice both entangles and prolongs dispute. As for instance, if there was a debate proposed betwixt a protestant and a papist, whether there be such a place as Purgatory? Let them remember that they both agree in this point, that Christ has made satisfaction or atonement for sin, and upon this ground let them both stand, while they search out the controverted doctrine of Purgatory by way of conference or debate.

VI. The question should be cleared from all doubtful terms and needless additions; and all things that belong to the question should be expressed in plain and intelligible language. This is so necessary a thing, that without it men will be exposed to such sort of ridiculous contests as was found one day between the two unlearned combatants Sartor and Sutor, who assaulted and defended the doctrine of transubstantiation with much zeal and violence: but Latino happening to come into their company, and inquiring the subject of their dispute, asked each of them what he meant by that long hard word transubstantiation. Sutor readily informed him that he understood—bowing at the name of Jesus: but Sartor assured him that he meant nothing but bowing at the high altar. "No wonder, then," said Latino, "that you cannot agree when you neither understand one another, nor the word about which you contend." I think the whole family of the Sartors and Sutors would be wiser if they avoided such kind of debates till they understood the terms better. But alas! even their wives carry on such conferences: the other day one was heard in the street explaining to her less learned neighbour the meaning of metaphysical science; and she assured her, that as physics were medicines for the body, so metaphysics were physics for the soul; upon this they went on to dispute the point—how far the divine excelled the doctor.

> Auditum admissi risum teneatis, amici?
> Ridentem dicere verum quid vetat?
>
> Can it be faulty to repeat
> A dialogue that walk'd the street?
> Or can my gravest friends forbear
> A laugh, when such disputes they hear?

VII. And not only the sense and meaning of the words used in the question should be settled and adjusted between the disputants, but the precise point of inquiry should be distinctly fixed; the question in debate should be limited precisely to its special extent, or declared to be taken in its more general sense. As for instance, if two men are contending whether civil government be of divine right or not: here it must be observed, the question is not whether monarchy in one man, or a republic in multitudes of the people, or an aristocracy in a few of the chief, is appointed of God as necessary; but whether civil government in its most general sense, or in any form whatsoever, is derived from the will and appointment of God. Again, the point of inquiry should be limited further. Thus the question is, not whether government comes from the will of God by the light of divine revelation, for that is granted; but whether it is derived from the will of God by the light of reason too. This sort of specification or limitation of the question hinders and prevents the disputants from wandering away from the precise point of inquiry.

It is this trifling humour or dishonest artifice of changing the question, and wandering away from the first point of debate, which gives endless length to disputes, and causes both disputants to part without any satisfaction. And one chief occasion of it is this: when one of the combatants feels his cause run low and fail, and is just ready to be confuted and demolished, he is tempted to step aside to avoid the blow, and betakes him to a different question: thus, if his adversary be not well aware of him, he begins to entrench himself in a new fastness, and holds out the siege with a new artillery of thoughts and words. It is the pride of man which is the spring of this evil, and an unwillingness to yield up their own opinions even to be overcome by truth itself.

VIII. Keep this always therefore upon your mind as an everlasting rule of conduct in your debates to find out truth, that a resolute design, or even a warm affectation of victory, is the bane of all real improvement, and an effectual bar against the admission of the truth which you profess to seek. This works with a secret, but a powerful and mischievous influence in every dispute, unless we are much upon our guard. It appears in frequent conversation; every age, every sex, and each party of mankind, are so fond of being in the right, that they know not how to renounce this unhappy prejudice, this vain love of victory.

When truth with bright evidence is ready to break in upon a disputant, and to overcome his objections and mistakes, how swift and ready is the mind to engage wit and fancy, craft and subtlety, to cloud and perplex and puzzle the truth, if possible! How eager is he to throw in some impertinent question to divert from the main subject! How swift to take hold of some occasional word, thereby to lead the discourse off from the point in hand! So much afraid is human nature of parting with its errors, and being overcome by truth. Just thus a hunted hare calls up all the shifts that nature hath taught her: she treads back her mazes, crosses and confounds her former track, and uses all possible methods to divert the scent, when she is in danger of being seized and taken. Let puss practise what nature teaches; but would one imagine that any rational being should take such pains to avoid truth, and to escape the improvement of its understanding?

IX. When you come to a dispute in order to find out truth, do not presume that you are certainly possessed of it beforehand. Enter the debate with a sincere design of yielding to reason, on which side soever it appears. Use no subtle arts to cloud and entangle the question; hide not yourself in doubtful words and phrases; do not affect little shifts and subterfuges to avoid the force of an argument; take a generous pleasure to espy the first rising beams of truth, though it be on the side of your opponent; endeavour to remove the little obscurities that hang about it, and suffer and encourage it to break out into open and convincing light; that while your opponent perhaps may gain the better of your reasonings, yet you yourself may triumph over error; and I am sure that is a much more valuable acquisition and victory.

X. Watch narrowly in every dispute, that your opponent does not lead you unwarily to grant some principle of the proposition, which will bring with it a fatal consequence, and lead you insensibly into his sentiment, though it be far astray from the truth; and by this wrong step you will be, as it were, plunged into dangerous errors before you are aware. Polonides, in free conversation, led Incauto to agree with him in this plain proposition: That the blessed God has too much justice in any case to punish* any being who is in itself innocent: till he not only allowed it with an unthinking alacrity, but asserted it in most universal and unguarded terms. A little after, Polonides came in discourse to commend the virtues, the innocence, and the piety of our blessed Saviour; and thence inferred, it was impossible that God should ever punish so holy a person, who was never guilty of any crime: then Incauto espied the snare, and found himself robbed and defrauded of the great doctrine of the atonement by the death of Christ, upon which he had placed his immortal hopes according to the gospel. This taught him to bethink himself what a dangerous concession he had made in so universal a manner, that God would never punish any being who was innocent; and he saw it needful to recall his words, or to explain them better, by adding this restriction or limitation, viz. unless this innocent being were some way involved in another's sin, or stood as a voluntary surety for the guilty: by this limitation he secured the great and blessed doctrine of the sacrifice of Christ for the sins

* The word punish here signifies, to bring some natural evil upon a person on account of moral evil done.

of men, and learnt to be more cautious in his concessions for the time to come.

Two months ago Fatalio had almost tempted his friend Fidens to leave off prayer, and to abandon his dependence on the providence of God in the common affairs of life, by obtaining of him a concession of the like kind. Is it not evident to reason, says Fatalio, that God's immense scheme of transactions in the universe was contrived and determined long before you and I were born? Can you imagine, my dear Fidens, that the blessed God changes his original contrivances, and makes new interruptions in the course of them, so often as you and I want his aid, to prevent the little accidents of life, or to guard us from them? Can you suffer yourself to be persuaded that the great Creator of this world takes care to support a bridge which was quite rotten, and to make it stand firm a few minutes longer till you had rode over it? Or, will he uphold a falling tower, while we two were passing by it, that such worms as you and I are might escape the ruin?

But you say, you prayed for his protection in the morning, and he certainly hears prayer. I grant he hears it: but are you so fond and weak, said he, as to suppose that the universal Lord of all had such a regard to a word or two of your breath, as to make alterations in his own eternal scheme upon that account. Nor is there any other way whereby his providence can preserve you in answer to prayer, but by creating such perpetual interruptions and changes in his own conduct, according to your daily behaviour.

I acknowledge, says Fidens, there is no other way to secure the doctrine of divine providence in all these common affairs; and therefore I begin to doubt whether God does or ever will exert himself so particularly in our little concerns.

Have a care, good Fidens, that you yield not too far: take heed lest you have granted too much to Fatalio. Pray let me ask of you, could not the great God, who grasps and surveys all future and distant things in one single view, could not he from the beginning foresee your morning prayer for his protection, and appoint all second causes to concur for the support of that crazy bridge, or to make that old tower stand firm till you had escaped the danger? Or could not he cause all the mediums to work so as to make it fall before you came near it? Can he not appoint all his own transactions in the universe, and every event in the natural world, in a way of perfect correspondence with his own foreknowledge of all the events, actions, and appearances of the moral world in every part of it? Can he not direct every thing in nature, which is but his servant, to act in perfect agreement with his eternal prescience of our sins, or of our piety? And hereby all the glory of providence, and our necessary dependence upon it by faith and prayer, are as well secured, as if he interposed to alter his own scheme every moment.

Let me ask again; did not he in his own counsels or decrees appoint thunders and lightnings and earthquakes, to burn up and destroy Sodom and Gomorrah, and turn them into a dead sea, just at the time when the iniquities of those cities were raised to their supreme height? Did he not ordain the fountains of the deep to be broken up, and overwhelming rains to fall from heaven, just when a guilty world deserved to be drowned; while he took care of the security of righteous Noah, by an ark which should float upon that very deluge of waters? Thus he can punish the criminal when he pleases, and reward the devout worshipper in the proper season by his original and eternal schemes of appointment, as well as if he interposed every moment anew. Take heed, Fidens, that you be not tempted away, by such sophisms of Fatalio, to withhold prayer from God, and to renounce your faith in his providence.

Remember this short and plain caution of the subtle errors of men. Let a snake but once thrust in his head at some small unguarded fold of your garment, and he will insensibly and unavoidably wind his whole body into your bosom, and give you a pernicious wound.

XI. On the other hand, when you have found your opponent make any such concession as may turn to your real advantage in maintaining the truth, be wise and watchful to observe it, and make a happy improvement of it. Rhapsodus has taken a great deal of pains to detract from the honour of Christianity, by sly insinuations that the sacred writers are perpetually promoting virtue and piety by promises and threatenings; whereas neither the fear of future punishment, nor the hope of future reward, can possibly be called good affections, or such as are the acknowledged springs and sources of all actions truly good. He adds further, that this fear, or this hope, cannot consist in reality with virtue or goodness, if it either stands as essential to any moral performance or as a considerable motive to any good action; and thus he would fain lead Christians to be ashamed of the gospel of Christ, because of its future and eternal promises and threatenings, as being inconsistent with his notion of virtue; for he supposes virtue should be so beloved and practised for the sake of its own beauty and loveliness, that all other motives arising from rewards or punishments, fear or hope, do really take away just so much from the very nature of virtue as their influence reaches to; and no part of those good practices are really valuable, but what arises from the mere love of virtue itself, without any regard to punishment or reward.

But observe, in two pages afterwards, he grants that —this principle of fear of future punishment, and hope of future reward, how mercenary and servile soever it may be accounted, is yet in many circumstances a great advantage, security, and support to virtue; especially where there is danger of the violence of rage or lust, or any counter-working passion to control and overcome the good affections of the mind.

Now the rule and the practice of Christianity, or the gospel, as it is closely connected with future rewards and punishments, may be well supported by this concession. Pray, Rhapsodus, tell me, if every man in this present life, by the violence of some counter-working passion, may not have his good affections to virtue controlled or overcome? May not, therefore, his eternal fears and hopes be a great advantage, security, and support to virtue in so dangerous a state and situation, as our journey through this world towards a better? And this is all that the defence of Christianity necessarily requires.

And yet further let me ask our rhapsodist, If you have nothing else, sir, but the beauty and excellency and loveliness of virtue to preach and flourish upon, before such sorry and degenerate creatures as the bulk of mankind are, and you have no future rewards or punishments with which to address their hopes and fears, how many of these vicious wretches will you ever reclaim from all their variety of profaneness, intemperance, and madness? How many have you ever actually reclaimed by this smooth soft method, and these fine words? What has all that reasoning and rhetoric done which have been displayed by your predecessors the heathen moralists, upon this excellency and beauty of virtue? What has it been able to do towards the reforming of a sinful world? Perhaps now and then a man of better natural mould has been a little refined, and perhaps also there may have been here and there a man restrained or recovered from injustice or knavery, from drunkenness and lewdness, and vile debaucheries, by this fair reasoning and philosophy: but have the passions of revenge and envy, of ambition and pride, and the inward secret vices of the mind been mortified merely by this philosophical language? Have any of these men been made new creatures, men of real piety and love to God?

Go dress up all the virtues of human nature in all the beauties of your oratory, and declaim aloud on the praise of social virtue, and the amiable qualities of goodness, till your heart or your lungs ache, among the looser herds of mankind, and you will ever find, as your heathen fathers have done before, that the wild passions and appetites of men are too violent to be restrained by such mild and silken language. You may as well build up a fence of straw and feathers to resist a cannon ball, or try to quench a flaming granado with a shell of fair water, as hope to succeed in these attempts. But an eternal heaven and an eternal hell carry divine force and power with them: this doctrine, from the mouth of Christian preachers, has begun the reformation of multitudes; this gospel has recovered thousands among the nations from iniquity and death. They have been awakened by these awful scenes to begin religion, and afterwards their virtue has improved itself into superior and more refined principles and habits by divine grace, and risen to high and eminent degrees, though not to a consummate state. The blessed God knows human nature much better than Rhapsodus doth, and has throughout his word appointed a more proper and more effectual method of address to it by the passions of hope and fear, by punishments and rewards.

If you read on four pages further in these writings, you will find the author makes another concession. He allows that the master of a family, using proper rewards and gentle punishments towards his children, teaches them goodness, and by this help instructs them in a virtue which they afterwards practise upon other grounds, and without thinking of a penalty or a bribe; and this, says he, is what we call a liberal education and a liberal service.

This new concession of that author may also be very happily improved in favour of Christianity.—What are the best of men in this life? They are by no means perfect in virtue: we are all but children here under the great master of the family, and he is pleased, by hopes and fears, by mercies and corrections, to instruct us in virtue, and to conduct us onward towards the sublimer and more perfect practice of it in the future world, where it shall be performed, as in his own language, perhaps—without thinking of penalties or bribes. And since he hath allowed that this conduct may be called a liberal education, and a liberal service, let Christianity then be indulged the title of a liberal education also, and it is admirably fitted for such frail and sinful creatures, while they are training up towards the sublimer virtues of the heavenly state.

XII. When you are engaged in a dispute with a person of very different principles from yourself, and you cannot find any ready way to prevail with him to embrace the truth by principles which you both freely acknowledge, you may fairly make use of his own principles to show him his mistake, and thus convince or silence him from his own concessions.

If your opponent should be a Stoic philosopher or a Jew, you may pursue your argument in defence of some Christian doctrine or duty against such a disputant, by axioms or laws borrowed either from Zeno or Moses. And though you do not enter into the inquiry how many of the laws of Moses are abrogated, or whether Zeno was right or wrong in his philosophy, yet if from the principles and concessions of your opponent, you can support your argument for the gospel of Christ, this has been always counted a fair treatment of an adversary, and it is called *argumentum ad hominem*, or *ratio ex concessis*. St. Paul sometimes makes use of this sort of disputation, when he talks with Jews or heathen philosophers; and at last he silences if not convinces them: which is sometimes necessary to be done against an obstinate and clamorous adversary, that just honour might be paid to truths which he knew were divine, and that the only true doctrine of salvatoin might be confirmed and propagated among sinful and dying men.

XIII. Yet great care must be taken, lest your debates break in upon your passions, and awaken them to take part in the controversy. When the opponent pushes hard, and gives just and mortal wounds to our own opinons, our passions are very apt to feel the strokes, and to rise in resentment and defence. Self is so mingled with the sentiments which we have chosen, and has such a tender feeling of all the opposition which is made to them, that personal brawls are very ready to come in as seconds, to succeed and finish the dispute of opinions. Then noise, and clamour, and folly, appear in all their shapes, and chase reason and truth out of sight.

How unhappy is the case of frail and wretched mankind in this dark or dusky state of strong passion and glimmering reason! How ready are we, when our passions are engaged in the dispute, to consider more what loads of nonsense and reproach we can lay upon our opponent, than what reason and truth require in the controversy itself! Dismal are the consequences mankind are too often involved in by this evil principle; it is this common and dangerous practice that carries the heart aside from all that is fair and honest in our search after truth, or the propagation of it in the world. One would wish from one's very soul that none of the Christian fathers had been guilty of such follies as these.

But St. Jerome fairly confesses this evil principle, in his apology for himself to Pammachius, "that he had not so much regarded what was exactly to be spoken in the controversy he had in hand, as what was fit to lay a load on Jovinian." And, indeed, I fear this was the vile custom of many of the writers even in the church affairs of those times. But it will be a double scandal upon us, in our more enlightened age, if we will allow ourselves in a conduct so criminal and dishonest. Happy souls, who keep such a sacred dominion over their inferior and animal powers, and all the influences of pride and secular interest, that the sensitive tumults, or these vicious influences, never rise to disturb the superior and better operations of the reasoning mind!

XIV. These general directions are necessary, or at least useful, in all debates whatsoever, whether they arise in occasional conversation, or are appointed at any certain time or place: whether they are managed with or without any formal rules to govern them. But there are three sorts of disputation in which there are some forms and orders observed, and which are distinguished by these three names, viz. Socratic, Forensic, and Academic, *i. e.* the disputes of the schools.

Concerning each of these it may not be improper to discourse a little, and give a few particular directions or remarks about them.

CHAPTER XI.

THE SOCRATICAL WAY OF DISPUTATION.

I. This method of dispute derives its name from Socrates, by whom it was practised, and by other philosophers in his age, long before Aristotle invented the particular forms of syllogism in mood and figure, which are now used in scholastic disputations.

II. The Socratical way is managed by questions and answers in such a manner as this, viz. If I would lead a person into the belief of a heaven or hell, or a future state of rewards and punishments, I might begin in some such manner of inquiry, and suppose the most obvious and easy answers.

Q. Does not God govern the world?

A. Surely he that made it governs it.

Q. Is not God both a good and a righteous governor?

A. Both these characters doubtless belong to him.

Q. What is the true notion of a good and righteous governor?

A. That he punishes the wicked and rewards the good.

Q. Are the good always rewarded in this life?

A. No surely; for many virtuous men are miserable here, and greatly afflicted.

Q. Are the wicked always punished in this life?

A. No certainly; for many of them live without sorrow, and some of the vilest of men are often raised to great riches and honour.

Q. Wherein then doth God make it appear that he is good and righteous?

A. I own there is but little appearance of it on earth.

Q. Will there not be a time, then, when the tables shall be turned, and the scene of things changed, since God governs mankind righteously?

A. Doubtless there must be a proper time, wherein God will make that goodness and that righteousness to appear.

Q. If this be not before their death, how can it be done?

A. I can think of no other way but by supposing man to have some existence after this life.

Q. Are you not convinced then that there must be a state of reward and punishment after death?

A. Yes surely; I now see plainly, that the goodness

and righteousness of God, as governor of the world, necessarily require it.

III. Now the advantages of this method are very considerable.

1. It represents the form of a dialogue or common conversation, which is a much more easy, more pleasant, and a more sprightly way of instruction, and more fit to excite the attention, and sharpen the penetration of the learner, than solitary reading or silent attention to a lecture. Man, being a sociable creature, delights more in conversation, and learns better this way, if it could always be wisely and happily practised.

2. This method hath something very obliging in it, and carries a very humble and condescending air, when he that instructs seems to be the inquirer, and seeks information from him who learns.

3. It leads the learner into the knowledge of truth as it were by his own invention, which is a very pleasing thing to human nature; and by questions pertinently and artificially proposed, it does as effectually draw him on to discover his own mistakes, which he is much more easily persuaded to relinquish when he seems to have discovered them himself.

4. It is managed in a great measure in the form of the most easy reasoning, always arising from something asserted or known in the foregoing answer, and so proceeding to inquire something unknown in the following question, which again makes way for the next answer. Now such an exercise is very alluring and entertaining to the understanding, while its own reasoning powers are all along employed, and that without labour or difficulty, because, the querist finds out and proposes all the intermediate ideas or middle terms.

IV. There is a method very nearly akin to this, which has much obtained of late, viz. writing controversies by questions only, or confirming or refuting any position, or persuading to or dehorting from any practice, by the mere proposal of queries. The answer to them is supposed to be so plain and so necessary, that they are not expressed, because the query itself carries a convincing argument in it, and seems to determine what the answer must be.

V. If Christian catechisms could be framed in the manner of a Socratical dispute by question and answer, it would wonderfully enlighten the minds of children, and it would improve their intellectual and reasoning powers, at the same time that it leads them into the knowledge of religion: and it is upon one account well suited to the capacity of children; for the questions may be pretty numerous, and the querist must not proceed too swiftly towards the determination of his point proposed, that he may with more ease, with brighter evidence, and with surer success, draw the learner on to assent to those principles, step by step, from whence the final conclusion will naturally arise. The only inconvenience would be this, that if children were to reason out all their way entirely into the knowledge of every part of their religion, it would draw common catechisms into too large a volume for their leisure, attention, or memory.

Yet those who explain their catechisms to them may, by due application and forethought, instruct them in this manner.

CHAPTER XII.

OF FORENSIC DISPUTES.

I. The forum was a public place in Rome where lawyers and orators made their speeches before the proper judge in matters of property or in criminal cases, to accuse or excuse, to complain or defend: thence all sorts of disputations in public assemblies or courts of justice, where several persons make their distinct speeches for or against any person or thing whatsoever, but more especially in civil matters, may come under the name of Forensic disputes.

II. This is practised not only in the courts of judicature, where a single person sits to judge of the truth or goodness of any cause, and to determine according to the weight of reasons on either side; but it is used also in political senates or parliaments, ecclesiastical synods, and assemblies of various kinds.

In these assemblies, generally one person is chosen chairman or mediator, not to give a determination to the controversy, but chiefly to keep the several speakers to the rules of order and decency in their conduct: but the final determination of the questions arises from the majority of opinions or votes in the assembly, according as they are or ought to be swayed by the superior weight of reason appearing in the several speeches that are made.

III. The method of proceeding is usually in some such form as this. The first person who speaks, when the court is set, opens the case either more briefly or at large, and proposes the case to the judge or the chairman, or moderator of the assembly, and gives his own reasons for his opinion in the case proposed.

IV. This person is succeeded by one, or perhaps two, or several more, who paraphrase on the same subject, and argue on the same side of the question: they confirm what the first has spoken, and urge new reasons to enforce the same: then those who are of a different opinion stand up and make their several speeches in succession, opposing the cause which others have maintained, giving their reasons against it, and endeavouring to refute the arguments whereby the first speakers have supported it.

V. After this, one and another raises up to make their replies, to vindicate or to condemn, to establish or to confute what has been offered before on each side of the question; till at last, according to the rules, orders, or customs of the court or assembly, the controversy is decided, either by a single judge, or the suffrages of the assembly.

VI. Where the question or matter in debate consists of several parts, after it is once opened by the first or second speaker, sometimes those who follow take each of them a particular part of the debate, according to their inclination or their prior agreement, and apply themselves to argue upon that single point only, that so the whole complexion of the debate may not be thrown into confusion by the variety of subjects, if every speaker should handle all the subjects of debate.

VII. Before the final sentence of determination is given, it is usual to have the reasons and arguments, which have been offered on both sides, summed up and represented in a more compendious manner; and this is done either by the appointed judge of the court, or the chairman, or some noted person in the assembly, that so judgment may proceed upon the fullest survey of the whole subject, that as far as possible in human affairs nothing may be done contrary to truth or justice.

VIII. As this is a practice in which multitudes of gentlemen, besides those of the learned professions, may be engaged, at least, in their maturer years of life, so it would be a very proper and useful thing to introduce this custom into our academies, viz. to propose cases, and let the students debate them in a forensic manner in the presence of their tutors. There was something of this kind practised by the Roman youth in their schools, in order to train them up for orators, both in the forum and in the senate. Perhaps Juvenal gives some hints of it when he says,

> . . . . et nos,
> Consilium dedimus Syllæ, privatus ut altum
> Dormiret. . . . . *Sat.* 1.
>
> Where with men boys I strove to get renown,
> Advising Sylla to a private gown,
> That he might sleep the sounder.

Sometimes these were assigned to the boys as single subjects of a theme or declamation: so the same poet speaks sarcastically to Hannibal:

> . . . . . . I demens, et sævas curre per Alpes,
> Ut pueris placeas et declamatio fias. *Sat.* 10.
>
> Go climb the rugged Alps, ambitious fool.
> To please the boys, and be a theme at school.

See more of this matter in Kennet's Antiquities of Rome, in the second Essay on the Roman education.

CHAPTER XIII.

OF ACADEMIC, OR SCHOLASTIC DISPUTATION.

The common methods in which disputes are managed in schools of learning are these, viz.

I. The tutor appoints a question in some of the sciences, to be debated amongst his students: one of them undertakes to affirm or to deny the question, and to defend his assertion or negation, and to answer all objections against it; he is called the respondent: and the rest of the students in the same class, or who pursue the same science, are the opponents, who are appointed to dispute or raise objections against the proposition thus affirmed or denied.

II. Each of the students successively in their turn become the respondent or the defender of that proposition, while the rest oppose it also successively in their turns.

III. It is the business of the respondent to write a thesis in Latin, or short discourses on the question proposed; and he either affirms or denies the question, according to the opinion of the tutor, which is supposed to be the truth, and he reads it at the beginning of the dispute.

IV. In his discourse (which is written with as great accuracy as the youth is capable of) he explains the terms of the question, frees them from all ambiguity, fixes their sense, declares the true intent and meaning of the question itself, separates it from other questions with which it may have been complicated, and distinguishes it from other questions which may happen to be akin to it, and then pronounces in the negative or affirmative concerning it.

V. When this is done, then, in the second part of his discourse, he gives his own strongest arguments to confirm the proposition he has laid down, *i. e.* to vindicate his own side of the question; but he does not usually proceed to represent the objections against it, and to solve or answer them; for it is the business of the other students to raise objections in disputing.

VI. Note, in some schools the respondent is admitted to talk largely upon the question, with many flourishes and illustrations, to introduce great authorities from ancient and modern writings for the support of it, and to scatter Latin reproaches in abundance on all those who are of a different sentiment. But this is not always permitted; nor should it indeed ever be indulged, lest it teach youth to reproach instead of to reason.

VII. When the respondent has read over his thesis in the school, the junior student makes an objection, and draws it up into the regular form of a syllogism: the respondent repeats the objection, and either denies the major or minor proposition directly, or he distinguishes upon some word or phrase in the major or minor, and shows in what sense the proposition may be true, but that sense does not affect the question: and then declares, that in the sense which affects the present question, the proposition is not true, and consequently he denies it.

VIII. Then the opponent proceeds by another syllogism to vindicate the proposition that is denied: again the respondent answers by denying or distinguishing.

Thus the disputation goes on in a series or succession of syllogisms and answers, till the objector is silenced, and has no more to say.

IX. When he can go no further, the next student begins to propose his objection, and then the third and the fourth, even to the senior, who is the last opponent.

X. During this time the tutor sits in the chair as president or moderator, to see that the rules of disputation and decency be observed on both sides; and to admonish each disputant of any irregularity in their conduct. His work is also to illustrate and explain the answer or distinction of the respondent where it is obscure, to strengthen it where it is weak, and to correct it where it is false: and when the respondent is pinched with a strong objection, and is at loss for an answer, the moderator assists him, and suggests some answer to the objection of the opponent, in defence of the question, according to his opinion or sentiment.

XI. In public disputes, where the opponents and respondents choose their own side of the question, the moderator's work is not to favour either disputant; but he only sits as president, to see that the laws of disputation be observed, and a decorum maintained.

XII. Now the laws of disputation relate either to the opponont or to the respondent, or to both.

The laws obliging the opponent are these.

1. That he must directly contradict the proposition of the respondent, and not merely attack any of the arguments whereby the respondent has supported that proposition; for it is one thing to confute a single argument of the respondent, and another to confute the thesis itself.

2. (Which is akin to the former) he must contradict or oppose the very sense and intention of the proposition as the respondent has stated it, and not merely oppose the words of the thesis in any other sense; for this would be the way to plunge the dispute into ambiguity and darkness, to talk beside the question, to wrangle about words, and to attack a proposition different from what the respondent has espoused, which is called *ignoratio elenchi*.

3. He must propose his *argumenta* in a plain, short, and syllogistic form, according to the rules of logic, without flying to fallacies or sophisms, and, as far as may be, he should use categorical syllogisms.

4. Though the respondent may be attacked either upon a point of his own concession, which is called *argumentum ex concessis*, or by reducing him to an absurdity, which is called *reductio ad absurdam*, yet it is the neatest, the most useful, and the best sort of disputation, where the opponent draws his objections from the nature of the question itself.

5. Where the respondent denies any proposition, the opponent, if he proceed, must directly vindicate and confirm that proposition, *i. e.* he must make that proposition the conclusion of his next syllogism.

6. Where the respondent limits or distinguishes any proposition, the opponent must directly prove his own proposition in that sense, and according to the member of the distinction in which the respondent denied it.

XIII. the laws that oblige the respondent are these.

1. To repeat the argument of the opponent in the very same words in which it was proposed, before he attempts to answer it.

2. If the syllogism be false in the logical form of it, he must discover the fault according to the rules of logic.

3. If the argument does not directly and effectually oppose his thesis, he must show this mistake, and make it appear that his thesis is safe, even though the argument of the opponent be admitted; or, at least, that the argument does only aim at it collaterally, or at a distance, and not directly overthrow it, or conclude against it.

4. Where the matter of the opponent's objection is faulty in any part of it, the respondent must grant what is true in it, he must deny what is false, he must distinguish or limit the proposition which is ambiguous or doubtful, and then, granting the sense in which it is true, he must deny the sense in which it is false.

5. If an hypothetic proposition be false, the respondent must deny the consequence; if a disjunctive, he must deny the disjunction; if a categoric or relative, he must simply deny it.

6. It is sometimes allowed for the respondent to use an indirect answer after he has answered directly; and he may also show how the opponent's argument may be retorted against himself.

XIV. The laws that oblige both disputants are these:

1. Sometimes it is necessary there should be a mention of certain general principles in which they both agree, relating to the question, that so they may not dispute on those things which either are or ought to have been first granted on both sides.

2. When the state of the controversy is well known, and plainly determined and agreed, it must not be altered by either disputant in the course of the disputation; and the respondent especially should keep a watchful eye on the opponent in this matter.

3. Let neither party invade the province of the other; especially let the respondent take heed that he does

not turn opponent, except in retorting the argument upon his adversary after a direct response; and even this is allowed only as an illustration or confirmation of his own response.

4. Let each wait with patience till the other has done speaking. It is a piece of rudeness to interrupt another in his speech.

Yet, though the disputants have not this liberty, the moderator may do it, when either of the disputants break the rules, and he may interpose so far as to keep them in order.

XV. It must be confessed there are some advantages to be attained by academical disputation. It gives vigour and briskness to the mind thus exercised, and relieves the languor of private study and meditation. It sharpens the wit, and all the inventive powers. It makes the thoughts active, and sends them on all sides to find arguments and answers both for opposition and defence. It gives opportunity of viewing the subject of discourse on all sides, and of learning what inconveniences, difficulties, and objections, attend particular opinions. It furnishes the soul with various occasions of starting such thoughts as otherwise would never have come into the mind. It makes a student more expert in attacking and refuting an error, as well as in vindicating a truth. It instructs the scholar in the various methods of warding off the force of objections, and of discovering and repelling the subtle tricks of sophisters. It procures also a freedom and readiness of speech, and raises the modest and diffident genius to a due degree of courage.

XVI. But there are some very grievous inconveniences that may sometimes overbalance all these advantages. For many young students, by a constant habit of disputing, grow impudent and audacious, proud and disdainful, talkative and impertinent, and render themselves intolerable by an obstinate humour of maintaining whatever they have asserted, as well as by a spirit of contradiction, opposing almost every thing that they hear. The disputation itself often awakens the passions of ambition, emulation, and anger; it carries away the mind from that calm and sedate temper which is so necessary to contemplate truth.

XVII. It is evident also, that by frequent exercises of this sort, wherein opinions true and false are argued, supported, and refuted on both sides, the mind of man is led by insensible degrees to an uncertainty and fluctuating temper, and falls into danger of a sceptical humour, which never comes to an establishment in any doctrines. Many persons, by this means, become much more ready to observe whatsoever is offered in searching out truth; they hardly wait till they have read or heard the sentiment of any person, before their heads are busily employed to seek out arguments against it. They grow naturally sharp in finding out difficulties; and by indulging this humour they converse with the dark and doubtful parts of a subject so long, till they almost render themselves incapable of receiving the full evidence of a proposition, and acknowledging the light of truth. It has some tendency to make a youth a carping critic, rather than a judicious man.

XVIII. I would add yet further, that in these disputations the respondent is generally appointed to maintain the supposed truth, that is, the tutor's opinion. But all the opponents are busy and warmly engaged in finding arguments against the truth. Now if a sprightly young genius happens to manage his arguments so well as to puzzle and gravel the respondent, and perhaps to perplex the moderator a little too, he is soon tempted to suppose his argument unanswerable, and the truth entirely to lie on his side. The pleasure which he takes in having found a sophism which has great appearance of reason, and which he himself has managed with such success, becomes perhaps a strong prejudice to engage his inward sentiments in favour of his argument, and in opposition to the supposed truth.

XIX. Yet perhaps it may be possible to reduce scholastic disputations under such a guard as, may, in some measure, prevent most of these abuses of them, and the unhappy events that too often attend them; for it is pity that an exercise which has some valuable benefits attending it, should be utterly thrown away, if it be possible to secure young minds against the abuse of it; for which purpose some of these directions may seem proper.

XX. General directions for scholastic disputes:

1. Never dispute upon mere trifles, things that are utterly useless to be known, under a vain pretence of sharpening the wit; for the same advantage may be derived from solid and useful subjects, and thus two happy ends may be attained at once. Or if such disputations are always thought dangerous in important matters, let them be utterly abandoned.

2. Do not make infinite and unsearchable things the matter of dispute, nor such propositions as are made up of mere words without ideas, lest it lead young persons into a most unhappy habit of talking without a meaning, and boldly to determine upon things that are hardly within the reach of human capacity.

3. Let not obvious and known truths, or some of the most plain and certain propositions, be bandied about in a disputation, for a mere trial of skill; for he that opposes them in this manner will be in danger of contracting a habit of opposing all evidence, will acquire a spirit of contradiction, and pride himself in a power of resisting the brightest light, and fighting against the strongest proofs; this will insensibly injure the mind, and tends greatly to a universal scepticism.

Upon the whole, therefore, the most proper subjects of dispute seem to be, those very questions which are not of the very highest importance and certainty, nor of the meanest and trifling kind; but rather the intermediate questions between these two, and there is a large sufficiency of them in the sciences. But this I put as a mere proposal, to be determined by the more learned and prudent.

4. It would be well if every dispute could be so ordered as to be a means of searching out truth, and not to gain a triumph. Then each disputant might come to the work without bias and prejudice: with a desire of truth, and not with ambition of glory and victory.

Nor should the aim and design of the disputant be to avoid artfully and escape the difficulties which the opponent offers, but to discuss them thoroughly, and solve them fairly, if they are capable of being solved.

Again, let the opponent be solicitous not to darken and confound the responses that are given him by fresh subtleties; but let him bethink himself whether they are not a just answer to the objection, and be honestly ready to perceive and accept them, and yield to them.

5. For this end let both the respondent and opponent use the clearest and most distinct and expressive language in which they can clothe their thoughts. Let them seek and practise brevity and perspicuity on both sides, without long declamations, tedious circumlocutions, and rhetorical flourishes.

If there happen to be any doubt or obscurity on either side, let neither the one nor the other ever refuse to give a fair explication of the words they use.

6. They should not indulge ridicule, either of persons or things, in their disputations. They should abstain from all banter and jest, laughter and merriment. These are things that break in upon that philosophical gravity, sedateness, and serenity of temper which ought to be observed in every search after truth. However an argument on some subjects may be sometimes clothed with a little pleasantry, yet a jest or witticism should never be used instead of an argument, nor should it ever be suffered to pass for a real and solid proof.

But especially if the subject be sacred or divine, and have nothing in it comical or ridiculous, all ludicrous turns, and jocose or comical airs, should be entirely excluded, lest young minds become tinctured with a silly and profane sort of ridicule, and learn to jest and trifle with the awful solemnities of religion.

7. Nor should sarcasm and reproach, or insolent language, ever be used among fair disputants. Turn not off from things to speak of persons. Leave all noisy contests, all immodest clamours, brawling language, and especially all personal scandal and scurrility, to the meanest part of the vulgar world. Let your manner be all candour and gentleness, patient and ready to hear, humbly zealous to inform and be informed: you should be free and pleasant in every answer and behaviour,

rather like well bred gentlemen in polite conversation, than like noisy and contentious wranglers.

8. If the opponent sees victory to incline to his side, let him be content to show the force of his argument to the intelligent part of the company, without too importunate and petulant demands of an answer, and without insulting over his antagonist, or putting the modesty of the respondent to the blush. Nor let the respondent triumph over the opponent when he is silent and replies no more. On which side soever victory declares herself, let neither of them manage with such unpleasing and insolent airs, as to awaken those evil passions of pride, anger, shame, or resentment on either side which alienate the mind from truth, render it obstinate in the defence of an error, and never suffer it to part with any of its old opinions.

In short, when truth evidently appears on either side, let them learn to yield to conviction. When either party is at a nonplus, let them confess the difficulty, and desire present assistance, or further time and retirement to consider of the matter, and not rack their present invention to find out little shifts to avoid the force and evidence of truth.

9. Might it not be a safer practice in order to attain the best ends of disputation, and to avoid some of the ill effects of it, if the opponents were sometimes engaged on the side of truth, and produced their arguments in opposition to error? And what if the respondent was appointed to support the error, and defend it as well as he could, till he was forced to yield at least to those arguments of the opponent which appear to be really just, and strong, and unanswerable?

In this practice, the thesis of the respondent should only be a fair stating of the question with some of the chief objections against the truth proposed and solved.

Perhaps this practice might not so easily be perverted and abused to raise a cavilling, disputive, and sceptical temper in the minds of youth.

I confess, in this method which I now propose, there would be one amongst the students, viz. the respondent, always engaged in the supposed error; but all the rest would be exercising their talents in arguing for the supposed truth: whereas, in the common methods of disputation in the schools, especially where the students are numerous, each single student is perpetually employed to oppose the truth, and vindicate error, except once in a long time, when it comes to his turn to be respondent.

10. Upon the whole it seems necessary that these methods of disputation should be learned in the schools, in order to teach students better to defend truth, and to refute error, both in writing and conversation, where the scholastic forms are utterly neglected.

But after all, the advantage which youth may gain by disputations depends much on the tutor or moderator: he should manage with such prudence, both in the disputation and at the end of it, as to make all the disputants know the very point of controversy wherein it consists; he should manifest the fallacy of sophistical objections, and confirm the solid arguments and answers. This might teach students how to make the art of disputation useful for the searching out the truth and the defence of it, that it may not be learned and practised only as an art of wrangling, which reigned in the schools several hundred years, and divested the growing reason of youth of its best hopes and improvements.

CHAPTER XIV.

OF STUDY OR MEDITATION.

I. It has been proved and established in some of the foregoing chapters, that neither our own observations, nor our reading the labours of the learned, nor the attendance on the best lectures of instruction, nor enjoying the brightest conversation, can ever make a man truly knowing and wise, without the labours of his own reason in surveying, examining, and judging concerning all subjects upon the best evidence he can acquire. A good genius, or sagacity of thought, a happy judgment, a capacious memory, and large opportunities of observation and converse, will do much of themselves towards the cultivation of the mind, where they are well improved; but where, to the advantage of learned lectures, living instructions, and well chosen books, diligence and study are superadded, this man has all human aids concurring to raise him to a superior degree of wisdom and knowledge.

Under the preceding heads of discourse it has been already declared how our own meditation and reflection should examine, cultivate, and improve all other methods and advantages of enriching the understanding. What remains in this chapter is to give some further occasional hints how to employ our own thoughts, what sort of subjects we should meditate on, and in what manner we should regulate our studies, and how we may improve our judgment, so as in the most effectual and compendious way to attain such knowledge as may be most useful for every man in his circumstances of life, and particularly for those of the learned professions.

II. The first direction for youth is this—learn betimes to distinguish between words and things. Get clear and plain ideas of the things you are set to study. Do not content yourselves with mere words and names, lest your laboured improvements only amass a heap of unintelligible phrases, and you feed upon husks instead of kernels. This rule is of unknown use in every science.

But the greatest and most common danger is in the sacred science of theology, where settled terms and phrases have been pronounced divine and orthodox, which yet have no meaning in them. The scholastic divinity would furnish us with numerous instances of this folly; and yet for many ages all truth and all heresy have been determined by such senseless tests, and by words without ideas: such Shibboleths as these have decided the secular fates of men: and bishoprics or burning mitres or faggots have been the rewards of different persons, according as they pronounced these consecrated syllables, or not pronounced them. To defend them was all piety, and pomp, and triumph; to despise them, or to doubt or to deny them, was torture and death. A thousand thank-offerings are due to that Providence which has delivered our age and our nation from these absurd iniquities! O that every specimen and shadow of this madness were banished from our schools and churches in every shape!

III. Let not young students apply themselves to search out deep, dark, and abstruse matters, far above their reach, or spend their labour in any peculiar subjects, for which they have not the advantages of necessary antecedent learning, or books, or observations. Let them not be too hasty to know things above their present powers, nor plunge their inquiries at once into the depths of knowledge, nor begin to study any science in the middle of it; this will confound rather than enlighten the understanding; such practices may happen to discourage and jade the mind by an attempt above its power; it may balk the understanding, and create an aversion to future dilligence, and perhaps by despair may forbid the pursuit of that subject for ever afterwards: as a limb overstrained by lifting a weight above its power may never recover its former agility and vigour; or if it does, the man may be frighted from ever exerting its strength again.

IV. Nor yet let any student, on the other hand, fright himself at every turn with insurmountable difficulties, nor imagine that the truth is wrapt up in impenetrable darkness. These are formidable spectres which the understanding raises sometimes to flatter its own laziness. Those things which in a remote and confused view seem very obscure and perplexed may be approached by gentle and regular steps, and may then unfold and explain themselves at large to the eye. The hardest problems in geometry, and the most intricate schemes or diagrams, may be explicated and understood step by step; every great mathematician bears a constant witness to this observation.

V. In learning any new thing, there should be as little as possible first proposed to the mind at once, and that being understood and fully mastered, proceed then to the next adjoining part yet unknown. This is a slow, but safe and sure way to arrive at knowledge. If the mind apply itself at first to easier subjects, and things near akin to what is already known, and then advance to the more remote and knotty parts of knowledge by slow degrees, it would be able in this manner to cope with great difficulties, and prevail over them with amazing and happy success.

Mathon happened to dip into the last two chapters of a new book of geometry and mensuration as soon as he saw it, and was frighted with the complicated diagrams which he found there, about the frustums of cones and pyramids, &c. and some deep demonstrations among conic sections; he shut the book again in despair, and imagined none but a Sir Isaac Newton was ever fit to read it. But his tutor happily persuaded him to begin the first pages about lines and angles; and he found such surprising pleasure in three weeks time in the victories he daily obtained, that at last he became one of the chief geometers of his age.

VI. Engage not the mind in the intense pursuit of too many things at once; especially such as have no relation to one another. This will be ready to distract the understanding, and hinder it from attaining perfection in any one subject of study. Such a practice gives a slight smattering of several sciences, without any solid and substantial knowledge of them, and without any real and valuable improvement; and though two or three sorts of study may be usefully carried on at once, to entertain the mind with variety, that it may not be overtired with one sort of thoughts, yet a multitude of subjects will too much distract the attention, and weaken the application of the mind to any one of them.

Where two or three sciences are pursued at the same time, if one of them be dry, abstracted, and unpleasant, as logic, metaphysics, law, languages, let another be more entertaining and agreeable, to secure the mind from weariness and aversion to study. Delight should be intermingled with labour as far as possible, to allure us to bear the fatigue of dry studies the better. Poetry, practical mathematics, history, &c. are generally esteemed entertaining studies, and may be happily used for this purpose. Thus while we relieve a dull and heavy hour by some alluring employments of the mind, our very diversions enrich our understandings, and our pleasure is turned into profit.

XII. In the pursuit of every valuable subject of knowledge, keep the end always in your eye, and be not diverted from it by every petty trifle you meet with in the way. Some persons have such a wandering genius that they are ready to pursue every incidental theme or occasional idea, till they have lost sight of the original subject. These are the men who, when they are engaged in conversation, prolong their story by dwelling on every incident, and swell their narrative with long parentheses, till they have lost their first designs; like a man who is sent in quest of some great treasure, but he steps aside to gather every flower he finds, or stands still to dig up every shining pebble he meets with in his way, till the treasure is forgotten and never found.

VIII. Exert your care, skill, and diligence, about every subject and every question, in a just proportion to the importance of it, together with the danger and bad consequences of ignorance or error therein. Many excellent advantages flow from this one direction:

1. This rule will teach you to be very careful in gaining some general and fundamental truth both in philosophy, and religion, and in human life; because they are of the highest moment, and conduct our thoughts with ease into a thousand inferior and particular propositions. Such is that great principle in natural philosophy—the doctrine of gravitation, or mutual tendency of all bodies towards each other, which Sir Isaac Newton has so well established, and from which he has drawn the solution of a multitude of appearances in the heavenly bodies as well as on earth.

Such is that golden principle of morality which our blessed Lord has given us—Do that to others which you think just and reasonable that others should do to you, which is almost sufficient in itself to solve all cases of conscience which relate to our neighbour.

Such are those principles in religion—that a rational creature is accountable to his Maker for all his actions—that the soul of man is immortal—that there is a future state of happiness and of misery depending on our behaviour in the present life, on which all our religious practices are built or supported.

We should be very curious in examining all propositions that pretend to this honour of being general principles: and we should not without just evidence admit into this rank mere matters of common fame, or commonly received opinions; no, nor the general determination of the learned, or the established articles of any church or nation, &c. for there are many learned presumptions, many synodical and national mistakes, many established falsehoods, as well as many vulgar errors, wherein multitudes of men have followed one another for whole ages almost blindfold. It is of great importance for every man to be careful that these general principles are just and true; for one error may lead us into thousands, which will naturally follow, if once a leading falsehood be admitted.

2. This rule will direct us to be more careful about practical points than mere speculations, since they are commonly of much greater use and consequence: therefore the speculations of algebra, the doctrine of infinities, and the quadrature of curves in mathematical learning, together with all the train of theorems in natural philosophy, should by no means entrench upon our studies of morality and virtue. Even in the science of divinity itself, the sublimest speculations of it are not of that worth and value, as the rules of duty towards God and towards men.

3. In matters of practice we should be most careful to fix our end right, and wisely to determine the scope at which we aim, because that is to direct us in the choice and use of all the means to attain it. If our end be wrong, all our labour in the means will be vain, or perhaps so much the more pernicious as they are better suited to attain that mistaken end. If mere sensible pleasure, or human grandeur, or wealth, be our chief end, we shall choose means contrary to piety and virtue, and proceed apace towards real misery.

4. This rule will engage our best powers and deepest attention in the affairs of religion, and things that re-

late to a future world: for those propositions which extend only to the interest of the present life, are but of small importance when compared with those that have influence upon our everlasting concernments.

5. And even in the affairs of religion, if we walk by the conduct of this rule, we shall be much more laborious in our inquiries into the necessary and fundamental articles of faith and practice, than the lesser appendices of Christianity. The great doctrines of repentance towards God, faith in our Lord Jesus Christ, with love to men, and universal holiness, will employ our best and brightest hours and meditations, while the mint, anise, and cummin, the gestures, and vestures, and fringes of religion, will be regarded no farther than they have a plain and evident connexion with faith and love, with holiness and peace.

6. This rule will make us solicitous not only to avoid such errors, whose influence would spread wide into the whole scheme of our own knowledge and practice, but such mistakes also whose influence would be yet more extensive and injurious to others as well as to ourselves: perhaps to many persons or many families, to a whole church, a town, a country, or a kingdom. Upon this account, persons who are called to instruct others, who are raised to any eminence either in church or state, ought to be careful in settling their principles in matters relating to the civil, the moral, or the religious life, lest a mistake of theirs should diffuse wide mischief, should draw along with it most pernicious consequences, and perhaps extend to following generations.

These are some of the advantages which arise from the eighth rule, viz. Pursue every inquiry and study in proportion to its real value and importance.

IX. Have a care lest some beloved notion, or some darling science, so far prevail over your mind as to give a sovereign tincture to all your other studies, and discolour all your ideas, like a person in the jaundice, who spreads a yellow scene with his eyes over all the objects which he meets. I have known a man of peculiar skill in music, and much devoted to that science, who found out a great resemblance of the Athanasian doctrine of the Trinity in every single note, and he thought it carried something of argument in it to prove that doctrine. I have read of another who accommodated the seven days of the first week of creation to seven notes of music, and thus the whole creation became harmonious.

Under this influence, derived from mathematical studies, some have been tempted to cast all their logical, their metaphysical, and their theological and moral learning into the method of mathematicians, and bring every thing relating to those abstracted, or those practical sciences, under theorems, problems, postulates, scholiums, corollaries, &c. whereas, the matter ought always to direct the method; for all subjects or matters of thought cannot be moulded or subdued to one form. Neither the rules for the conduct of the understanding, nor the doctrines nor duties of religion and virtue, can be exhibited naturally in figures and diagrams. Things are to be considered as they are in themselves; their natures are inflexible, and their natural relations unalterable; and therefore, in order to conceive them aright, we must bring our understandings to things, and not pretend to bend and strain things to comport with our fancies and forms.

X. Suffer not any beloved study to prejudice your mind so far in favour of it as to despise all other learning. This is a fault of some little souls, who have got a smattering of astronomy, chymistry, metaphysics, history, &c. and for want of a due acquaintance with other sciences, make a scoff at them all in comparison of their favourite science. Their understandings are hereby cooped up in narrow bounds, so that they never look abroad into other provinces of the intellectual world, which are more beautiful, perhaps, and more fruitful than their own: if they would search a little into other sciences, they might not only find treasures of new knowledge, but might be furnished also with rich hints of thought, and glorious assistances to cultivate that very province to which they have confined themselves.

Here I would always give some grains of allowance to the sacred science of theology, which is incomparably superior to all the rest, as it teaches us the knowledge of God, and the way to his eternal favour. This is that noble study which is every man's duty, and every one who can be called a rational creature is capable of it.

This is that science which would truly enlarge the minds of men, were it studied with that freedom, that unbiased love of truth, and that sacred charity which it teaches; and if it were not made, contrary to its own nature, the occasion of strife, faction, malignity, a narrow spirit, and unreasonable impositions on the mind and practice. Let this, therefore, stand always chief.

XI. Let every particular study have due and proper time assigned it, and let not a favourite science prevail with you to lay out such hours upon it, as ought to be employed upon the more necessary and more important affairs or studies of your profession. When you have, according to the best of your discretion, and according to the circumstances of your life, fixed proper hours for particular studies, endeavour to keep to those rules; not, indeed, with a superstitious preciseness, but with some good degrees of a regular constancy. Order and method in a course of study saves much time, and makes large improvements. Such a fixation of certain hours will have a happy influence to secure you from trifling and wasting away your minutes in impertinence.

XII. Do not apply yourself to any one study at one time longer than the mind is capable of giving a close attention to it without weariness or wandering. Do not over fatigue the spirits at any time, lest the mind be seized with a lassitude, and thereby be tempted to nauseate and grow tired of a particular subject before you have finished it.

XIII. In the beginning of your application to any new subject be not too uneasy under present difficulties that occur, nor too importunate and impatient for answers and solutions to any questions that arise. Perhaps a little more study, a little further acquaintance with the subject, a little time and experience, will solve those difficulties, untie the knot, and make your doubts vanish: especially if you are under the instruction of a tutor, he can inform you that your inquiries are perhaps too early, and that you have not yet learned those principles upon which the solution of such a difficulty depends.

XIV. Do not expect to arrive at certainty in every subject which you pursue. There are a hundred things wherein we mortals in this dark and imperfect state must be content with probability, where our best light and reasonings will reach no farther. We must balance arguments as justly as we can, and where we cannot find weight enough on either side to determine the scale with sovereign force and assurance, we must content ourselves, perhaps, with a small preponderation. This will give us a probable opinion, and those probabilities are sufficient for the daily determination of a thousand actions in human life, and many times even in matters of religion.

It is admirably well expressed by a late writer—"When there is a great strength of argument set before us, if we will refuse to do what appears most fit for us, till every little objection is removed, we shall never take one wise resolution as long as we live."

Suppose I had been honestly and long searching what religion I should choose, and yet I could not find that the argument in defence of Christianity arose to complete certainty, but went only so far as to give me a probable evidence of the truth of it; though many difficulties still remain, yet I should think myself obliged to receive and practise that religion, for the God of nature and reason has bound us to assent and act according to the best evidence we have, even though it be not absolute and complete; and as he is our supreme judge, his abounding goodness and equity will approve and acquit the man whose conscience honestly and willingly seeks the best light, and obeys it as far as he can discover it.

But in matters of great importance in religion, let him join all due diligence with earnest and humble prayer for divine aid in his inquiries; such prayer and such diligence as eternal concerns require, and such as he may plead with courage before the judge of all.

XV. Endeavour to apply every speculative study as far as possible, to some practical use, that both yourself and others may be the better for it. Inquiries even in natural philosophy should not be mere amusement, and much less in the affairs of religion. Researches into the springs of natural bodies and their motions should lead men to invent happy methods for the ease and convenience of human life; or at least they should be improved to awaken us to admire the wonderous wisdom and contrivances of God our creator in all the works of nature.

If we pursue mathematical speculations, they will inure us to attend closely to any subject, to seek and gain clear ideas, to distinguish truth from falsehood, to judge justly, and to argue strongly; and these studies do more directly furnish us with all the various rules of those useful arts of life, viz. measuring, building, sailing, &c.

Even our very inquiries and disputations about vacuum or space, and atoms, about incommensurable quantities, and finite divisibility of matter, and eternal duration, which seems to be purely speculative, will show us some good practical lessons, will lead us to see the weakness of our nature, and should teach us humility in arguments of divine subjects and matters of sacred revelation. This should guard us against rejecting any doctrine which is expressly and evidently revealed, though we cannot fully understand it. It is good sometimes to lose and bewilder ourselves in such studies for this very reason, and to attain this practical advantage, this improvement in true modesty and spirit.

XVI. Though we should always be ready to change our sentiments of things upon just conviction of their falsehood, yet there is not the same necessity of changing our accustomed methods of reading or study and practice, even though we have not been led at first into the happiest method. Our thought may be true, though we may have hit upon an improper order of thinking. Truth does not always depend upon the most convenient method. There may be a certain form and order in which we have long accustomed ourselves to range our ideas and notions, which may be best for us now, though it was not originally best in itself. The inconveniences of changing may be much greater than the conveniences we could obtain by a new method

As for instance, if a man in his younger days has ranged all his sentiments in theology in the method of Ames's Medulla Theologiæ, or Bishop Usher's Body of Divinity, it may be much more natural and easy for him to continue to dispose all his further acquirements in the same order, though perhaps neither of those treatises are in themselves written in the most perfect method. So when we have long fixed our cases of shelves in a library, and ranged our books in any particular order, viz. according to their languages, or according to their subjects, or according to the alphabetical names of the authors, we are perfectly well acquainted with the order in which they now stand, and we can find any particular book which we seek, or add a new book which we have purchased, with much greater ease than we can do in finer cases of shelves where the books were ranged in any different manner whatsoever; any different position of the volumes would be new and strange, and troublesome to us, and would not countervail the inconveniences of a change.

So if a man of forty years old has been taught to hold his pen awkwardly in his youth, and yet writes sufficiently well for all the purposes of his station, it is not worth while to teach him now the most accurate methods of learning that instrument; for this would create him more trouble without equal advantage, and perhaps he might never attain to write better after he has placed his fingers perfectly right with this new accuracy.

CHAPTER XV.

OF FIXING THE ATTENTION.

A STUDENT should labour, by all proper methods, to acquire a study fixation of thought. Attention is a very necessary thing in order to improve our minds. The evidence of truth does not always appear immediately, nor strike the soul at first sight. It is by long attention and inspection that we arrive at evidence, and it is for want of it we judge falsely of many things. We make haste to determine upon a slight and a sudden view, we confirm our guesses which arise from a glance, we pass a judgment while we have but a confused or obscure perception, and thus plunge ourselves into mis takes. This is like a man who, walking in a mist, or being at a great distance from any visible object (suppose a tree, a man, a horse, or a church,) judges much amiss of the figure, and situation, and colours of it, and sometimes takes one for the other; whereas, if he would but withhold his judgment till he came nearer to it, or stay till clearer light comes, and then would fix his eyes longer upon it, he would secure himself from those mistakes.

Now, in order to gain a greater facility of attention, we may observe these rules:—

I. Get a good liking to the study of knowledge you would pursue. We may observe, that there is not much difficulty in confining the mind to contemplate what we have a great desire to know; and especially if they are matters of sense, or ideas which paint themselves upon the fancy. It is but acquiring a hearty good will and resolution to search out and survey the various properties and parts of such objects, and our attention will be engaged, if there be any delight or diversion in the study or contemplation of them. Therefore mathematical studies have a strange influence towards fixing the attention of the mind, and giving a steadiness to a wandering disposition, because they deal much in lines, figures, and numbers, which affect and please the sense and imagination. Histories have a strong tendency the same way, for they engage the soul by a variety of sensible occurrences; when it hath begun, it knows not how to leave off; it longs to know the final event, through a natural curiosity that belongs to mankind. Voyages and travels, and accounts of strange countries and strange appearances, will assist in this work. This sort of study detains the mind by the perpetual occurrence and expectation of something new, and that which may gratefully strike the imagination.

II. Sometimes we may make use of sensible things and corporeal images for the illustration of those notions, which are more abstracted and intellectual. Therefore diagrams greatly assist the mind in astronomy and philosophy; and the emblems of virtues and vices may happily teach children, and pleasingly impress those useful moral ideas on young minds, which perhaps might be conveyed to them with much more difficulty by mere moral and abstracted discourses.

I confess, in this practice of representing moral subjects by pictures, we should be cautious lest we so far immerse the mind in corporeal images, as to render it unfit to take in an abstracted and intellectual idea, or cause it to form wrong conceptions of immaterial things. This practice, therefore, is rather to be used at first, in order to get a fixed habit of attention, and in some cases only; but it can never be our constant way and method of pursuing all moral, abstracted, and spiritual themes.

III Apply yourself to those studies, and read those authors who draw out their subjects into a perpetual chain of connected reasonings, wherein the following parts of the discourse are naturally and easily derived from those which go before. Several of the mathematical sciences, if not all, are happily useful for this purpose. This will render the labour of study delightful to a rational mind, and will fix the powers of the understanding with strong attention to their proper operations by the very pleasure of it. *Labor ipse voluptas* is a happy proposition wheresoever it can be applied.

IV. Do not choose your constant place of study by the finery of the prospects, or the most various and entertaining scenes of sensible things. Too much light, or a variety of objects which strike the eye or the ear, especially while they are ever in motion or often changing, have a natural and powerful tendency to steal away the mind too often from its steady pursuit of any subject which we contemplate; and thereby the soul gets a habit of silly curiosity and impertinence, of trifling and wandering. Vagario thought himself furnished with the best closet for his studies among the beauties, gaieties, and diversions of Kensington or Hampton Court; but after seven years professing to pursue learning, he was a mere novice still.

V. Be not in too much haste to come to the determination of a difficult or important point. Think it worth your waiting to find out truth. Do not give your assent up to either side of a question too soon, merely on this account, that the study of it is long and difficult. Rather be contented with ignorance for a season, and continue in suspense till your attention, and meditation, and due labour, have found out sufficient evidence on one side. Some are so fond to know a great deal at once, and love to talk of things with freedom and boldness before they truly understand them, that they scarcely ever allow themselves attention enough to search the matter through and through.

VI. Have a care of indulging the more sensual passions and appetites of animal nature; they are great enemies to attention. Let not the mind of a student be under the influence of any warm affection to things of sense, when he comes to engage in the search of truth, or the improvement of his understanding. A person under the power of love, or fear, or anger, great pain, or deep sorrow, hath so little government of his soul, that he cannot keep it attentive to the proper subject of his meditation. The passions call away the thoughts with incessant importunity towards the object that excited them; and if we indulge the frequent rise and roving of passions, we shall thereby procure an unsteady and unattentive habit of mind.

Yet this one exception must be admitted, viz. If we can be so happy as to engage any passion of the soul on the side of the particular study which we are pursuing, it may have great influence to fix the attention more strongly to it.

VII. It is, therefore, very useful to fix and engage the mind in the pursuit of any study by a consideration of the divine pleasures of truth and knowledge—by a sense of our duty to God—by a delight in the exercise of our intellectual faculties—by the hope of future service to our fellow creatures, and glorious advantage to ourselves both in this world and that which is to come. These thoughts, though they may move our affections, yet they do it with a proper influence: these will rather assist and promote our attention, than disturb or divert it from the subject of our present and proper meditations.

A soul inspired with the fondest love of truth, and the warmest aspirations after sincere felicity and celestial beatitude, will keep all its powers attentive to the incessant pursuit of them: passion is then refined and consecrated to its divinest purposes.

CHAPTER XVI.

OF ENLARGING THE CAPACITY OF THE MIND.

THERE are three things which in an especial manner go to make up that amplitude or capacity of mind which is one of the noblest characters belonging to the understanding.

1. When the mind is ready to take in great and sublime ideas without pain or difficulty.

2. When the mind is free to receive new and strange ideas, upon just evidence, without great surprise or aversion.

3. When the mind is able to conceive or survey many ideas at once without confusion, and to form a true judgment derived from that extensive survey.

The person who wants either of these characters may, in that respect, be said to have a narrow genius. Let us diffuse our meditations a little upon this subject.

I. That is an ample and capacious mind which is ready to take in vast and sublime ideas without pain or difficulty. Persons who have never been used to converse with any thing but the common, little, and obvious affairs of life, have acquired such a narrow or contracted habit of soul, that they are not able to stretch their intellects wide enough to admit large and noble thoughts; they are ready to make their domestic, daily, and familiar images of things the measure of all that is, and all that can be.

Talk to them of the vast dimensions of the planetary worlds; tell them that the star called Jupiter is a solid globe, two hundred and twenty times bigger than our earth; that the sun is a vast globe of fire, above a thousand times bigger than Jupiter, that is, two hundred and twenty thousand times bigger than the earth; that the distance from the earth to the sun is eighty-one millions of miles; and that a cannon bullet shot from the earth would not arrive at the nearest of the fixed stars in some hundreds of years: they cannot bear the belief of it; but hear all these glorious labours of astronomy as a mere idle romance.

Inform them of the amazing swiftness of the motion of some of the smallest or the biggest bodies in nature; assure them, acording to the best philosophy, that the planet Venus (i. e. our morning or evening star, which is near as big as our earth,) though it seems to move from its place but a few yards in a month, does really fly seventy thousand miles in an hour; tell them that the rays of light shoot from the sun to our earth at the rate of one hundred and eighty thousand miles in the second of a minute; they stand aghast at such sort of talk, and believe it no more than the tales of giants fifty yards high, and the rabbinical fables of Leviathan, who every day swallows a fish of three miles long, and is thus preparing himself to be the food and entertainment of the blessed at the feast of Paradise.

These unenlarged souls are in the same manner disgusted with the wonders which the microscope has discovered concerning the shape, the limbs, and motions of ten thousand little animals, whose united bulk would not equal a pepper-corn: they are ready to give the lie to all the improvements of our senses by the invention of a variety of glasses, and will scarcely believe any thing beyond the testimony of their naked eye without the assistance of art.

Now, if we would attempt in a learned manner to relieve the minds that labour under this defect:

1. It is useful to begin with some first principles of geometry, and lead them onward by degrees to the doctrine of quantities which are incommensurable, or which

will admit of no common measure, though it be ever so small. By this means they will see the necessity of admitting the infinite divisibility of quantity or matter.

This same doctrine may also be proved to their understandings, and almost to their senses, by some easier arguments in a more obvious manner. As the very opening and closing of a pair of compasses will evidently prove, that if the smallest supposed part of matter or quantity be put between the points, there will be still less and less distances or quantities all the way between the legs, till you come to the head or joint; wherefore there is no such thing possible as the smallest quantity. But a little acquaintance with true philosophy and mathematical learning would soon teach them there are no limits either as to the extension of space or to the division of body, and would lead them to believe there are bodies amazingly great or small beyond their present imagination.

2. It is proper also to acquaint them with the circumference of our earth, which may be proved by very easy principles of geometry, geography, and astronomy, to be about twenty-four thousand miles round, as it has been actually found to have this dimension by mariners, who have sailed round it. Then let them be taught, that in every twenty-four hours either the sun and stars must all move round this earth, or the earth must turn round upon its own axis. If the earth itself revolve thus, then each house or mountain near the equator must move at the rate of a thousand miles in an hour: but if, as they generally suppose, the sun or stars move round the earth, then (the circumference of their several orbits or spheres being vastly greater than this earth) they must have a motion prodigiously swifter than a thousand miles an hour. Such a thought as this will by degrees enlarge their minds, and they will be taught even upon their own principles of the diurnal revolutions of the heavens, to take in some of the vast dimensions of the heavenly bodies, their spaces and motions.

3. To this should be added the use of telescopes, to help them to see the distant wonders in the skies; and microscopes, which discover the minutest parts of little

animals, and reveal some of the finer and most curious works of nature. They should be acquainted also with some other noble inventions of modern philosophy, which have a great influence to enlarge the human understanding, of which I shall take occasion to speak more under the next head.

4. For the same purpose they may be invited to read those parts of Milton's admirable poem, entitled Paradise Lost, where he describes the armies and power of angels, the wars and the senate of devils, the creation of this earth, together with the description of Heaven, Hell, and Paradise.

It must be granted that poesy often deals in these vast and sublime ideas. And even if the subject or matter of the poem doth not require such amazing and extensive thoughts, yet tropes and figures, which are some of the main powers and beauties of poesy, do so gloriously exalt the matter, as to give a sublime imagination its proper relish and delight.

So when a boar is chased in hunting:

> His nostrils flames expire,
> And his red eyeballs roll with living fire.
> *Dryden.*

When Ulysses withholds and suppresses his resentment.

> His wrath comprest,
> Recoiling, mutter'd thunder in his breast.
> *Pope.*

But especially where the subject is grand, the poet fails not to represent it in all its grandeur.

So when the supremacy of a God is described:

> He sees, with equal eye, as God of all,
> A hero perish, or a sparrow fall;
> Atoms or systems into ruin hurl'd,
> And now a bubble burst, and now a world.
> *Pope.*

These sorts of writing have a natural tendency to enlarge the capacity of the mind, and make sublime ideas familiar to it. And instead of running always to the ancient heathen poesy with this design, we may with equal, if not superior advantage, apply ourselves to converse with some of the best of our modern poets, as well as with the writings of the prophets, and the poetical parts of the Bible, viz. the book of Job and the Psalms, in which sacred authors we shall find sometimes more sublime ideas, more glorious descriptions, more elevated language, than the fondest critics have ever found in any of the heathen versifiers either of Greece or Rome: for the Eastern writers use and allow much stronger figures and tropes than the Western.

Now there are many and great advantages to be derived from this sort of enlargement of the mind.

It will lead us into more exalted apprehensions of the great God our Creator than ever we had before. It will entertain our thoughts with holy wonder and amazement, while we contemplate that Being who created these various works of surprising greatness, and surprising smallness; who has displayed most inconceivable wisdom in the contrivance of all the parts, powers, and motions of these little animals invisible to the naked eye; who has manifested a most divine extent of knowledge, power, and greatness, in forming, moving, and managing the most extensive bulk of the heavenly bodies, and in surveying and comprehending all those unmeasurable spaces in which they move. Fancy, with all her images, is fatigued and overwhelmed in following the planetary worlds through such immense stages, such astonishing journeys as these are, and resigns its place to the pure intellect, which learns by degrees to take in such ideas as these, and to adore its Creator with new and sublime devotion.

And not only are we taught to form juster ideas of the great God by these methods, but this enlargement of the mind carries us on to nobler conceptions of his intelligent creatures. The mind that deals only in vulgar and common ideas is ready to imagine the nature and powers of man to come something near to God his maker, because we do not see or sensibly converse with any beings superior to ourselves. But when the soul has obtained a greater amplitude of thought, it will not then immediately pronounce every thing to be God which is above man. It then learns to suppose there may be as many various ranks of beings in the invisible world in a constant gradation superior to us, as we ourselves are superior to all the ranks of being beneath us in this visible world; even though we descend downward far below the ant and the worm, the snail and the oyster, to the least and to the dullest animated atoms which are discovered to us by microscopes.

By this means we shall be able to suppose what prodigious power angels, whether good or bad, must be furnished with, and prodigious knowledge, in order to oversee the realms of Persia and Græcia of old, or if any such superintended the affairs of Great Britain, France, Ireland, Germany, &c. in our days: what power and speed is necessary to destroy one hundred and eighty-five thousand armed men in one night in the Assyrian camp of Sennacherib, and all the first-born of the land of Egypt in another, both which are attributed to an angel.

By these steps we shall ascend to form more just ideas of the knowledge and grandeur, the power and glory of the man Jesus Christ, who is intimately united to God, and is one with him. Doubtless he is furnished with superior powers to all the angels in heaven, because he is employed in superior work, and appointed to be the Sovereign Lord of all the visible and invisible worlds. It is his human nature in which the Godhead dwells bodily, that is advanced to these honours, and to this empire: and perhaps there is little or nothing in the government of the kingdoms of nature and grace but what is transacted by the man Jesus, inhabited by the divine power and wisdom, and employed as a medium or conscious instrument of this extensive gubernation.

II. I proceed now to consider the next thing wherein the capacity or amplitude of the mind consists, and that is, when the mind is free to receive new and strange ideas and propositions upon just evidence without any great surprise or aversion. Those who confine themselves within the circle of their own hereditary ideas and opinions, and who never give themselves leave so much as to examine or believe any thing besides the dictates of their own family, or sect, or party, are justly charged with a narrowness of soul. Let us survey some instances of this imperfection, and then direct to the cure of it.

1. Persons who have been bred up all their days within the smoke of their father's chimney, or within the limits of their native town or village, are surprised at every new sight that appears, when they travel a few miles from home. The ploughman stands amazed at the shops, the trade, the crowds of people, the magnificent buildings, the pomp, and riches, and equipage of the court and city, and would hardly believe what was told him before he saw it. On the other hand, the cockney, travelling into the country, is surprised at many actions of the quadruped and winged animals in the field, and at many common practices of rural affairs.

If either of these happen to hear an account of the familiar and daily customs of foreign countries, they pronounce them at once indecent and ridiculous: so narrow are their understandings, and their thoughts so confined, that they know not how to believe any thing wise and proper besides what they have been taught to practise.

This narrowness of mind should be cured by hearing and reading the accounts of different parts of the world, and the histories of past ages, and of nations and countries distant from our own, especially the more polite parts of mankind. Nothing tends in this respect so much to enlarge the mind as travelling, i. e. making a visit to other towns, cities, or countries, besides those in which we were born and educated: and where our condition of life does not grant us this privilege, we must endeavour to supply the want of it by books.

2. It is the same narrowness of mind that awakens the surprise and aversion of some persons, when they hear of doctrines and schemes in human affairs, or in religion, quite different from what they have embraced. Perhaps they have been trained up from their infancy in one set of notions, and their thoughts have been confined to one single tract both in the civil or religious life, without ever hearing or knowing what other opin-

ions are current among mankind: or at least they have seen all other notions besides their own represented in a false and malignant light; whereupon they judge and condemn at once every sentiment but what their own party receives; and they think it a piece of justice and truth to lay heavy censures upon the practice of every sect in Christianity or politics. They have so rooted themselves in the opinions of their party, that they cannot hear an objection with patience, nor can they bear a vindication, or so much as an apology, for any set of principles beside their own; all the rest is nonsense or heresy, folly or blasphemy.

This defect also is to be relieved by free conversation with persons of different sentiments: this will teach us to bear with patience a defence of opinions contrary to our own. If we are scholars, we should also read the objections against our own tenets, and view the principles of other parties, as they are represented in their own authors, and not merely in the citations of those who would confute them. We should take an honest and unbiassed survey of the force of reasoning on all sides, and bring all to the test of unprejudiced reasoning and divine revelation. Note, this is not to be done in a rash and self-sufficient manner; but with an humble dependance on divine wisdom and grace, while we walk among snares and dangers.

By such a free converse with persons of different sects (especially those who differ only in particular forms of Christianity, but agree in the great and necessary doctrines of it) we shall find that there are persons of good sense and virtue, persons of piety and worth, persons of much candour and goodness, who belong to different parties, and have imbibed sentiments opposite to each other. This will soften the roughness of an unpolished soul, and enlarge the avenues of our charity towards others, and incline us to receive them into all the degrees of unity and affection which the word of God requires.

3. I might borrow further illustrations both of this freedom and this aversion to receive new truths from modern astronomy and natural philosophy. How much is the vulgar part of the world surprised at the talk of

the diurnal and annual revolutions of the earth! They have ever been taught by their senses, and their neighbours, to imagine the earth stands fixed in the centre of the universe, and that the sun, with all the planets and fixed stars, are whirled round this little globe once in twenty-four hours: not considering that such a diurnal motion, by reason of the distance of some of those heavenly bodies, must be almost infinitely swifter, and more inconceivable, than any which the modern astronomers attribute to them. Tell these persons that the sun is fixed in the centre, that the earth, with all the planets, roll round the sun in their several periods, and that the moon rolls round the earth in a lesser circle, while, together with the earth, she is carried round the sun; they cannot admit a syllable of this new and strange doctrine, and they pronouce it utterly contrary to all sense and reason.

Acquaint them that there are four moons also perpetually rolling round the planet Jupiter, and carried along with him in his periodical circuit round the sun, which little moons were never known till the year 1610, when Galileo discovered them by his telescope: inform them that Saturn has five moons of the same kind attending him; and that the body of that planet is encompassed with a broad flat circular ring, distant from the planet twenty-one thousand miles, and twenty-one thousand miles broad; they look upon these things as tales and fancies, and will tell you that the glasses do but delude your eyes with vast images; and even when they themselves consult their own eyesight in the use of these tubes, the narrowness of their mind is such, that they will scarcely believe their senses when they dictate ideas so new and strange.

And if you proceed further, and attempt to lead them into a belief that all these planetary worlds are habitable, and it is probable they are replenished with intellectual beings dwelling in bodies, they will deride the folly of him that informs them; for they resolve to believe there are no habitable worlds but this earth, and no spirits dwelling in bodies besides mankind; and it is well if they do not fix the brand of heresy on the man who is leading them out of their long imprisonment, and loosing the fetters of their souls.

There are many other things relating to mechanical experiments, and to the properties of the air, water, fire, iron, the loadstone, and other minerals and metals, as well as the doctrine of the sensible qualities, viz. colours, sounds, tastes, &c. which this rank of men cannot believe for want of a greater amplitude of mind.

The best way to convince them is by giving them some acquaintance with the various experiments in philosophy, and proving by ocular demonstration the multiform and amazing operations of the air-pump, the loadstone, the chymical furnace, optical glasses, and mechanical engines. By this means the understanding will stretch itself by degrees, and when they have found there are so many new and strange things that are most evidently true, they will not be so forward to condemn every new proposition in any of the other sciences, or in the affairs of religion or civil life.

III. The capacity of the understanding includes yet another qualification in it, and that is, an ability to receive many ideas at once without confusion. The ample mind takes a survey of several objects with one glance, keeps them all within sight and present to the soul, that they may be compared together in their mutual respects; it forms just judgments, and it draws proper inferences from this comparison, even to a great length of argument, and a chain of demonstrations.

The narrowness that belongs to human souls in general is a great imperfection and impediment to wisdom and happiness. There are but few persons who can contemplate or practise several things at once; our faculties are very limited, and while we are intent upon one part or property of a subject, we have but a slight glimpse of the rest, or we lose it out of sight. But it is a sign of a large and capacious mind, if we can with one single view take in a variety of objects; or at least when the mind can apply itself to several objects with so swift a succession, and in so few moments, as attains almost the same ends as if it were all done in the same instant.

This is a necessary qualification in order to great knowledge and good judgment; for there are several things in human life, in religion, and in the sciences, which have various circumstances, appendices, and relations attending them; and without a survey of all those ideas which stand in connexion with and relation to each other, we are often in danger of passing a false judgment on the subject proposed. It is for this reason there are so numerous controversies found among the learned and unlearned world, in matters of religion, as well as in the affairs of civil government. The notions of sin, and duty to God and our fellow creatures; of law, justice, authority, and power; of covenant, faith, justification, redemption, and grace; of church, bishop, presbyter, ordination, &c. contain in them such complicated ideas, that when we are to judge of any thing concerning them, it is hard to take into our view at once all the attendants or consequents that must and will be concerned in the determination of a single question: and yet, without a due attention to many or most of these, we are in danger of determining that question amiss.

It is owing to the narrowness of our minds that we are exposed to the same peril in the matters of human duty and prudence. In many things which we do, we ought not only to consider the mere naked action itself, but the persons who act, the persons towards whom, the time when, the place where, the manner how, the end for which the action is done, together with the effects that must or that may follow, and all other surrounding circumstances: these things must necessarily be taken into our view, in order to determine whether the action, which is indifferent in itself, be either lawful or unlawful, good or evil, wise or foolish, decent or indecent, proper or improper, as it is so circumstantiated.

Let me give a plain instance for the illustration of this matter. Mario kills a dog, which, considered merely in itself, seems to be an indifferent action: now the dog was Timon's, and not his own; this makes it look unlawful. But Timon bid him do it; this gives it an appearance of lawfulness again. It was done at church, and in time of divine service; these circumstances added, cast on it an air of irreligion. But the dog flew at Mario, and put him in danger of his life; this relieves the seeming impiety of the action. Yet Mario might have escaped by flying thence; therefore the action appears to be improper. But the dog was known to be mad; this further circumstance makes it almost necessary that the dog should be slain, lest he might worry the assembly, and do much mischief. Yet again, Mario killed him with a pistol, which he happened to have in his pocket since yesterday's journey; now hereby the whole congregation was terrified and discomposed, and divine service was broken off: this carries an appearance of great indecency and impropriety in it: but after all, when we consider a further circumstance, that Mario, being thus violently assaulted by a mad dog, had no way of escape, and had no other weapon about him, it seems to take away all the colours of impropriety, indecency, or unlawfulness, and to allow that the preservation of one or many lives will justify the act as wise and good. Now all these concurrent appendices of the action ought to be surveyed, in order to pronounce with justice and truth concerning it.

There are a multitude of human actions in private life, in domestic affairs, in traffic, in civil governments, in courts of justice, in schools of learning, &c. which have so many complicated circumstances, aspects, and situations, with regard to time and place, persons and things, that it is impossible for any one to pass a right judgment concerning them, without entering into most of these circumstances, and surveying them extensively, and comparing and balancing them all aright.

Whence by the way I may take occasion to say, how many thousands are there who take upon them to pass their censures on the personal and the domestic actions of others, who pronounce boldly on the affairs of the public, and determine the justice or madness, the wisdom or folly of national administrations, of peace and war, &c. whom neither God nor men ever qualified for such a post of judgment! They were not capable of entering into the numerous concurring springs of action, nor had they ever taken a survey of the twentieth part of the circumstances which were necessary for such judgments or censures.

It is the narrowness of our minds, as well as the vices of the will, that oftentimes prevents us from taking a full view of all the complicated and concurring appendices that belong to human actions; thence it comes to pass that there is so little right judgment, so little justice, prudence, or decency, practised among the bulk of mankind; thence arise infinite reproaches and censures; alike foolish and unrighteous. You see, therefore, how needful and happy a thing it is to be possessed of some measure of this amplitude of soul, in order to make us very wise, or knowing, or just, or prudent, or happy.

I confess this sort of amplitude or capacity of mind is in a great measure the gift of nature, for some are born with much more capacious souls than others.

The genius of some persons is so poor and limited, that they can hardly take in the connexion of two or three propositions, unless it be in matters of sense, and which they have learned by experience: they are utterly unfit for speculative studies; it is hard for them to discern the difference betwixt right and wrong in matters of reason on any abstracted subjects; these ought never to set up for scholars, but apply themselves to those arts and professions of life which are to be learned at an easier rate, by slow degrees and daily experience.

Others have a soul a little more capacious, and they can take in the connexion of a few propositions pretty well; but if the chain of consequences be a little prolix, here they stick and are confounded. If persons of this make ever devote themselves to science, they should be well assured of a solid and strong constitution of body, and well resolved to bear the fatigue of hard labour and diligence in study: if the iron be bent, King Solomon tells us, we must put more strength.

But, in the third place, there are some of so bright and happy a genius, and so ample a mind, that they can take in a long train of propositions, if not at once, yet in a very few moments, and judge well concerning the dependance of them. They can survey a variety of

13

complicated ideas without fatigue or disturbance; and a number of truths offering themselves as it were at one view to their understanding, doth not perplex or confound them. This makes a great man.

Now, though there may be much owing to nature in this case, yet experience assures us, that even a lower degree of this capacity and extent of thought may be increased by diligence and application, by frequent exercise, and the observation of such rules as these:

I. Labour by all means to gain an attentive and patient temper of mind, a power of confining and fixing your thoughts so long on any one appointed subject, till you have surveyed it on every side and in every situation, and run through the several powers, parts, properties and relations, effects and consequences of it. He whose thoughts are very fluttering and wandering, and cannot be fixed attentively to a few ideas successively, will never be able to survey many and various objects distinctly at once, but will certainly be overwhelmed and confounded with the multiplicity of them. The rules for fixing the attention in the former chapter are proper to be consulted here.

II. Accustom yourself to clear and distinct ideas in every thing you think of. Be not satisfied with obscure and confused conceptions of things, especially where clearer may be obtained; for one obscure or confused idea, especially if it be of great importance in the question, intermingled with many clear ones, and placed in its variety of aspects towards them, will be in danger of spreading confusion over the whole scene of ideas, and thus may have an unhappy influence to overwhelm the understanding with darkness and pervert the judgment. A little black paint will shamefully tincture and spoil twenty gay colours.

Consider yet further, that if you content yourself frequently with words instead of ideas, or with cloudy and confused notions of things, how impenetrable will that darkness be, and how vast and endless that confusion which must surround and involve the understanding, when many of these obscure and confused ideas come to be set before the soul at once; and how impossible will it be to form a clear and just judgment about them.

III. Use all diligence to acquire and treasure up a large store of ideas and notions: take every opportunity to add something to your stock; and by frequent recollection fix them in your memory; nothing tends to confirm and enlarge the memory like a frequent review of its possessions. Then the brain being well furnished with various traces, signatures, and images, will have a rich treasure always ready to be proposed or offered to the soul, when it directs its thought towards any particular subject. This will gradually give the mind a faculty of surveying many objects at once, as a room that is richly adorned and hung round with a great variety of pictures strikes the eye almost at once with all that variety, especially if they have been well surveyed one by one at first: this makes it habitual and more easy to the inhabitants to take in many of those painted scenes with a single glance or two.

Here note, that by acquiring a rich treasure of notions, I do not mean only single ideas, but also propositions, observations, and experiences, with reasonings and arguments upon the various subjects that occur among natural and moral, common or sacred affairs; that when you are called to judge concerning any question, you will have some principles of truth, some useful axioms and observations, always ready at hand to direct and assist your judgment.

IV. It is necessary that we should as far as possible entertain and lay up our daily new ideas in a regular order, and range the acquisitions of our souls under proper heads, whether of divinity, law, physics, mathematics, morality, politics, trade, domestic life, civility, decency, &c. whether of cause, effect, substance, mode, power, property, body, spirit, &c. We should inure our minds to method and order continually; and when we take in any fresh ideas, occurrences, and observations, we should dispose of them in their proper places, and see how they stand and agree with the rest of our notions on the same subjects: as a scholar would dispose of a new book on a proper shelf among its kindred authors; or as an officer at the post-house in London disposes of every letter he takes in, placing it in the box that belongs to the proper road or county.

In any of these cases, if things lay all in a heap, the addition of any new object would increase the confusion; but method gives a speedy and short survey of them with ease and pleasure. Method is of admirable advantage to keep our ideas from a confused mixture, and to preserve them ready for every use. The science of ontology, which distributes all beings, and all the affections of being, whether absolute or relative, under proper classes, is of good service to keep our intellectual acquisitions in such order as that the mind may survey them at once.

V. As method is necessary for the improvement of the mind, in order to make your treasure of ideas most useful, so in all your further pursuits of truth and acquirements of rational knowledge, observe a regular progressive method. Begin with the most simple, easy, and obvious ideas; then by degrees join two, and three, and more of them together: thus the complicated ideas, growing up under your eye and observation, will not give the same confusion of thought as they would do if they were all offered to the mind at once, without your observing the original and formation of them. An eminent example of this appears in the study of arithmetic. If a scholar, just admitted into the school, observes his master performing an operation in the rule of division, his head is at once disturbed and confounded with the manifold comparisons of the numbers of the divisor and dividend, and the multiplication of the one and subtraction of it from the other; but if he begin regularly at addition, and so proceed by subtraction and multiplication, he will then in a few weeks be able to take in an intelligent survey of all those operations in division, and to practise them himself with ease and pleasure, each of which at first seemed all intricacy and confusion.

An illustration of the like nature may be borrowed from geometry and algebra, and other mathematical practices: how easily does an expert geometrician with one glance of his eye take in a complicated diagram, made up of many lines and circles, angles, and arches! How readily does he judge of it, whether the demonstration designed by it be true or false! It was by degrees he arrived at this stretch of understanding; he began with a single line or a point; he joined two lines in an angle; he advanced to triangles and squares, polygons and circles; thus the powers of his understanding were stretched and augmented daily, till, by diligence and application, he acquired this extensive faculty of mind.

But this advantage does not belong only to mathematical learning. If we apply ourselves at first in any science to clear and single ideas, and never hurry ourselves on to the following and more complicated parts of knowledge, till we thoroughly understand the foregoing, we may practice the same method of enlarging the capacity of the soul with success in any one of the sciences, or in the affairs of life and religion.

Beginning with A, B, C, and making syllables out of letters, and words out of syllables, has been the foundation of all that glorious superstructure of arts and sciences which have enriched the minds and libraries of the learned world in several ages. These are the first steps by which the ample and capacious souls among mankind have arrived at that prodigious extent of knowledge, which renders them the wonder and glory of the nation where they live. Though Plato and Cicero, Descartes and Mr. Boyle, Mr. Locke and Sir Isaac Newton, were doubtless favoured by nature with a genius of uncommon amplitude; yet, in their early years, and first attempts of science, this was but limited and narrow, in comparison of what they attained at last. But how vast and capacious were those powers which they afterwards acquired by patient attention and watchful observation, by the pursuit of clear ideas, and a regular method of thinking!

VI. Another means of acquiring this amplitude and capacity of mind, is a perusal of difficult entangled questions, and of the solution of them in any science. Speculative and casuistical divinity will furnish us with many such cases and controversies. There are some such difficulties in reconciling several parts of the Epistles of St. Paul, relating to the Jewish law and the Christian gospel; a happy solution whereof will require such an extensive view of things, and the reading of these happy solutions will enlarge this faculty in younger students. In moral and political subjects, Puffendorff's Law of Nature and Nations, and several determinations therein will promote the same amplitude of mind. An attendance on public trials, and arguments in the civil courts of justice, will be of good advantage for this purpose: and after a man has studied the general principles of the law of nature, and the laws of England, in proper books, the reading the reports of adjudged cases, collected by men of great sagacity and judgment, will richly improve his mind toward acquiring this desirable amplitude and extent of thought, and more especially in persons of that profession.

CHAPTER XVII.

OF IMPROVING THE MEMORY.

Memory is a distinct faculty of the mind of man, very different from perception, judgment, and reasoning, and its other powers. Then we are said to remember any thing, when the idea of it arises in the mind with a consciousness at the same time that we have had this idea before. Our memory is our natural power of retaining what we learn, and of recalling it on every occasion. Therefore we can never be said to remember any thing, whether it be ideas or propositions, words or things, notions or arguments, of which we have not had some former idea or perception, either by sense or imagination, thought or reflection; but whatsoever we learn from observation, books, or conversation, &c. it must all be laid up and preserved in the memory, if we would make it really useful.

So necessary and so excellent a faculty is the memory of man, that all other abilities of the mind borrow from hence their beauty and perfection; for the other capacities of the soul are almost useless without this. To what purpose are all our labours in knowledge and wisdom, if we want memory to preserve and use what we have acquired? What signify all other intellectual and spiritual improvements, if they are lost as soon as they are obtained? It is memory alone that enriches the mind, by preserving what our labour and industry daily collect. In a word, there can be neither knowledge, nor arts, nor sciences, without memory; nor can there be any improvement of mankind in virtue or morals, or the practice of religion, without the assistance and influence of this power. Without memory the soul of man would be but a poor, destitute, naked being, with an everlasting blank spread over it, except the fleeting ideas of the present moment.

Memory is very useful to those who speak as well as to those who learn; it assists the teacher and the orator, as well as the scholar or the hearer. The best speeches and instructions are almost lost, if those who hear them immediately forget them. And those who are called to speak in public are much better heard and accepted, when they can deliver their discourse by the help of a lively genius and a ready memory, than when they are forced to read all that they would communicate to their hearers. Reading is certainly a heavier way of the conveyance of our sentiments; and there are very few mere readers who have the felicity of penetrating the soul and awakening the passions of those who hear, by such a grace and power of oratory, as the man who seems to talk every word from his very heart, and pours out the riches of his own knowledge upon the people round about him by the help of a free and copious memory. This gives life and spirit to every thing that is spoken, and has a natural tendency to make a deeper impression on the minds of men: it awakens the dullest spirits, causes them to receive a discourse with more affection and pleasure, and adds a singular grace and excellency both to the person and his oration.

A good judgment and a good memory are very different qualifications. A person may have a very strong, capacious, and retentive memory, where the judgment is very poor and weak: as sometimes it happens in those who are but one degree above an idiot, who have manifested an amazing strength and extent of memory, but have hardly been able to join or disjoin two or three ideas in a wise and happy manner to make a solid rational proposition.

There have been instances of others who have had but a very tolerable power of memory, yet their judgment has been of a much superior degree, just and wise, solid and excellent.

Yet it must be acknowledged, that where a happy memory is found in any person, there is one good foundation laid for a wise and just judgment of things, wheresoever the natural genius has any thing of sagacity and brightness to make a right use of it. A good judgment must always in some measure depend upon a survey and comparison of several things together in the mind, and determining the truth of some doubtful proposition by that survey and comparison. When the mind has, as it were, set all those various objects present before it, which are necessary to form a true proposition or judgment concerning any thing, it then determines that such and such ideas are to be joined or disjoined, to be affirmed or denied; and this is a consistency and correspondence with all those other ideas and propositions which any way relate or belong to the same subject. Now there can be no such comprehensive survey of many things without a tolerable degree of memory; it is by reviewing things past we learn to judge of the future: and it happens sometimes that if one needful or important object or idea be absent, the judgment concerning the thing inquired will thereby become false or mistaken.

You will inquire then, How comes it to pass that there are some persons who appear in the world of business, as well as in the world of learning, to have a good judgment, and have acquired the just character of prudence and wisdom, and yet have neither a very bright genius or sagacity of thought, nor a very happy memory, so that they cannot set before their minds at once a large scene of ideas in order to pass a judgment?

Now we may learn from Penseroso some accounts of this difficulty. You shall scarcely ever find this man forward in judging and determining things proposed to him; but he always takes time, and delays, and suspends, and ponders things maturely, before he passes his judgment: then he practises a slow meditation, ruminates on the subject, and thus perhaps in two or three nights and days rouses and awakens those several ideas, one after another, as he can, which are necessary in order to judge aright of the thing proposed, and makes them pass before his review in succession: this he doth to relieve the want both of a quick sagacity of thought and of a ready memory and speedy recollection; and this caution and practice lays the foundation of his just judgment and wise conduct. He surveys well before he judges.

Whence I cannot but take occasion to infer one good rule of advice to persons of higher as well as lower genius, and of large as well as narrow memories, viz. That they do not too hastily pronounce concerning matters of doubt or inquiry, where there is not an urgent necessity of present action. The bright genius is ready to be so forward as often betrays itself into great errors in judgment, speech, and conduct, without a continual guard upon itself, and using the bridle of the tongue. And it is by this delay and precaution that many a person of much lower natural abilities shall often excel persons of the brightest genius in wisdom and prudence.

It is often found that a fine genius has but a feeble memory: for where the genius is bright, and the imagination vivid, the power of memory may be too much neglected and lose its improvement. An active fancy readily wanders over a multitude of objects, and is continually entertaining itself with new flying images; it runs through a number of new scenes or new pages with pleasure, but without due attention, and seldom suffers itself to dwell long enough upon any one of them, to make a deep impression thereof upon the mind, and commit it to lasting remembrance. This is one plain and obvious reason why there are some persons of very bright parts and active spirits, who have but short and narrow powers of remembrance: for having riches of their own, they are not solicitous to borrow.

And as such a quick and various fancy and invention may be some hinderance to the attention and memory, so a mind of a good retentive ability, and which is ever crowding its memory with things which it learns and reads continually, may prevent, restrain, and cramp the invention itself. The memory of Lectorides is ever ready, upon all occasions, to offer to his mind something out of other men's writings or conversations, and is presenting him with the thoughts of other persons perpetually: thus the man who had naturally a good flowing invention, does not suffer himself to pursue his own thoughts. Some persons who have been blessed by nature with sagacity and no contemptible genius, have too often forbid the exercise of it, by tying themselves down to the memory of the volumes they have read, and the sentiments of other men contained in them.

Where the memory has been almost constantly employing itself in scraping together new acquirements, and where there has not been a judgment sufficient to distinguish what things were fit to be recommended and treasured up in the memory, and what things were idle, useless, or needless, the mind has been filled with a wretched heap of hodgepotch of words or ideas; and the soul may be said to have had large possessions, but no true riches.

I have read in some of Mr. Milton's writings a very beautiful simile, whereby he represents the books of the Fathers, as they are called in the Christian Church. Whatsoever, saith he, Old Time with his huge drag-net has conveyed down to us along the stream of ages, whether it be shells or shell-fish, jewels or pebbles, sticks or straws, sea-weeds or mud, these are the ancients, these are the fathers. The case is much the same with the memorial possessions of the greatest part of mankind. A few useful things, perhaps, mixed and confounded with many trifles, and all manner of rubbish, fill up their memories and compose their intellectual possessions. It is a great happiness therefore to distinguish things aright, and to lay up nothing in the memory but what has some just value in it, and is worthy to be numbered as a part of our treasure.

Whatsoever improvements arise to the mind of man from the wise exercise of his own reasoning powers, these may be called his proper manufactures; and whatsoever he borrows from abroad, these may be termed his proper treasures; both together make a wealthy and a happy mind.

How many excellent judgments and reasonings are framed in the mind of a man of wisdom and study in a length of years! How many worthy and admirable notions has he been possessed of in life, both by his own reasonings, and by his prudent and laborious collections in the course of his reading! But, alas! how many thousands of them vanish away again and are lost in empty air, for want of a stronger and more retentive memory! When a young practitioner in the law was once said to contest a point of debate with that great lawyer in the last age, Serjeant Maynard, he is reported to have answered him, "Alas! young man, I have forgot much more law than ever thou hast learnt or read."

What an unknown and unspeakable happiness would it be to a man of judgment, and who is engaged in the pursuit of knowledge, if he had but a power of stamping all his own best sentiments upon his memory in some indelible characters; and if he could but imprint every valuable paragraph and sentiment of the most excellent authors he has read, upon his mind, with the same speed and facility with which he read them! If a man of good genius and sagacity could but retain and survey all those numerous, those wise and beautiful ideas at once, which have ever passed through his thoughts upon any one subject, how admirably would he be furnished to pass a just judgment about all present objects and occurrences! What a glorious entertainment and pleasure would felicitate his spirit, if he could grasp all these in a single survey, as the skilful eye of a painter runs over a fine and complicate piece of history wrought by the hand of a Titian or a Raphael, views the whole scene at once, and feeds himself with the extensive delight! But these are joys that do not belong to mortality.

Thus far I have indulged some loose and unconnected thoughts and remarks with regard to the different powers of wit, memory, and judgment. For it was very difficult to throw them into a regular form or method without more room. Let us now with more regularity treat of the memory alone.

"Though the memory be a natural faculty of the mind of man, and belongs to spirits which are not incarnate—though the mind itself is immaterial—a principle superadded to matter, yet the brain is the instrument which it employs in all its operations. Though it is not matter, yet it works by means of matter, and its operations are materially affected by the condition of the brain, its principal organ. Through the medium of the brain and nervous system the mind obtains a knowledge of the external world. The memory receives impressions of facts and events, and treasures up their images; and it also becomes the retentive receptacle of the ideas and conclusions derived from meditation and reflection.

The immaturity of the brain in early life renders it incapable of becoming the instrument of powerful mental actions, and the images which are then impressed upon the memory are chiefly those of facts and events. The memory grows from the period of infancy, and may be greatly improved by proper exercise, or injured by sloth.

The improvement of the memory requires the cultivation of habits of attention, or of intense application of the mind to whatever is, at the time, its more immediate object of pursuit. Slight impressions are soon forgotten, but whatever is impressed upon the mind by fixed attention and close thought, is indelibly stamped upon the memory, and becomes as durable as the mind itself.

Many persons of advanced age will tell long stories of things which occurred during the early period of their lives, and were so deeply engraven upon the memory as to be retained in their most minute particulars through a long succession of years.

The memory is more or less affected by various diseases of the body; chiefly from injuries of the head, affections of the brain, fever, and diseases of extreme debility. Numerous cases are on record of persons who, from the influence of disease, have recovered a knowledge of things long forgotten; and of others who have lost all knowledge of persons and things. A man who was born in France, but had spent most of his life in England, and entirely lost the habit of speaking French, received an injury on the head, and, during the illness which followed, always spoke in the French language. Another, when recovering from an injury of the head, spoke the Welsh language, which he learned in childhood, but had subsequently entirely forgotten. Another entirely lost his mental faculties during a severe illness. For several weeks subsequent to his recovery he remembered nothing, and understood nothing; but at the expiration of two or three months he gradually recovered his memory and other faculties.

Impressions which are deeply engraven upon the mind appear never to be effaced; but the power of calling them up is sometimes lost, until sickness or some other cause restores that power. The faculties of the mind are greatly assisted or injured by the condition of the brain, which in most aged people relaxes its energies, and a want of close attention to passing events prevents lasting impressions from being made on the memory.

The brain being the chief instrument of the mind, whatever tends to promote a healthful and vigorous condition of that organ may help to preserve the memory; but excess of wine, or luxury of any kind, as well as excess in study and application to the business of life, may injure the memory by overstraining and weakening the brain."

A good memory has these several qualifications.

1. It is ready to receive and admit, with great ease, the various ideas both of words and things which are learned or taught. 2. It is large and copious to treasure up these ideas in great number and variety. 3. It is strong and durable to retain for a considerable time those words or thoughts which are committed to it. 4. It is faithful and active to suggest and recollect, upon every proper occasion, all those words or thoughts which have been recommended to its care, or treasured up in it.

Now in every one of these qualifications a memory may be injured or may be improved: yet I shall not insist distinctly on these particulars, but only in general propose a few rules or directions whereby this noble faculty of memory, in all its branches and qualifications, may be preserved or assisted, and show what are the practices that both by reason and experience have been found of happy influence to this purpose.

There is one great and general direction which belongs to the improvement of other powers as well as of the memory, and that is, to keep it always in due and proper exercise. Many acts by degrees form a habit, and thereby the ability or power is strengthened, and made more ready to appear again in action. Our memories should be used and inured from childhood to bear a moderate quantity of knowledge let into them early, and they will thereby become strong for use and service. As any limb well and duly exercised grows stronger, the nerves of the body are corroborated thereby. Milo took up a calf, and daily carried it on his shoulders; as the calf grew, his strength grew also, and he at last arrived at firmness of joints enough to bear the bull.

Our memories will be in a great measure moulded and formed, improved or injured, according to the exercise of them. If we never use them, they will be almost lost. Those who are wont to converse or read but a few things only, will retain but a few in their memory; those who are used to remember things but for an hour, and charge their memories with it no longer, will retain them but an hour before they vanish. And let words be remembered as well as things, that so you may acquire a *copia verborum* as well as *rerum*, and be more ready to express your mind on all occasions.

Yet there should be a caution given in such cases: the memory of a child or any infirm person should not be overburdened; for a limb or a joint may be overstrained by being too much loaded, and its natural power never be recovered. Teachers should wisely judge of the power and constitution of youth, and impose no more on them than they are able to bear with cheerfulness and improvement.

And particularly they should take care that the memory of the learner be not too much crowded with a tumultuous heap or overbearing multitude of documents or ideas at one time; this is the way to remember nothing; one idea effaces another. An overgreedy grasp does not retain the largest handful. But it is the exercise of memory with a due moderation, that is one general rule towards the improvement of it.

The particular rules are such as these:

1. Due attention and diligence to learn and know things, which we would commit to our remembrance, is a rule of great necessity in this case. When the attention is strongly fixed to any particular subject, all that is said concerning it makes a deeper impression upon the mind. There are some persons who complain they cannot remember divine or human discourses which they hear, when, in truth, their thoughts are wandering half the time, or they hear with such coldness and indifferency, and a trifling temper of spirit, that it is no wonder the things which are read or spoken make but a slight impression on the mind, and get no firm footing in the seat of memory, but soon vanish and are lost.

It is needful, therefore, if we would maintain a long remembrance of the things which we read, or hear, that we should engage our delight and pleasure in those subjects, and use the other methods which are before prescribed in order to fix the attention. Sloth, indolence, and idleness, will no more bless the mind with intellectual riches, than it will fill the hand with gain, the field with corn, or the purse with treasure.

Let it be added also, that not only the slothful and the negligent deprive themselves of proper knowledge for the furniture of their memory, but such as appear to have active spirits, who are ever skimming over the surface of things with a volatile temper, will fix nothing in their mind. Vario will spend whole mornings in running over loose and unconnected pages, and with fresh curiosity is ever glancing over new words and ideas that strike his present fancy; he is fluttering over a thousand objects of art and science, and yet treasures up but little knowledge. There must be the labour and the diligence of close attention to particular subjects of thought and inquiry, which only can impress what we read or think of upon the remembering faculty of man.

2. Clear and distinct apprehension of the things which we commit to memory is necessary in order to make them stick and dwell there. If we would remember words, or learn the names of persons or things, we should have them recommended to our memory by a clear and distinct pronunciation, spelling, or writing. If we would treasure up the ideas of things, notions, propositions, arguments, and sciences, these should be recommended also to our memory by a clear and distinct perception of them. Faint, glimmering, and confused ideas will vanish like images seen in twilight. Every thing which we learn should be conveyed to the understanding in the plainest expressions, without any ambiguity, that we may not mistake what we desire to remember. This is a general rule, whether we would employ the memory about words or things, though it must be confessed that mere sounds and words are much harder to get by heart than the knowledge of things and real images.

For this reason take heed (as I have often before warned) that you do not take up with words instead of things, nor mere sounds instead of real sentiments and ideas. Many a lad forgets what has been taught him, merely because he never well understood it; he never clearly and distinctly took in the meaning of those sounds and syllables which he was required to get by heart.

This is one true reason why boys make so poor a proficiency in learning the Latin tongue under masters who teach them by grammars and rules written in Latin, of which I have spoken before. And this is a common case with children when they learn their catechisms in their early days. The language and the sentiments conveyed in those catechisms are far above the understanding of creatures of that age, and they have no tolerable ideas under the words. This makes the answers much harder to be remembered, and in truth they learn nothing but words without ideas; and if they are ever so perfect in repeating the words, yet they know nothing of divinity.

And for this reason it is a necessary rule in teaching children the principles of religion, that they should be expressed in very plain, easy, and familiar words, brought as low as possible down to their understandings, according to their different ages and capacities, and thereby they will obtain some useful knowledge when the words are treasured up in their memory, because at the same time they will treasure up those divine ideas too.

3. Method and regularity in the things we commit to memory, is necessary in order to make them take more effectual possession of the mind, and abide there long. As much as systematical learning is decried by some vain and humorous triflers of the age, it is certainly the happiest way to furnish the mind with a variety of knowledge.

Whatsoever you would trust to your memory, let it be disposed in a proper method, connected well together, and referred to distinct and particular heads or classes, both general and particular. An apothecary's boy will much sooner learn all the medicines in his master's shop, when they are ranged in boxes or on shelves according to their distinct natures, whether herbs, drugs, or minerals, whether leaves or roots, whether chymical or galenical preparations, whether simple or compound, &c. and when they are placed in some order according to their nature, their fluidity, or their consistence, &c. in phials, bottles, gallipots, cases, drawers, &c.; so the genealogy of a family is more easily learnt when you begin at some great-grandfather as the root, and distinguish the stock, the large boughs, the lesser branches, the twigs, and the buds, till you come down to the present infants of the house. And, indeed, all sorts of arts and sciences taught in a method something of this kind are more happily committed to the mind or memory.

I might give another plain simile to confirm the truth of this. What horse or carriage can take up and bear away all the various rude and unwieldy loppings of a branchy tree at once? But if they are divided yet further, so as to be laid close, and bound up in a more uniform manner into several faggots, perhaps those loppings may be all carried at one single load or burden.

The mutual dependance of things on each other help the memory of both. A wise connexion of the parts of a discourse, in a rational method, gives great advantage to the reader or hearer in order to his remembrance of it. Therefore many mathematical demonstrations in a long train may be remembered much better than a heap of sentences which have no connexion. The book of Proverbs, at least from the tenth chapter and onwards, is much harder to remember than the book of Psalms, for this reason; and some Christians have told me that they remember what is written in the Epistle to the Romans, and that to the Hebrews, much better than many others of the sacred Epistles, because there is more exact method and connexion observed in them.

He that would learn to remember a sermon which he hears, should acquaint himself by degrees with the method in which the several important parts of it are delivered. It is a certain fault in a multitude of preachers, that they utterly neglect method in their harangues; or at least they refuse to render their method visible and sensible to the hearers. One would be tempted to think it was for fear lest their auditors should remember too much of their sermons, and prevent their preaching them three or four times over: but I have candour enough to persuade myself that the true reason is, they imagine it to be a more modish way of preaching without particulars: I am sure it is a much more useless one. And it would be of great advantage both to the speaker and hearer to have discourses for the pulpit cast into a plain and easy method, and the reasons or inferences ranged in a proper order, and that under the words, first, secondly, and thirdly, however they may be now fancied to sound unpolite or unfashionable; but Archbishop Tillotson did not think so in his days.

4. A frequent review, and careful repetition of the things we would learn, and an abridgment of them in a narrow compass for this end, has a great influence to fix them in the memory; therefore it is that the rules of grammar, and useful examples of the variation of words,

and the peculiar forms of speech in any language, are so often appointed by the masters as lessons for the scholars to be frequently repeated; and they are contracted into tables for frequent review, that what is not fixed in the mind at first, may be stamped upon the memory by a perpetual survey and rehearsal.

Repetition is so very useful a practice, that Mnemon, even from his youth to his old age, never read a book without making some small points, dashes, or hooks, in the margin, to mark what parts of the discourse were proper for review: and when he came to the end of a section or chapter, he always shut his book, and recollected all the sentiments or expressions he had remarked, so that he could give a tolerable analysis and abstract of every treatise he had read, just after he had finished it. Thence he became so well furnished with a rich variety of knowledge.

Even when a person is hearing a sermon or a lecture, he may give his thoughts leave now and then to step back so far as to recollect the several heads of it from the beginning, two or three times before the lecture or sermon is finished: the omission or the loss of a sentence or two among the amplifications is richly compensated by preserving in the mind the method and order of the whole discourse in the most important branches of it.

If we would fix in the memory the discourses we hear, or what we design to speak, let us abstract them into brief compends, and review them often. Lawyers and divines have need of such assistances: they write down short notes or hints of the principal heads of what they desire to commit to their memory in order to preach or plead, for such abstracts or epitomes may be reviewed much sooner, and the several amplifying sentiments or sentences will be more easily invented or recollected in their proper places. The art of shorthand is of excellent use for this as well as for other purposes. It must be acknowledged, that those who scarcely ever take a pen in their hand to write short notes or hints of what they are to speak or learn, who never try to cast things into method, or to contract the survey of them in order to commit them to their memory, had need have a double degree of that natural power of retaining and recollecting what they read, or hear, or intend to speak.

Do not plunge yourself into other businesses or studies, amusements or recreations, immediately after you have attended upon instruction, if you can well avoid it. Get time if possible to recollect the things you have heard, that they may not be washed all away from the mind by a torrent of other occurrences or engagements, nor lost in the crowd or clamour of other loud or importunate affairs.

Talking over the things which you have read with your companions on the first proper opportunity you have for it, is a most useful manner of review or repetition, in order to fix them upon the mind. Teach them your younger friends, in order to establish your own knowledge while you communicate it to them. The animal powers of your tongue and of your ear, as well as your intellectual faculties, will all join together to help the memory. Hermetas studied hard in a remote corner of the land, and in solitude, yet he became a very learned man. He seldom was so happy as to enjoy suitable society at home, and therefore he talked over to the fields and the woods in the evening what he had been reading in the day, and found so considerable advantage by this practice that he recommended it to all his friends, since he could set his probatum to it for seventeen years.

5. Pleasure and delight in the things we learn give great assistance towards the remembrance of them. Whatsoever therefore we desire that a child should commit to his memory, make it as pleasant to him as possible; endeavour to search his genius and his temper, and let him take in the instructions you give him or the lessons you appoint him, as far as may be, in a way suited to his natural inclination. Fabellus would never learn any moral lessons till they were moulded into the form of some fiction or fable like those of Æsop, or till they put on the appearance of a parable, like those wherein our blessed Saviour taught the ignorant world; then he remembered well the emblematical instructions that were given him, and learnt to practice the moral

sense and meaning of them. Young Spectorius was taught virtue by setting before him a variety of examples of the various good qualities in human life; and he was appointed daily to repeat some story of this kind out Valerius Maximus. The same lad was early instructed to avoid the common vices and follies of youth in the same manner. This is akin to the method whereby the Lacedæmonians trained up their children to hate drunkenness and intemperance, viz. by bringing a drunken man into their company, and showing them what a beast he had made of himself. Such visible and sensible forms of instruction will make long and useful impressions upon the memory.

Children may be taught to remember many things in a way of sport and play. Some young creatures have learnt their letters and syllables, and the pronouncing and spelling of words, by having them pasted or written upon many little flat tablets or dies. Some have been taught vocabularies of different languages, having a word in one tongue written on one side of these tablets, and the same word in another tongue on the other side of them.

There might be also many entertaining contrivances for the instruction of children in several things relating to geometry, geography, and astronomy, in such alluring and illusory methods, which would make a most agreeable and lasting impression on their minds.

6. The memory of useful things may receive considerable aid if they are thrown into verse; for the numbers and measures, and rhyme, according to the poesy of different languages, have a considerable influence upon mankind, both to make them receive with more ease the things proposed to their observation, and preserve them longer in their remembrance. How many are there of the common affairs of human life which have been taught in early years by the help of rhyme, and have been like nails fastened in a sure place, and riveted by daily use!

So the number of the days of each month are engraven on the memory of thousands by these four lines:—

Thirty days hath September,
June, and April, and November;
February twenty-eight alone;
All the rest have thirty-one.

So lads have been taught frugality by surveying and judging of their own expences by these three lines:—

Compute the pence but of one day's expence,
So many pounds, and angels, groats, and pence,
Are spent in one whole year's circumference.

For the number of days in a year is three hundred and sixty-five, which number of pence makes one pound, one angel, one groat, and one penny.

So have rules of health been prescribed in the book called *Schola Sdlernitani*, and many a person has preserved himself doubtless from evening gluttony, and the pains and diseases consequent upon it, by these two lines:—

Ex magna cœna stomacho fit maxima pœna:
Ut sis nocte levis, sit tibi cœna brevis.

Englished:—

To be easy all night
Let your supper be light;
Or else you'll complain
Of a stomach in pain.

And a hundred proverbial sentences in various languages are formed into rhyme or a verse, whereby they are made to stick upon the memory of old and young.

It is from this principle that moral rules have been cast into a poetic mould from all antiquity. So the golden verses of the Pythagoreans in Greek; Cato's distiches *De Moribus* in Latin; Lilly's precepts to scholars, called *Qui Mihi*, with many others; and this has been done with very good success. A line or two of this kind, recurring on the memory, have often guarded youth from a temptation to vice and folly, as well as put them in mind of their present duty.

It is for this reason also that the genders, declensions, and variations of nouns and verbs have been taught in verse, by those who have complied with the prejudice of long custom, to teach English children the Latin tongue by rules written in Latin: and truly those rude heaps of words and terminations of an unknown tongue would have never been so happily learnt by heart by a hundred thousand boys without this smoothing artifice; nor indeed do I know any thing else can be said with good reason to excuse or relieve the obvious absurdities of this practice.

7 When you would remember new things or words, endeavour to associate and connect them with some words or things which you have well known before, and which are fixed and established in your memory. This association of ideas is of great importance and force, and may be of excellent use in many instances of human life. One idea which is familiar to the mind, connected with others which are new and strange, will bring those new ideas into easy remembrance. Maronides had got the first hundred lines of Virgil's Æneis printed upon his memory so perfectly, that he knew not only the order and number of every word, but each verse also; and by this means he would undertake to remember two or three hundred names of persons or things, by some rational or fantastic connexion between some word in the verse, and some letter, syllable, property, or accident of the name or thing to be remembered, even though they had been repeated but once or twice at most in his hearing. Animato practised much the same art of memory, by getting the Latin names of twenty-two animals into his head according to the alphabet, viz. asinus, basilicus, canis, draco, elephas, felis, gryphus, hircus, iuvenis, leo, mulus, noctua, ovis, panthera, quadrupes, rhinoceros, simia, taurus, ursus, xiphius, hyæna or yæna, zibetta. Most of these he divided also into four parts, viz. head and body, feet, fins, or wings, and tail, and by some arbitrary or chimerical attachments of each of these to a word or thing, which he desired to remember, he committed them to the care of his memory, and that with good success.

It is also by this association of ideas that we may better imprint any new idea upon the memory, by joining with it some circumstance of the time, place, company, &c. wherein we first observed, heard, or learned it. If we would recover an absent idea, it is useful to recollect those circumstances of time, place, &c. The substance will many times be recovered and brought to the thoughts by recollecting the shadow: a man recurs to our fancy by remembering his garment, his size or stature, his office or employment, &c. A beast, bird, or fish, by its colour, figure or motion, by the cage, court-yard, or cistern wherein it was kept.

To this head also we may refer that remembrance of names and things which may be derived from our recollection of their likeness to other things which we know; either their resemblance in name, character, form, accident; or any thing that belongs to them. An idea or word which has been lost or forgotten, has been often recovered by hitting upon some other kindred word or idea which has the nearest resemblance to it, and that in the letters, syllables, or sound of the name, as well as properties of the thing.

If we would remember Hippocrates, or Galen, or Paracelsus, think of a physician's name beginning with H, G, or P. If we will remember Ovidius Naso, we may represent a man with a large nose; if Plato, we may think upon a person with large shoulders; if Crispus, we shall fancy another with curled hair; and so of other things.

And sometimes a new or strange idea may be fixed in the memory by considering its contrary or opposite. So if we cannot hit on the word Goliath, the remembrance of David may recover it; or the name of a Trojan may be recovered by thinking of a Greek, &c.

8. In such cases wherein it may be done, seek after a local memory, or a remembrance of what you have read by the side or page of where it is written or printed; whether the right or the left, whether at the top, the middle, or the bottom, whether at the beginning of a chapter or a paragraph, or the end of it. It has been some advantage, for this reason, to accustom one's self to books of the same edition; and it has been of constant and special use to divines and private Christians to be furnished with several Bibles of the same edition; that wheresoever they are, whether in their chamber,

parlour, or study, in the younger or elder years of life, they may find the chapters and verses standing in the same parts of the page.

This is also a great convenience to be observed by printers in the new editions of grammars, psalms, Testaments, &c. to print every chapter, paragraph, or verse, in the same part of the page as the former, that so it may yield a happy assistance to those young learners who find, and even feel, the advantage of a local memory.

9. Let every thing we desire to remember be fairly and distinctly written and divided into periods, with large characters in the beginning, for by this means we shall the more readily imprint the matter and words on our minds, and recollect them with a glance, the more remarkable the writing appears to the eye. This sense conveys the ideas to the fancy better than any other; and what we have seen is not so soon forgotten as what we have only heard. What Horace affirms of the mind or passions may be said also of the memory:—

> Segnius irritant animos demissa per aurem,
> Quam quæ sunt oculis subjecta fidelibus, et quæ
> Ipse sibi tradit spectator.

Applied thus in English:

> Sounds which address the year are lost and die
> In one short hour; but that which strikes the eye
> Lives long upon the mind; the faithful sight
> Engraves the knowledge with a beam of light.

For the assistance of weak memories the first letters or words of every period, in every page, may be written in distinct colours; yellow, green, red, black, &c.; and if you observe the same order of colours in the following sentences, it will be still the better. This will make a greater impression, and may much aid the memory.

Under this head we may take notice of the advantage which the memory gains by having the several objects of our learning drawn out into schemes and tables; matters of mathematical science and natural philosophy are not only let into the understanding, but preserved in the memory by figures and diagrams. The situation of the several parts of the earth are better learned by one day's conversing with a map or a sea-chart, than by merely reading the description of their situation a hundred times over in books of geography. So the constellations in astronomy, and their position in the heavens, are more easily remembered by hemispheres of the stars well drawn. It is by having such sort of memorials, figures, and tables, hung round our studies or places of residence or resort, that our memory of these things will be greatly assisted and improved, as I have shown at large in the twentieth chapter, of the use of sciences.

I might add here also, that once writing over what we design to remember, and giving due attention to what we write, will fix it more in the mind than reading it five times. And in the same manner, if we had a plan of the naked lines of longitude and latitude projected on the meridian printed for this use, a learner might much more speedily advance himself in the knowledge of geography by his own drawing the figures of all the parts of the world upon it by imitation, than by many days survey of a map of the world so printed.—The same also may be said concerning the constellations of heaven, drawn by the learner on a naked projection of the circles of the sphere upon the plane of the equator.

10. It has sometimes been the practice of men to imprint names or sentences on their memory by taking the first letters of every word of that sentence, or of those names, and making a new word of them. So the name of the Maccabees is borrowed from the first letters of the Hebrew words, which make that sentence Mi Camoka Bealim Jehovah, i. e. Who is like thee among the gods? which was written on their banners. Jesus Christ our Saviour has been called a fish, in Greek ΙΧΘΥΣ by the fathers, because these are the first letters in those Greek words, Jesus Christ, God's Son, the Saviour. So the word Vibgyor teaches us to remember the order of the seven original colours, as they appear by the sunbeams cast through a prism on white paper, or formed by the sun in a rainbow, according to the different refrangibility of the rays, viz. violet, indigo, blue, green, yellow, orange, and red.

In this manner the Hebrew grammarians teach their students to remember the letters which change their natural pronunciation by the inscription of a dagesh, by gathering these six letters, beth, gimel, daleth, caph, pe, and thau, into the word Begadchepat; and that they might not forget the letters named Quiescent, viz. a, h, v, and i, they are joined in the word Ahevi. So the universal and particular propositions in logic are remembered by the words Barbara, Celarent, Darii, &c.

Other artificial helps to memory may be just mentioned here.

Dr. Grey, in his book called Memoria Technica, has exchanged the figures 1, 2, 3, 4, 5, 6, 7, 8, 9, for some consonants, b, d, t, f, l, y, p, k, n, and some vowels, a, e, i, o, u, and several diphthongs, and thereby formed words that denote numbers, which may be more easily remembered: and Mr. Lowe has improved his scheme in a small pamphlet called Mnemonics Delineated; whereby in seven leaves he has comprised almost an infinity of things, in science and in common life, and reduced them to a sort of measure like Latin verse; though the words may be supposed to be very barbarous, being such a mixture of vowels and consonants as are very unfit for harmony.

But after all, the very writers on this subject have confessed that several of those artificial helps of memory are so cumbersome as not to be suitable to every temper or person; nor are they of any use for the delivery of a discourse by memory, nor of much service in learning the sciences: but they may be sometimes practised for the assisting our remembrance of certain sentences, numbers, and names.

CHAPTER XVIII.

OF DETERMINING A QUESTION.

I. When a subject is proposed to your thoughts, consider whether it be knowable at all, or no; and then whether it be not above the reach of your inquiry and knowledge in the present state; and remember, that it is great waste of time to busy yourselves too much amongst unsearchables: the chief use of these studies is to keep the mind humble, by finding its own ignorance and weakness.

II. Consider again whether the matter be worthy of your inquiry at all; and then how far it may be worthy of your present search and labour according to your age, your time of life, your station in the world, your capacity, your profession, your chief design and end. There are many things worth inquiry to one man, which are not so to another; and there are things that may deserve the study of the same person in one part of life, which would be improper or impertinent at another. To read books of the art of preaching, or disputes about church discipline, are proper for a theological student in the end of his academical studies, but not at the beginning of them. To pursue mathematical studies very largely may be useful for a professor of philosophy, but not for a divine.

III. Consider whether the subject of your inquiry be easy or difficult; whether you have sufficient foundation or skill, furniture and advantage for the pursuit of it. It would be madness for a young statuary to attempt at first to carve a Venus or a Mercury, and especially without proper tools. And it is equal folly for a man to pretend to make great improvements in natural philosophy without due experiments.

IV. Consider whether the subject be any ways useful or no before you engage in the study of it: often put this question to yourselves, *Cui Bono?* To what purpose? What end will it attain? Is it for the glory of God, for the good of men, for your own advantage, for the removal of any natural or moral evil, for the attainment of any natural or moral good? Will the profit be equal to the labour? There are many subtle impertinences learned in the schools; many painful trifles, even among the mathematical theorems and problems; many difficiles nugæ, or laborious follies of various kinds, which some ingenious men have been engaged in. A due reflection upon these things will call the mind away from vain amusements, and save much time.

V. Consider what tendency it has to make you wiser and better, as well as to make you more learned; and those questions which tend to wisdom and prudence in our conduct among men, as well as piety toward God, are doubtless more important, and preferable beyond all those inquiries which only improve our knowledge in mere speculations.

VI. If the question appear to be well worth your diligent application, and you are furnished with the necessary requisites to pursue it, then consider whether it be dressed up and entangled in more words than is needful, and contain or include more complicated ideas than is necessary; and if so, endeavour to reduce it to a greater simplicity and plainness, which will make the inquiry and argument easier and plainer all the way.

VII. If it be stated in an improper, obscure, or irregular form, it may be meliorated by changing the phrase, or transposing the parts of it; but be careful always to keep the grand and important point of inquiry the same in your new stating the question. Little tricks and deceits of sophistry, by sliding in or leaving out such words as entirely change the question should be abandoned and renounced by all fair disputants and honest searchers after truth.

The stating a question with clearness and justice goes a great way many times towards the answering it. The greatest part of true knowledge lies in a distinct perception of things which are in themselves distinct; and some men give more light and knowledge by the bare stating of the question with perspicuity and justice, than others by talking of it in gross confusion for whole hours together. To state a question is but to separate and disentangle the parts of it from one another, as well as from every thing which does not concern the question, and then lay the disentangled parts of the question in due order and method: oftentimes, without more ado, this fully resolves the doubt, and shows the mind where the truth lies, without argument or dispute.

VIII. If the question relate to an axiom, or first principle of truth, remember that a long train of consequences may depend upon it; therefore it should not be suddenly admitted or received.

It is not enough to determine the truth of a proposition, much less to raise it to the honour of an axiom or first principle, to say that it has been believed through many ages, that it has been received by many nations, that it is almost universally acknowledged, or nobody denies it, that it is established by human laws, or that temporal penalties or reproaches will attend the disbelief of it.

IX. Nor is it enough to forbid any proposition the title of axiom, because it has been denied by some persons, and doubted of by others; for some persons have been unreasonably credulous, and others have been as unreasonably sceptical. Then only should a proposition be called an axiom, or a self-evident truth, when, by a moderate attention to the subject and predicate, their connexion appears in so plain a light, and so clear an evidence, as needs no third idea, or middle term, to prove them to be connected.

X. While you are in search after truth in questions of a doubtful nature, or such as you have not yet thoroughly examined, keep up a just indifference to either side of the question, if you would be led honestly into the truth: for a desire or inclination leaning to either side biasses the judgment strangely: whereas by this indifference for every thing but truth, you will be excited to examine fairly instead of presuming, and your assent will be secured from going beyond your evidence.

XI. For the most part people are born to their opinions, and never question the truth of what their family, or their country, or their party profess. They clothe their minds as they do their bodies, after the fashion in vogue, nor one of a hundred ever examined their principles. It is suspected of lukewarmness to suppose examination necessary; and it will be charged as a tendency to apostasy, if we go about to examine them. Persons are applauded for presuming they are in the right, and, as Mr. Locke saith, he that considers and inquires into the reason of things is counted a foe to orthodoxy, because possibly he may deviate from some of the received doctrines. And thus men, without any industry or acquisition of their own (lazy and idle as they are) inherit local truths, i. e. the truths of that place where they live, and are inured to assent without evidence.

This hath a long and unhappy influence; for if a man can bring his mind once to be positive and fierce for propositions whose evidence he hath never examined, and that in matters of the greatest concernment, he will naturally follow this short and easy way of judging and believing in cases of less moment, and build all his opinions upon insufficient grounds.

XII. In determining a question, especially when it is a matter of difficulty and importance, do not take up with partial examination, but turn your thoughts on all sides, to gather in all the light you can towards the solution of it. Take time, and use all the helps that are to be attained, before you fully determine, except only where present necessity of action calls for speedy determination.

If you would know what may be called a partial examination, take these instances, viz.

When you examine an object of sense or inquire into some matter of sensation at too great a distance from the object, or in an inconvenient situation of it, or under any indisposition of the organs, or any disguise whatsoever relating to the medium or the organ of the object itself, or when you examine it by one sense only, where others might be employed; or when you inquire into it by sense only, without the use of the understanding, and judgment, and reason.

If it be a question which is to be determined by reason and argument, then your examination is partial when you turn the question only in one light, and do not turn it on all sides: when you look upon it only in its relations and aspects to one sort of object, and not to another; when you consider only the advantages of it, and the reasons for it, and neglect to think of the reasons against it, and never survey its inconveniences too; when you determine on a sudden, before you have given yourself a due time for weighing all circumstances, &c.

Again, if it be a question of fact, depending upon the report or testimony of men, your examination is but partial when you inquire only what one man or a few say, and avoid the testimony of others; when you only ask what those report who were not eye or ear witnesses, and neglect those who saw and heard it; when you content yourself with mere loose and general talk about it, and never enter into particulars; or when there are many who deny the fact, and you never concern yourself about their reasons for denying it, but resolve to believe only those who affirm it.

There is yet a further fault in your partial examination of any question, when you resolve to determine it by natural reason only where you might be assisted by supernatural revelation; or when you decide the point by some word or sentence, or by some part of revelation without comparing it with other parts, which might give further light, and better help to determine the meaning.

It is also a culpable partiality, if you examine some doubtful or pretended vision or revelation without the use of reason, or without the use of that revelation which is undoubted and sufficiently proved to be divine. These are all instances of imperfect examination: and we should never determine a question by one or two lights, where we may have the advantage of three or four.

XIII. Take heed lest some darling notion, some favourite hypothesis, some beloved doctrine, or some common but unexamined opinion, be made a test of the truth or falsehood of all other propositions about the same subject. Dare not build much upon such a notion or doctrine till it be very fully examined, accurately adjusted, and sufficiently confirmed. Some persons, by indulging such a practice, have been led into long ranks of errors; they have found themselves involved in a train of mistakes, by taking up some petty hypothesis or principle, either in philosophy, politics, or religion, upon slight and insufficient grounds, and establishing that as a test and rule by which to judge of all other things.

XIV. For the same reason, have a care of suddenly determining any one question, on which the determination of any kindred or parallel cases will easily or naturally follow. Take heed of receiving any wrong turn in your early judgment of things; be watchful as far as possible against any false bias, which may be given to the understanding, especially in younger years. The indulgence of some one silly opinion, or the giving credit to one foolish fable, lays the mind open to be imposed upon by many. The ancient Romans were taught to believe that Romulus and Remus, the founders of their state and empire, were exposed in the woods, and nursed by a wolf: this story prepared their minds for the reception of any tales of the like nature relating to other countries. Trojus Pompeius would enforce the belief, that one of the ancient kings of Spain was also nursed and suckled by a hart, from the fable of Romulus and Remus. It was by the same influence they learned to give up their hopes and fears to omens and soothsaying, when they were once persuaded that the greatness of their empire, and the glory of Romulus their founder, were predicted by the happy omen of twelve vultures appearing to him when he sought where to build the city. They readily received all the following legends, of prodigies, auguries, and prognostics, for many ages together, with which Livy has furnished his huge history.

So the child who is once taught to believe any one occurrence to be a good or evil omen, or any day of the month or week to be lucky or unlucky, hath a wide inroad made on the soundness of his understanding in the following judgments of his life; he lies ever open to all the silly impressions and idle tales of nurses, and imbibes many a foolish story with greediness, which he must unlearn again if ever he become acquainted with truth and wisdom.

XV. Have a care of interesting your warm and religious zeal in those matters which are not sufficiently evident in themselves, or which are not fully and thoroughly examined and proved; for this zeal, whether right or wrong, when it is once engaged, will have a powerful influence to establish your own minds in those doctrines which are really doubtful, and to stop up all the avenues of further light. This will bring upon the soul a sort of sacred awe and dread of heresy, with a divine concern to maintain whatever opinion you have espoused as divine, though perhaps you have espoused it without any just evidence, and ought to have renounced it as false and pernicious.

We ought to be zealous for the most important points of our religion, and to contend earnestly for the faith once delivered to the saints; but we ought not to employ this sacred fervour of spirit in the service of any article till we have seen it made out with plain and strong conviction, that it is a necessary or important point of faith or practice, and is either an evident dictate of the light of nature, or an assured article of revelation. Zeal must not reign over the powers of our understanding, but obey them: God is the God of light and truth, a God of reason and order, and he never requires mankind to use their natural faculties amiss for the support of his cause. Even the most mysterious and sublime doctrines of revelation are not to be believed without a just reason for it; nor should our pious affections be engaged in the defence of them till we have plain and convincing proof that they are certainly revealed, though perhaps we may never in this world attain to such clear and distinct ideas of them as we desire.

XVI. As a warm zeal ought never to be employed in the defence of any revealed truth, till our reason be well convinced of the revelation; so neither should wit and banter, jest and ridicule, ever be indulged to oppose or assault any doctrines of professed revelation, till reason has proved they are not really revealed; and even then these methods should be used very seldom, and with the utmost caution and prudence. Raillery and wit were never made to answer our inquiries after truth, and to determine a question of rational controversy; though they may sometimes be serviceable to expose to contempt those inconsistent follies which have been first abundantly refuted by argument, they serve indeed only to cover nonsense with shame, when reason has first proved it to be mere nonsense.

It is therefore a silly and most unreasonable test which some of our deists have introduced to judge of divine revelation, viz. to try if it will bear ridicule and laughter. They are effectually beaten in all their combats at the weapons of men, that is, reason and argument; and it would not be unjust (though it is a little uncourtly) to say that they would now attack our religion with the talents of a vile animal, that is, grin and grimace.

I cannot think that a jester or a monkey, a droll or a puppet, can be proper judges or deciders of controversy. That which dresses up all things in disguise is not likely to lead us into any just sentiments about them. Plato or Socrates, Cæsar or Alexander, might have a fool's coat clapped upon any of them, and perhaps, in this disguise, neither the wisdom of the one, nor the majesty of the other, would secure them from a sneer; this treatment would never inform us whether they were kings or slaves, whether they were fools or philosophers. The strongest reasoning, the best sense, and the politest thoughts, may be set in a most ridiculous light by this grinning faculty: the most obvious axioms of eternal truth may be dressed in a very foolish form, and wrapped up in artful absurdities by this talent; but they are truth, and reason, and good sense still. Euclid, with all his demonstrations, might be so covered and overwhelmed with banter, that a beginner in the mathematics might be tempted to doubt whether his theorems were true or no, and to imagine they could never be useful. So weaker minds might be easily prejudiced against the noblest principles of truth and goodness; and the younger part of mankind might be beat off from the belief of the most serious, the most rational and important points, even of natural religion, by the impudent jests of a profane wit. The moral duties of the civil life, as well as the articles of Christianity, may be painted over with the colours of folly, and exposed upon a stage, so as to ruin all social and personal virtue among the gay and thoughtless part of the world.

XVII. It should be observed also, that these very men cry out loudly against the use of all severe railing and reproach in debates, and all penalties and persecutions of the state, in order to convince the minds and consciences of men, and determine points of truth and error.

Now I renounce these penal and smarting methods of conviction as much as they do, and yet I think still these are every whit as wise, as just, and as good for this purpose as banter and ridicule. Why should public mockery in print, or a merry joke upon a stage, be a better test of truth than severe railing sarcasm, and public persecutions and penalties? Why should more light be derived to the understanding by a song of scurrilous mirth, or a witty ballad, than there is by a rude cudgel? When a professor of any religion is set up to be laughed at, I cannot see how this should help us to judge of the truth of his faith any better than if he were scourged. The jeers of a theatre, the pillory, and the whippingpost are very near akin. When the person or his opinion is made the jest of the mob, or his back the shambles of the executioner, I think there is no more conviction in the one than in the other.

XVIII. Besides, supposing it is but barely possible that the great God should reveal his mind and will to men by miracle, vision, or inspiration, it is a piece of contempt and profane insolence to treat any tolerable or rational appearance of such a revelation with jest and laughter, in order to find whether it be divine or not. And yet, if this be a proper test of revelation, it may be properly applied to the true as well as the false, in order to distinguish it. Suppose a royal proclamation was sent to a distant part of the kingdom, and some of the subjects should doubt whether it came from the king or no; is it possible that wit and ridicule should ever decide the point? Or would the prince ever think himself treated with just honour to have his proclamation canvassed in this manner on a public stage, and become the sport of buffoons, in order to determine the question, Whether it is the word of a king or no?

Let such sort of writers go on at their dearest peril, and sport themselves in their own deceivings; let them at their peril make a jest at the Bible, and treat the sacred articles of Christianity with scoff and merriment: but then let them lay aside all their pretences to reason as well as religion; and as they expose themselves by such writings to the neglect and contempt of men, so let them prepare to meet the majesty and indignation of God without timely repentance.

XIX. In reading philosophical, moral, or religious controversies, never raise your esteem of any opinion by the assurance and zeal wherewith the author asserts it, nor by the highest praises he bestows upon it; nor, on the other hand, let your esteem of an opinion be abated, nor your aversion to it raised by the supercilious contempt cast upon it by a warm writer, nor by the sovereign airs with which he condemns it. Let the force of argument alone influence your assent or dissent. Take care that your soul be not warped or biassed on one side or the other by any strains of flattering or abusive language; for there is no question whatsoever but what hath some such sort of defenders and opposers. Leave those writers to their own follies who practise thus upon the weakness of their readers without argument; leave them to triumph in their own fancied possessions and victories: it is oftentimes found that their possessions are but a heap of errors, and their boasted victories are but overbearing noise and clamour to silence the voice of truth.

In philosophy and religion the bigots of all parties are generally the most positive, and deal much in this sort of argument. Sometimes these are the weapons of pride, for a haughty man supposes all his opinions to be infallible, and imagines the contrary sentiments are ever ridiculous and not worthy of notice. Sometimes these ways of talking are the mere arms of ignorance: the men who use them know little of the opposite side of the question, and therefore they exult in their own vain pretences to knowledge, as though no man of sense could oppose their opinions. They rail at an objection against their own sentiments, because they can find no other answer to it but railing. And men of learning, by their excessive vanity, have been sometimes tempted into the same insolent practice as well as the ignorant.

Yet let it be remembered too, that there are some truths so plain and evident, that the opposition to them is strange, unaccountable, and almost monstrous: and in vindication of such truths a writer of good sense may sometimes be allowed to use a degree of assurance, and pronounce them strongly with an air of confidence, while he defends them with reasons of convincing force.

XX. Sometimes a question may be proposed which is of so large and extensive a nature, and refers to such a multitude of subjects, as ought not in justice to be determined at once by a single argument or answer: as if one should ask me, Are you a professed disciple of the Stoics or the Platonists? Do you receive an assent to the principles of Gassendus, Descartes, or Sir Isaac Newton? Have you chosen the hypothesis of Tycho or Copernicus? Have you devoted yourself to the sentiments of Arminius, or Calvin? Are your notions episcopal, presbyterian, or independent, &c.? I think it may be very proper in such cases not to give an answer in the gross, but rather to enter into a detail of particulars, and explain one's own sentiments. Perhaps there is no man, nor set of men upon earth, whose sentiments I entirely follow. God has given me reason to judge for myself; and though I may see sufficient ground to agree to the greatest part of the opinions of one person or party, yet it does by no means follow that I should receive them all. Truth does not always go by the lump, nor does error tincture and spoil all the articles of belief that some one party professes.

Since there are difficulties attend every scheme of human knowledge, it is enough for me in the main to incline to that side which has the fewest difficulties; and I would endeavour, as far as possible, to correct the mistakes or the harsh expressions of one party, by softening and reconciling methods, by reducing the extremes, and by borrowing some of the best principles or phrases from another. Cicero was one of the greatest men of antiquity, and gives us an account of the various opinions of philosophers in his age; but he himself was of the eclectic sect, and chose out of each of them such positions as in his wisest judgment came nearest to the truth.

XXI. When you are called in the course of life or religion to judge and determine concerning any question, and to affirm or deny it, take a full survey of the objections against it, as well as the arguments for it, as far as your time and circumstances admit, and see on which side the preponderation falls. If either the objections against any proposition, or the arguments for the defence of it, carry in them most undoubted evidence, and are plainly unanswerable, they will and ought to constrain the assent, though there may be many seeming probabilities on the other side, which at first sight would flatter the judgment to favour it. But where the reasons on both sides are very near of equal weight, there suspension or doubt is our duty, unless in cases wherein present determination or practice is required, and there we must act according to the present appearing preponderation of reasons.

XXII. In matters of moment and importance, it is our duty indeed to seek after certain and conclusive arguments (if they can be found) in order to determine a question; but where the matter is of little consequence, it is not worth our labour to spend much time in seeking after certainties; it is sufficient here, if probable reasons offer themselves. And even in matters of greater importance, especially where daily practice is necessary, and where we cannot attain any sufficient or certain grounds to determine a question on either side, we must then take up with such probable arguments as we can arrive at. But this general rule should be observed, viz. to take heed that our assent be no stronger, or rise no higher in the degree of it, than the probable argument will support.

XXIII. There are many things even in religion, as well as in philosophy and civil life, which we believe with very different degrees of assent; and this is, or should be, always regulated according to the different degrees of evidence which we enjoy: and perhaps there are a thousand gradations in our assent to the things we believe, because there are thousands of circumstances relating to different questions, which increase or diminish the evidence we have concerning them, and that in matters both of reason and revelation.

I believe there is a God, and that obedience is due to him from every reasonable creature; this I am most fully assured of, because I have the strongest evidence, since it is the plain dictate both of reason and revelation.

Again, I believe there is a future resurrection of the dead, because scripture tells us so in the plainest terms, though reason says nothing of it. I believe also, that the same matter of our bodies which died (in part at least) shall arise; but I am not so fully assured of this circumstance, because the revelation of it is not quite so clear and express. Yet further, I believe that the good men who were acquainted here on earth shall know each other in heaven; but my persuasion of it is not absolutely certain, because my assent to it arises only from circumstantial reasonings of men upon what God has told us, and therefore my evidences are not strong beyond a possibility of mistake. This direction cannot be too often repeated, that our assent ought always to keep pace with our evidence; and our belief of any proposition should never rise higher than the proof or evidence we have to support it, nor should our faith run faster than right reason can encourage it.

XXIV. Perhaps it will be objected here, Why then does our Saviour, in the histories of the Gospel, so much commend a strong faith, and lay out both his miraculous benefits and his praises upon some of those poor creatures of little reasoning who professed an assured belief of his commission and power to heal them?

I answer, the God of nature has given every man his own reason to be the judge of evidence to himself in particular, and to direct his assent in all things about which he is called to judge; and even the matters of revelation are to be believed by us because our reason pronounces the revelation to be true. Therefore the great God will not, or cannot, in any instance, require us to assent to any thing without reasonable or sufficient evidence; nor to believe any proposition more strongly than what our evidence for it will support. We have therefore abundant ground to believe, that those persons of whom our Saviour requires such strong faith, or whom he commends for their strong faith, had as strong and certain evidence of his power and commission from the credible and incontestable reports they had heard of his miracles, which were wrought on purpose to give evidence to his commission.* Now in such a case, both this strong faith and the open profession of it were very worthy of public encouragement and praise from our Saviour, because of the great and public opposition which the magistrates, and the priests, and the doctors of the age made against Jesus the man of Nazareth, when he appeared as the Messiah.

And besides all this it may be reasonably supposed, with regard to some of those strong exercises of faith which are required and commended, that these believers had some further hints of inward evidence and immediate revelation from God himself; as when St. Peter confesses Christ to be the Son of God, Matt. xvi. 16, 17, our blessed Saviour commends him saying, "Blessed art thou, Simon Barjona;" but he adds, "Flesh and blood hath not revealed it unto thee, but my Father who is in heaven."

And the same may be said concerning the faith of miracles, the exercise whereof was sometimes required of the disciples and others, i. e. when by inward and divine influences God assured them such miracles should be wrought, their obedience to and compliance with these divine illuminations was expected and commended. Now this supernatural inspiration carried sufficient evidence with it to them, as well as to the ancient prophets, though we who never felt it are not so capable to judge and distinguish it.

XXV. What is said before concerning truth or doctrines, may be also confirmed concerning duties; the reason of both is the same; as the one are truths for our speculation, the others are truths for our practice. Duties which are expressly required in the plain lan-

*When our Saviour gently reproves Thomas for his unbelief, John, xx. 29, he does it in these words, "Because thou hast seen me, Thomas, thou hast believed: blessed are they who have not seen, and yet have believed," i. e. Blessed are they who, though they have not been favoured with the evidence of their senses as thou hast been, yet have been convinced by the reasonable and sufficient moral evidence of the well grounded report of others, and have believed in me upon that evidence. Of this moral evidence Mr. Ditton writes exceedingly well in his book of the Resurrection of Christ.

guage of Scripture, or dictated by the most evident reasoning upon first principles, ought to bind our consciences more than those which are but dubiously inferred, and that only from occasional occurrences, incidents, and circumstances: as for instance, I am certain that I ought to pray to God; my conscience is bound to this, because there are most evident commands for it to be found in Scripture, as well as to be derived from reason. I believe also, that I may pray to God either by a written form or without one, because neither reason nor revelation expressly requires either of these modes of prayer at all times, or forbids the other. I cannot, therefore, bind my conscience to practise the one so as utterly to renounce the other; but I would practice either of them as my reason and other circumstances direct me.

Again, I believe that Christians ought to remember the death of Christ by the symbols of bread and wine; and I believe there ought to be pastors in a Christian church some way ordained or set apart to lead the worship, and to bless and distribute the elements; but the last of these practices is not so expressly directed, prescribed, and required in Scripture as the former; and, therefore, I feel my conscience evidently bound to remember the death of Christ with some society of Christians or other, since it is a most plain command, though their methods of ordaining a pastor be very different from other men, or from my own opinion; or whether the person who distributes these elements be only an occasional or a settled administrator; since none of these things are plainly determined in Scripture. I must not omit or neglect an express command, because some unnecessary circumstances are dubious. And I trust I shall receive approbation from the God of nature, and from Jesus my judge at the last day, if I have endeavoured in this manner to believe and practice every thing in proportion to the degree of evidence which God has given me about it, or which he has put me into a capacity to seek and obtain in the age and nation wherein I live.

Query, Whether the obstinate deists and the fatalists of Great Britain will find sufficient apology from this principle? But I leave them to venture the awful experiment.

XXVI. We may observe these three rules in judging of probabilities which are to be determined by reason, relating either to things past or things to come.

1. That which agrees most with the constitution of nature carries the greatest probability in it, where no other circumstance appears to counterpoise it: as if I let loose a greyhound within sight of a hare upon a large plain, there is great probability the greyhound will seize her; that a thousand sparrows will fly away at the sight of a hawk among them.

2. That which is most conformable to the constant observations of men, or to experiment frequently repeated, is most likely to be true; as that a winter will not pass away in England without some frost and snow; that if you deal out great quantities of strong liquor to the mob, there will be many drunk; that a large assembly of men will be of different opinions in any doubtful point; that a thief will make his escape out of prison if the doors of it are unguarded at midnight.

3. In matters of fact, which are past or present, where neither nature, nor observation, nor custom, gives us any sufficient information on either side of the question, there we may derive a probability from the attestation of wise and honest men, by word or writing, or the concurring witnesses of multitudes who have seen and known what they relate, &c. This testimony in many cases will arise to the degree of moral certainty. So we believe that the plant tea grows in China; and that the emperor of the Turks lives at Constantinople; that Julius Cæsar conquered France, and that Jesus our Saviour lived and died in Judea; that thousands were converted to the Christian faith in a century after the death of Christ; and that the books which contain the Christian religion are certain histories and epistles which were written above a thousand years ago. There is an infinite variety of such propositions which can admit of no reasonable doubt, though they are not matters which are directly evident to our own senses or our mere reasoning powers.

XXVII. When a point hath been well examined, and our own judgment settled upon just arguments in our manly age, and after a large survey of the merits of the cause, it would be a weakness for us always to continue fluttering in suspense We ought therefore to stand firm in such well established principles, and not be tempted to change and alter for the sake of every difficulty, or every occasional objection. We are not to be carried about with every flying doctrine, like children tossed to and fro, and wavering with the wind. It is a good thing to have the heart established with grace, not with meats; that is, in the great doctrines of the gospel of grace, and in Jesus Christ, who is the same yesterday, to-day, and for ever; but it is not so necessary in the more minute matters of religion, such as meats and drink, forms and ceremonies, which are of less importance, and for which Scripture has not given such express directions. This is the advice of the great apostle, Eph. 14; Heb. xiii. 8, 9.

In short, those truths which are the springs of daily practice should be settled as soon as we can with the exercise of our best powers after the state of manhood: but those things wherein we may possibly mistake should never be so absolutely and finally established and determined as though we were infallible. If the papists of Great Britain had maintained such a resolute establishment and assurance in the days of King Henry VIII. or Queen Elizabeth, there never had been a reformation: nor would any heathen have been converted, even under the ministry of St. Paul, if their obstinate settlement in their idolatries had kept their eyes shut against all further light. Yet this should not hinder us from settling our most important principles of faith and practice, where reason shines with its clearest evidence, and the word of God plainly determines truth and duty.

XXVIII. But let us remember also, that though the Gospel be an infallible revelation, we are but fallible interpreters when we determine the sense even of some important propositions written there; and therefore, though we seem to be established in the belief of any particular sense of Scripture, and though there may be just calls of Providence to profess and subscribe it, yet there is no need that we should resolve or promise, subscribe or swear, never to change our mind (since it is possible, in the nature and course of things, we may meet with such a solid and substantial objection as may give us a quite different view of things from what we once imagined, and may lay before us sufficient evidence of the contrary.) We may happen to find a fairer light cast over the same Scriptures, and see reason to alter our sentiments even in some points of moment. *Sic sentio, sic sentiam*, i. e. so I believe, and so I will believe, is the prison of the soul for lifetime, and a bar against all the improvements of the mind. To impose such a profession on other men in matters not absolutely necessary, and not absolutely certain, is a criminal usurpation and tyranny over faith and conscience, and which none has power to require but an infallible dictator.

CHAPTER XIX.

OF INQUIRING INTO CAUSES AND EFFECTS.

SOME effects are found out by their causes, and some causes by their effects. Let us consider both these.

I. When we are inquiring into the cause of any particular effect or appearance, either in the world of nature, or in the civil or moral concerns of men, we may follow this method:

1. Consider what effects or appearances you have known of a kindred nature, and what have been the certain and real causes of them; for like effects have generally like causes, especially when they are found in the same sort of subjects.

2. Consider what are the several possible causes which may produce such an effect, and find out by some circumstances how many of those possible causes are excluded in this particular case: Thence proceed by degrees to the probable causes, till a more close attention and inspection shall exclude some of them also, and lead you gradually to the real and certain cause.

3. Consider what things preceded such an event or appearance, which might have any influence upon it; and though we cannot certainly determine the cause of any thing only from its going before the effect, yet among the many forerunners we may probably light upon the true cause by further and more particular inquiry.

4. Consider whether one cause be sufficient to produce the effect, or whether it does not require a concurrence of several causes; and then endeavour as far as possible to adjust the degrees of influence that each cause might have in producing the effect, and the proper agency and influence of each of them therein.

So in natural philosophy, if I would find what are principles or causes of that sensation which we call heat when I stand near the fire; here I shall find it is necessary that there be an agency of the particles of fire on my flesh, either mediately by themselves, or at least by the intermediate air; there must be a particular sort of motion and vellication impressed upon my nerves; there must be a derivation of that motion to the brain; and there must be an attention of my soul to this motion; if either of these are wanting, the sensation of heat will not be produced.

So in the moral world, if I inquire into the revolution of a state or kingdom, perhaps I find it brought about by the tyranny and folly of a prince, or by the disaffection of his own subjects; and this disaffection and opposition may arise either upon the account of impositions in religion, or injuries relating to their civil rights; or the revolution may be effected by the invasion of a foreign army, or by the opposition of some person at home or abroad that lays claim to the government, &c. or a herc who would guard the liberties of the people; or by many of these concurring together: then we must adjust the influences of each as wisely as we can, and not ascribe the whole event to one of them alone.

II. When we are inquiring into the effects of any particular cause or causes, we may follow this method:

1. Consider diligently the nature of every cause apart, and observe what effect every part or property of it will tend to produce.

2. Consider the causes united together in their several natures, and ways of operation: inquire how far the powers or properties of one will hinder or promote the effects of the other, and wisely balance the propositions of their influence.

3. Consider what the subject is, in or upon which the cause is to operate: for the same cause on different subjects will oftentimes produce different effects; as the sun which softens wax will harden clay.

4. Be frequent and diligent in making all proper experiments, in setting such causes at work, whose effects you desire to know, and putting together in an orderly manner such things as are most likely to produce some useful effects, according to the best survey you can take of all the concurring causes and circumstances.

5. Observe carefully all the events which happen either by an occasional concurrence of various causes, or by the industrious applications of knowing men: and when you see any happy effect certainly produced, and often repeated, treasure it up, together with the known causes of it, amongst your improvements.

6. Take a just survey of all the circumstances which attend the operation of any cause or causes, whereby any special effect is produced: and find out as far as possible how far any of those circumstances had a tendency either to obstruct or promote or change those operations, and consequently how far the effect might be influenced by them.

In this manner physicians practise and improve their skill. They consider the various known effects of particular herbs or drugs, they meditate what will be the effects of their composition, and whether the virtues of the one will exalt or diminish the force of the other, or correct any of its nocent qualities. Then they observe the native constitution, and the present temper or circumstances of the patient, and what is likely to be the effect of such a medicine on such a patient. And in all uncommon cases they make wise and cautious experiments, and nicely observe the effects of particular compound medicines on different constitutions and in different diseases, and by these treasures of just observations they grow up to an honourable degree of skill in the art of healing. So the preacher considers the doctrines and reasons, the precepts, the promises and threatenings of the word of God, and what are the natural effects of them upon the mind; he considers what is the natural tendency of such a virtue, or such a vice; he is well apprized that the representation of some of these things may convince the understanding, some may terrify the conscience, some may allure the slothful, and some encourage the desponding mind; he observes the temper of his hearers, or of any particular person that converses with him about things sacred, and he judges what will be the effects of each representation on such persons; he reviews and recollects what have been the effects of some special parts and methods of his ministry; and by a careful survey of all these he attains greater degrees of skill in his sacred employment.

Note—In all these cases we must distinguish those causes and effects which are naturally and necessarily connected with each other, from those which have only an accidental or contingent connexion. Even in those causes where the effect is but contingent, we may sometimes arrive at a very high degree of probability; yet we cannot arrive at such certainty as where the causes operate by an evident and natural necessity, and the effects necessarily follow the operation.—See more on this subject, Logic, Part II. chap. V. sect. 7.

CHAPTER XX.

OF THE SCIENCES, AND THEIR USE IN PARTICULAR PROFESSIONS.

I. The best way to learn any science is to begin with a regular system, or a short and plain scheme of that science, well drawn up into a narrow compass, omitting the deeper and more abstruse parts of it, and that also under the conduct and instruction of some skilful teacher. Systems are necessary to give an entire and comprehensive view of the several parts of any science, which may have a mutual influence toward the explication or proof of each other: whereas if a man deals always and only in essays and discourses on particular parts of a science, he will never obtain a distinct and just idea of the whole, and may perhaps omit some important part of it, after seven years reading of such occasional discourses.

For this reason young students should apply themselves to their systems much more than pamphlets. That man is never so fit to judge of particular subjects relating to any science, who has never taken a survey of the whole.

It is the remark of an ingenious writer, should a barbarous Indian, who had never seen a palace or a ship, view their separate and disjointed parts, and observe the pillars, doors, windows, cornices, and turrets of the one, or the prow and stern, the ribs and masts, the ropes and shrouds, the sails and tackle of the other, he would be able to form but a very lame and dark idea of either of those excellent and useful inventions. In like manner, those who contemplate only the fragments or pieces broken off from any science, dispersed in short unconnected discourses, and do not discern their relation to each other, and how they may be adapted, and by their union procure the delightful symmetry of a regular scheme, can never survey an entire body of truth, but must always view it as deformed and dismembered; while their ideas, which must be ever indistinct and often repugnant, will lie in the brain unsorted, and thrown together without order or coherence: such is the knowledge of those men who live upon the scraps of the sciences.

A youth of genius and lively imagination, of an active and forward spirit, may form within himself some alluring scenes and pleasing schemes in the beginning of a science, which are utterly inconsistent with some of the necessary and substantial parts of it which appear in the middle or the end. And if he never read and pass through the whole, he takes up and is satisfied with his own hasty pleasing schemes, and treasures these errors up amongst his solid acquisitions; whereas his own labour and study farther pursued would have shown him his early mistakes, and cured him of his self-flattering delusions.

Hence it comes to pass that we have so many half-scholars nowadays, and there is so much confusion and inconsistency in the notions and opinions of some persons, because they devote their hours of study entirely to short essays and pamphlets, and cast contempt upon systems under a pretence of greater politeness; whereas the true reason of this contempt of systematical learning is mere laziness and want of judgment.

II. After we are grown well acquainted with a short system or compendium of a science, which is written in the plainest and most simple manner, it is then proper to read a large regular treatise on that subject, if we design a complete knowledge and cultivation of it: and either while we are reading this larger system, or after we have done it, then occasional discourses and essays upon the particular subjects and parts of that science may be read with the greatest profit: for in these essays we may often find very considerable corrections and improvements of what these compends, or even the larger systems may have taught us, mingled with some mistakes.

And these corrections or improvements should be as remarks adjoined by way of note or commentary in their proper places, and superadded to the regular treatise we have read. Then a studious and judicious review of the whole will give us a tolerable acquaintance with that science.

III. It is a great happiness to have such a tutor, or such friends and companions at hand, who are able to inform us what are the best books written on any science, or any special part of it. For want of this advantage many a man has wasted his time in reading over perhaps some whole volumes, and learnt little more by it than to know that those volumes were not worth his reading.

IV. As for the languages, they are certainly best

learned in the younger years of life. The memory is then most empty and unfurnished, and ready to receive new ideas continually. We find that children, in two years time after they are born, learn to speak their native tongue.

V. The mere abstracted sciences, which depend more upon the understanding and judgment, and which deal much in abstracted ideas, should not be imposed upon children too soon; such are logic, metaphysics, ethics, politics, or the depths and difficulties of grammar and criticism. Yet it must be confessed the first rudiments of grammar are necessary, or at least very convenient to be known when a youth learns a new language; and some general easy principles and rules of morality and divinity are needful in order to teach a child his duty to God and man; but to enter far into abstracted reasonings on these subjects is beyond the capacity of children.

VI. There are several of the sciences that will more agreeably employ our younger years, and the general parts of them may be easily taken in by boys. The first principles and easier practices of arithmetic, geometry, plain trigonometry, measuring heights, depths, lengths, distances, &c. the rudiments of geometry and astronomy, together with something of mechanics, may be easily conveyed into the minds of acute young persons, from nine or ten years old and upward. These studies may be entertaining and useful to young ladies as well as to gentlemen, and to all those who are bred up to the learned professions. The fair sex may intermingle those with the operations of the needle and the knowledge of domestic life. Boys may be taught to join them with their rudiments of grammar, and their labour in the languages. And even those who never learn any language but their mother-tongue, may be taught these sciences with lasting benefit in early days.

That this may be done with ease and advantage, take these three reasons:

1. Because they depend so much upon schemes and numbers, images, lines, and fingers, and sensible things, that the imagination or fancy will greatly assist the

understanding, and render the knowledge of them much more easy.

2. These studies are so pleasant that they will make the dry labour of learning words, phrases, and languages more tolerable to boys in a Latin school by this most agreeable mixture. The employment of youth in these studies will tempt them to neglect many of the foolish plays of childhood, and they will find sweeter entertainment for themselves and their leisure hours by a cultivation of these pretty pieces of alluring knowledge.

3. The knowledge of these parts of science are both easy and worthy to be retained in the memory by all children when they come to manly years, for they are useful through all the parts of human life: they tend to enlarge the understanding early, and to give a various acquaintance with useful subjects betimes. And surely it is best, as far as possible, to train up children in the knowledge of those things which they should never forget rather than to let them waste years of life in trifles, or in hard words which are not worth remembering.

And here by the way I cannot but wonder that any author in our age should have attempted to teach any of the exploded physics of Descartes, or the nobler inventions of Sir Isaac Newton in his hypothesis of the heavenly bodies and their motions, in his doctrine of light and colours, and other parts of his physiology, or to instruct children in the knowledge of the theory of the heavens, earth and planets, without any figures or diagrams. Is it possible to give a boy or a young lady the clear, distinct, and proper apprehensions of these things, without lines and figures to describe them? Does not their understanding want the aid of fancy and images to convey stronger and juster ideas of them to the inmost soul? Or do they imagine that youth can penetrate into all these beauties and artifices of nature, without those helps which persons of maturer age find necessary for that purpose? I would not willingly name the books, because some of the writers are said to be gentlemen of excellent acquirements.

VII. After we have first learnt and gone through any of those arts and sciences which are to be explained by diagrams, figures, and schemes, such as geometry, geography, astronomy, optics, mechanics, &c. we may best preserve them in memory, by having those schemes and figures in large sheets of paper hanging always before the eye in closets, parlours, halls, chambers, entries, staircases, &c. Thus the learned images will be perpetually impressed upon the brain, and will keep the learning that depends upon them alive and fresh in the mind through the growing years of life: the mere diagrams and figures will ever recall to our thoughts those theorems, problems, and corollaries, which have been demonstrated by them.

It is incredible how much geography may be learnt this way by the two terrestrial hemispheres, and by particular maps and charts of the coast and countries of the earth happily disposed round about us. Thus we may learn also the constellations, by just projections of the celestial sphere, hung up in the same manner. And I must confess, for the bulk of learners of astronomy, I like that projection of the stars best which includes in it all the stars of our horizon, and therefore it reaches to the thirty-eighth and half degree of southern latitude, though its centre is the north pole. This gives us a better view of the heavenly bodies, as they appear every night to us, and it may be made use of with a little instruction, and with ease, to serve for a nocturnal, and show the true hour of the night.

But remember, if there be any colouring upon these maps or projections, it should be laid on so thin as not to obscure or conceal any part of the lines, figures, or letters; whereas most times they are daubed so thick with gay and glaring colours, and hung up so high above the reach of the eye that should survey and read them as though their only design were to make a gaudy show upon the wall, and they hung there merely to cover the naked plaster or wainscot.

Those sciences which may be drawn out into tables may be also thus hung up and disposed in proper places, such as brief abstracts of history, chronology, &c,; and indeed the schemes of any of the arts or sciences may be analyzed in a sort of skeleton, and represented upon tables, with various dependencies and connexions of their several parts and subjects that belong to them. Mr. Solomon Lowe has happily thrown the grammar of several languages into such tables; and a frequent review of these abstracts and epitomes would tend much to imprint them on the brain, when they have been once well learned; this would keep those learned traces always open, and assist the weakness of a labouring memory. In this manner may a scheme of the Scripture history be drawn out, and perpetuate those ideas in the mind with which our daily reading furnishes us.

VIII. Every man who pretends to the character of a scholar should attain some general and superficial ideas of most or all the sciences: for there is a certain connexion among the various parts of human knowledge, so that some notions borrowed from any one science may assist our acquaintance with any other, either by way of explication, illustration, or proof: though there are some sciences conjoined by a much nearer affinity than others.

IX. Let those parts of every science be chiefly studied at first, and reviewed afterwards, which have a more direct tendency to assist our proper profession, as men, or our general profession, as Christians, always observing what we have ourselves found most necessary and useful to us in the course of our lives. Age and experience will teach us to judge which of the sciences, and which parts of them, have been of greatest use and are most valuable; but in younger years of life we are not sufficient judges of this matter, and therefore should seek advice from others who are elder.

X. There are three learned professions among us, viz. divinity, law, and medicine. Though every man who pretends to be a scholar or a gentleman should so far acquaint himself with a superficial scheme of all the sciences, as not to stand amazed like a mere stranger at the mention of the common subjects that belong to them; yet there is no necessity for every man of learning to enter into their difficulties and deep recesses, nor to climb the heights to which some others have arrived. The knowledge of them in a proper measure may be happily useful to every profession, not only because all arts and sciences have a sort of communion and connexion with each other, but it is an angelic pleasure to grow in knowledge, it is a matter of honour and esteem, and renders a man more agreeable and acceptable in every company.

But let us survey several of them more particularly, with regard to the learned professions; and first, of the mathematics.

XI. Though I have so often commended mathematical studies, and particularly the speculations of arithmetic and geometry, as a means to fix a wavering mind, to beget a habit of attention, and to improve the faculty of reason; yet I would by no means be understood to recommend to all a pursuit of these sciences, to those extensive lengths to which the moderns have advanced them. This is neither necessary nor proper for any students, but those few who shall make those studies their chief profession and business of life, or those gentlemen whose capacities and turn of mind are suited to these studies, and have all manner of advantage to improve in them.

The general principles of arithmetic, algebra, geometry, and trigonometry, of geography, of modern astronomy, mechanics, statics, and optics, have their valuable and excellent uses, not only for the exercise and improvement of the faculties of the mind, but the subjects themselves are very well worth our knowledge in a moderate degree, and are often made of admirable service in human life. So much of these subjects as Dr. Wells has given us in his three volumes, entitled The Young Gentleman's Mathematics, is richly sufficient for the greatest part of scholars or gentlemen; though perhaps there may be some single treatises, at least on some of these subjects, which may be better written and more useful to be perused than those of that learned author.

But a penetration into the abstruse difficulties and depths of modern algebra and fluxions, the various methods of quadratures, the mensuration of all manner of curves, and their mutual transformation, and twenty other things that some modern mathematicians deal in, are not worth the labour of those who design either of the three learned professions, divinity, law, or physic, as the business of life. This is the sentence of a considerable man, viz. Dr. George Cheyne, who was a very good proficient and writer on these subjects: he affirms that they are but barren and airy studies, for a man entirely to live upon, and that for a man to indulge and riot in these exquisitely bewitching contemplations is only proper for public professors, or for gentlemen of estates, who have a strong propensity this way, and a genius fit to cultivate them.

But, says he, to own a great but grievous truth, though they may quicken and sharpen the invention; strengthen and extend the imagination, improve and refine the reasoning faculty, and are of use both in the necessary and the luxurious refinement of mechanical arts; yet having no tendency to rectify the will, to sweeten the temper, or mend the heart, they often leave a stiffness, a positiveness, a sufficiency on weak minds, which is much more pernicious to society, and to the interests of the great end of our being, than all their advantages can recompense. He adds further, concerning the launching into the depths of these studies, that they are apt to beget a secret and refined pride, an overweening and overbearing vanity, the most opposite temper to the true spirit of the Gospel. This tempts them to presume on a kind of omniscience in respect to their fellow creatures, who have not risen to their elevation; nor are they fit to be trusted in the hands of any but those who have acquired an humble heart, a lowly spirit, and a sober and teachable temper. See Dr. Cheyne's preface to his Essay on Health and Long Life.

XII. Some of the practical parts of geometry, astronomy, dialling, optics, statics, mechanics, &c. may be agreeable entertainments and amusements to students in every profession, at leisure hours, if they enjoy such circumstances of life as to furnish them with conveniences for this sort of improvement: but let them take great care lest they entrench upon more necessary employments, and so fall under the charge and censure of wasted time.

Yet I cannot help making this observation, that where

students, or indeed any young gentlemen have, in their early years, made themselves masters of a variety of elegant problems in the mathematical circle of knowledge, and gained the most easy, neat, and entertaining experiments in natural philosophy, with some short and agreeable speculations or practices, in any other of the arts and sciences, they have hereby laid a foundation for the esteem and love of mankind among those with whom they converse, in higher or lower ranks of life; they have been often guarded by this means from the temptation of innocent pleasures, and have secured both their own hours and the hours of their companions from running to waste in sauntering and trifles, and from a thousand impertinences in silly dialogues. Gaming and drinking, and many criminal and foolish scenes of talk and action, have been prevented by these innocent and improving elegancies of knowledge.

XIII. History is a necessary study in the supreme place for gentlemen who deal in politics. The government of nations, and distressful and desolating events which have in all ages attended the mistakes of politicians, should be ever present on their minds, to warn them to avoid the like conduct. Geography and chronology, which precisely inform us of the place or time where such transactions or events happened, are the eyes of history, and of absolute necessity in some measure to attend it.

But history, as far as relates to the affairs of the Bible, is as necessary to divines as to gentlemen of any profession. It helps us to reconcile many difficulties in Scripture, and demonstrates a divine Providence. Dr. Prideaux's Connexions of the Old and New Testament is an excellent treatise of this kind.

XIV. Among the smaller histories, biography, or the memoirs of the lives of great and good men, has a high rank in my esteem, as worthy of the perusal of every person who devotes himself to the study of divinity. Therein we frequently find our holy religion reduced to practice, and many parts of Christianity shining with a trancendent and exemplary light. We learn there how deeply sensible great and good men have been of the ruins of human nature by the first apostasy from God, and how they have toiled and laboured, and turned themselves on all sides, to seek a recovery in vain, till they have found the Gospel of Christ an all-sufficient relief. We are there furnished with effectual and unanswerable evidences that the religion of Jesus, with all its self-denials, virtues, and devotions, is a very practicable thing, since it has been carried to such a degree of honour by some wise and holy men. We have been there assured that the pleasures and satisfactions of the Christian life, in its present practice and future hopes, are not mere raptures of fancy and enthusiasm, when some of the strictest professors of reason have added the sanction of their testimony.

In short, the lives or memoirs of persons of piety, well written, have been of infinite and unspeakable advantage to the disciples and professors of Christianity, and have given us admirable instances and rules how to resist every temptation of a soothing or frowning world, how to practice important and difficult duties, how to love God above all, and to love our neighbour as ourselves, to live by the faith of the Son of God, and to die in the same faith, in sure and certain hope of a resurrection to eternal life.

XV. Remember that logic and ontology or metaphysics, are necessary sciences, though they have been greatly abused by scholastic writers, who have professed to teach them in former ages. Not only all students, whether they design the profession of theology, law, or physic, but all gentlemen should at least acquire a superficial knowledge of them. The introduction of so many subtleties, nice distinctions, and insignificant terms, without clear ideas, has brought a great part of the logic and metaphysics of the schools into just contempt. Their logic has appeared the mere art of wrangling, and their metaphysics the skill of splitting a hair, of distinguishing without a difference, and of putting long hard names upon common things, and sometimes upon a confused jumble of things which have no clear ideas belonging to them.

It is certain that an unknown heap of trifles and impertinences have been intermingled with these useful parts of learning, upon which account many persons in this polite age have made it a part of their breeding to throw a jest upon them; and to rally them well has been esteemed a more valuable talent than to understand them.

But this is running into wide extremes, nor ought these parts of science to be abandoned by the wise, because some writers of former ages have played the fool with them. True logic teaches us to use our reason well, and brings a light into the understanding: true metaphysics or ontology casts a light upon all the objects of thought and meditation, by ranging every being, with all the absolute and relative perfections and properties, modes and attendants of it, in proper rank and classes, and thereby it discovers the various relations of things to each other, and what are their general or special differences from each other, wherein a great part of human knowledge consists. And by this means it greatly conduces to instruct us in method, or the disposition of every thing into its proper rank and class of beings, attributes, or action.

XVI. If I were to say any thing of natural philosophy, I would venture to lay down my sentiments thus:

I think it must needs be very useful to a divine to understand something of natural science. The mere natural history of birds, beasts, and fishes, of insects, trees, and plants, as well as of meteors, such as clouds, thunder, lightnings, snow, hail, frost, &c. in all their common or uncommon appearances, may be of considerable use to one who studies divinity, to give him wider and more delightful views of the works of God, and to furnish him with lively and happy images and metaphors drawn from the large volume of nature, to display and represent the things of God and religion in the most beautiful and affecting colours.

And if the mere history of these things be useful for this purpose, surely it will be of further advantage to be led into the reasons, causes, and effects of these natural objects and appearances, and to know the established laws of nature, matter, and motion, whereby the great

God carries on his extensive works of providence from the creation to this day.

I confess the old Aristotelian scheme of this science will teach us very little that is worth knowing about these matters; but the later writers, who have explained nature and its operations in a more sensible and geometrical manner, are well worth the moderate study of a divine; especially those who have followed the principles of that wonder of our age and nation, Sir Isaac Newton. There is much pleasure and entertainment as well as real profit to be derived from those admirable improvements which have been advanced in natural philosophy in late years, by the assistance of mathematical learning, as well as from the multitude of experiments which have been made and are still making in natural subjects.

XVII. This is a science which indeed eminently belongs to the physician: he ought to know all the parts of human nature, what are the sound and healthy functions of an animal body, and what are the distempers and dangers which attend it; he should also be furnished with a large knowledge of plants and animals, and every thing which makes up the *materia medica*, or the ingredients of which medicines are made; and many other things in natural philosophy are subservient to his profession, as well as the kindred art of surgery.

XVIII. Questions about the powers and operations of nature may also sometimes come into the lawyer's cognizance, especially such as relate to assaults, wounds, murders, &c. I remember I have read a trial of a man for murder by drowning, wherein the judge on the bench heard several arguments concerning the lungs being filled or not filled with water, by inspiration or expiration, &c.; to all which he professed himself so much a stranger, as did not do him any great honour in public.

XIX. But I think no divine, who can obtain it, should be utterly destitute of this knowledge. By the assistance of this study he will be better able to survey the various monuments of creating wisdom in the heavens, the earth, the seas, with wonder and worship: and by the use of a moderate skill in this science, he may communicate so much of the astonishing works of God in the formation and government of this visible world, and so far instruct many of his hearers, as may assist the transfusion of the same ideas into their minds, and raise them to the same delightful exercises of devotion. O Lord, how manifold are thy works! in wisdom hast thou made them all! They are sought out by all that have pleasure in them.

Besides, it is worthy of the notice of every student in theology, that he ought to have some acquaintance with the principles of nature, that he may judge a little how far they will go; so that he may not be imposed upon to take every strange appearance in nature for a miracle, that he may reason the clearer upon the subject, that he may better confirm the miracles of Moses and of Christ, nor yield up his faith to any pretences of prodigy and wonder, which are either the occasional and uncommon operations of the elements, or the crafty sleights of men well skilled in philosophy and mechanical operations to delude the simple.

XX. The knowledge also of animal nature, and of the rational soul of man, and the mutual influence of these two ingredients of our composition upon each other, is worthy the study of a divine. It is of great importance to persons of this character and office to judge how far the animal powers have influence upon such and such particular appearances and practices of mankind; how far the appetites or passions of human nature are owing to the flesh and blood, or to the mind; how far they may be moderated, and how far they ought to be subdued; and what are the happiest methods of obtaining these ends. By this science also we may be better informed how far these passions or appetites are lawful, and how far they are criminal, by considering how far they are subject to the power of the will, and how far they may be changed and corrected by our watchfulness, care, and diligence.

It comes also very properly under the cognizance of this profession to be able in some measure to determine questions which may arise relating to real inspiration or prophecy, to wild enthusiasm, to fits of a convulsive kind, to melancholy or frenzy, &c. and what directions are proper to be given concerning any appearances of this nature.

XXI. Next to the knowledge of natural things, and acquaintance with the human nature and constitution, which is made up of soul and body, I think that natural religion properly takes its place. This consists of these two parts, viz. 1. The speculative or contemplative, which is the knowledge of God in his various perfections and in his relations to his rational creatures, so far as may be known by the light of nature, which heretofore used to be called the second part of metaphysics. It includes also, 2. That which is practical or active, that is, the knowledge of the several duties which arise from our relation to God, and our relation to our fellow creatures, and our proper conduct and government of ourselves; this has been used to be called ethics, or moral philosophy.

XXII. The knowledge of these things is proper for all men of learning; not only because it teaches them to obtain juster views of the several parts of revealed religion and of Christianity, which are built upon them, but because every branch of natural religion, and of moral duty, is contained and necessarily implied in all the revealed religions that ever God prescribed to the world. We may well suspect that religion does not come from God which renounces any part of natural duty.

Whether mankind live under the dispensation of the patriarchs, or of Moses, or the prophets, or of our Lord Jesus Christ, still we are bound to know the one true God, and to practise all that adoration and reverence, all that love to him, that faith in his perfections, with that obedience and submission to his will, which natural religion requires. We are still bound to exercise that justice, truth, and goodness towards our neighbours, that restraint and moderation of our own appetites and passions, and that regular behaviour towards ourselves and all our fellow creatures around us, which moral philosophy teaches. There is no sort of revealed religion that will dispense with these natural obligations;

and a happy acquaintance with the several appetites, inclinations, and passions of human nature, and the best methods to rule and restrain, to direct and govern them, are our constant business, and ought to be our everlasting study.

Yet I would lay down this caution, viz. That since students are instructed in the knowledge of the true God in their lectures on Christianity, and since among the Christian duties they are also taught all the moral dictates of the light of nature, or a complete scheme of ethics, there is no absolute necessity of learning these two parts of natural religion, as distinct sciences, separate and by themselves; but still it is of great importance for a tutor, while he is reading to his pupils these parts of the Christian religion, to give them notice how far the light of nature or mere reason will instruct us in these doctrines and duties, and how far we are obliged to divine relation and Scripture, for clearing up and establishing the firm foundations of the one, for affording us superior motives and powers to practice the other, for raising them to more exalted degrees, and building so glorious a superstructure upon them.

XXIII. The study of natural religion, viz. the knowledge of God and the rules of virtue and piety, as far as they are discovered by the light of nature, is needful to prove the truth of divine revelation or scripture, in the most effectual manner: but after the divine authority of Scripture is established, that will be a very sufficient spring from whence the bulk of mankind may derive their knowledge of divinity, or the Christian religion, in order to their own present faith and practice, and their future and eternal happiness. In this sense theology is a science necessary for every one that hopes for the favour of God and the felicity of another world; and it is of infinitely more importance than any of the arts and sciences which belong to any of the learned professions here on earth.

XXIV. Perhaps it will be thought necessary I should say something concerning the study of the civil law, or the law of nature and nations.

If we would speak with great justness and propriety,

subjection to the clergy in matters of this life and the life to come.

But to return, there are still so many forms of proceeding in judicature, and things called by Latin names in the profession of the law, and so many barbarous words with Latin terminations, that it is necessary lawyers should understand this language. Some acquaintance also with the old French tongue is needful for the same persons and professions, since the tenures of Lyttleton, which are a sort of Bible to the gentlemen of the long robe, were written in that language: and this tongue has been interwoven in some forms of the English law, from the days of William the Conqueror, who came from Normandy in France.

XXVIII. Physicians should be skilled in the Greek as well as in the Latin, because their great master Hippocrates wrote in that tongue, and his writings are still of good value and use. A multitude of the names, both of the parts of the body, of diseases, and of medicines are derived from the Greek language: and there are many excellent books of physic, both in the theoretical and practical parts of it which are delivered to the world in the Roman tongue, and of which that profession should not be ignorant.

XXIX. Such as intend the study of theology should be well acquainted also with the Latin, because it has been for many hundred years the language of the schools of learning: their disputations are generally limited to that language, and many and excellent books of divinity must be entirely concealed from the students, unless they are acquainted with Latin authors.

But those that design the sacred profession of theology should make it their labour of chief importance to be very conversant with their Bibles, both in the Old and New Testament: and this requires some knowledge of those original languages, Greek and Hebrew, in which the Scriptures were written. All that will pursue these studies with honour should be able to read the Old Testament tolerably in the Hebrew tongue; at least they should be so far acquainted with it as to find out the sense of a text by the help of a dictionary. But scarce any man should be thought worthy of the name of a solid divine, or a skilful teacher of the Gospel, in these days of light and liberty, unless he has pretty good knowledge of the Greek, since all the important points of the Christian religion are derived from the New Testament, which was first written in that language.

XXX. As for the Syriac and Arabic tongues, if one divine in thirty, or in three hundred, travel far into these regions, it is enough. A few learned men skilled in these languages will make sufficient remarks upon them for the service of the whole Christian world; which remarks may sometimes happen to be of use to those divines who are unacquainted with them in reading the Bible. But the advantage of these tongues is not of so great importance as it has been too often represented. My reader will agree with me, when he considers that the chief uses of them are these:

The Arabic is a language which has some kindred and affinity to the Hebrew, and perhaps we may now and then guess at the sense of some uncommon and doubtful Hebrew word, which is found but once or twice in the Bible, by its supposed affinity to the Arabic: but whatever conjectures may be made by some kindred of a Hebrew word to an Arabic root, yet there is no certainty to be gathered from it: for even words of the same language, which are undoubtedly of the same theme or primitive, will give us but very doubtful and sorry information concerning the true sense of kindred words which spring from the same theme.

Let me give a plain instance or two of this uncertainty. The word *strages* signifies slaughter; *stratum* is Latin for a bed; *stramen* is straw; and *stragulum* is a quilt or coverlid: they are all drawn and derived from *sterno;* which signifies to throw down, to kill, or to spread abroad. Let the critics tell me what certain sense they could put upon either of these four words by their mere cognation with each other, or their derivation from one common verb. Again, who can tell me the certain meaning and precise idea of the word honest in English, and assure me that it signifies a man of integrity, justice, and probity, though it is evidently derived from *honestus* in Latin? Whereas *honestus* has a very different idea, and signifies a man of some figure in the world, or a man of honour. Let any man judge then how little service toward explaining the Hebrew tongue can be furnished from all the language of Arabia. Surely a great part of the long learned fatigues and tiresome travels of men through this country is almost vain and useless to make the Hebrew Bible better understood.

As for the Syriac language, it is granted there may be some small advantage drawn from the knowledge of it, because there is a very ancient translation of the New Testament in that tongue; and perhaps this may sometimes give a proper and apposite meaning to a difficult and doubtful text, and offer a fair hint for recovering the true meaning of the Scripture from the perverse glosses of other writers. But there are several commentators and lexicographers who have been acquainted with the Syriac language, and have given us the chief of these hints in their writings on Scripture.

And after all, since none of these assistances can yield us a sufficient proof of a true interpretation, and give a certain sense of a text, who would be persuaded to waste any great number of his better hours in such dry studies, and in labours of so little profit?

XXXI. The Chaldean language, indeed, is much nearer to the Hebrew, and it is proper for a divine to have some acquaintance with it, because there are several verses or chapters of Ezra and Daniel which are written in that language: and the old Jewish targums or commentaries, which are written in the Chaldean tongue, may sometimes happen to cast a light upon a little doubtful Scripture of the Old Testament.

But it must be still owned that the knowledge of these Eastern tongues does not deserve to be magnified to such a degree as some of the proficients in them have indulged; wherein they have carried matters beyond all reason and justice, since scarce any of the most important subjects of the Gospel of Christ and the way of salvation can gain any advantage from them.

XXXII. The art of grammar comes now to be mentioned. It is a distinct thing from the mere knowledge of the languages; for all mankind are taught from their infancy to speak their common tongue, by a natural imitation of their mothers and nurses, and those who are round about them, without any knowledge of the art of grammar, and the various observations and rules that relate to it. Grammar indeed is nothing else but rules and observations drawn from the common speech of mankind in their several languages; and it teaches us to speak and pronounce, to spell and write with propriety and exactness, according to the custom of those in every nation who are or were supposed to speak and write their own language best. Now it is a shame for a man to pretend to science and study in any of the three learned professions, who is not in some measure acquainted with the propriety of those languages with which he ought to be conversant in his daily studies, and more especially in such as he may sometimes be called upon to write as well as read.

XXXIII. Next to grammar, we proceed to consider rhetoric.

Now rhetoric in general is the art of persuading, which may be distinguished into these three parts; viz. 1. Conveying the sense of the speaker to the understanding of the hearers in the clearest and most intelligible manner, by the plainest expressions and the most lively and striking representations of it, so that the mind may be thoroughly convinced of the thing proposed. 2. Persuading the will effectually to choose or refuse the thing suggested and represented. 3. Raising the passions in the most vivid and forcible manner, so as to set all the soul and every power of nature at work, to pursue or avoid the thing in debate.

To attain this end there is not only a great deal of art necessary in the representation of matters to the auditory, but also in the disposition or method of introducing these particular representations, together with the reasons which might convince, and the various methods which might persuade and prevail upon the hearers. There are certain seasons wherein a violent torrent of oration, in a disguised and concealed method, may be more effectual than all the nice forms of logic and reasoning. The figures of interrogation and exclamation have sometimes a large place and happy effect in this sort of discourse, and no figure of speech should be wanting here, where the speaker has art enough happily to introduce it.

There are many remarks and rules laid down by the teachers of this art to improve a young genius in those glorious talents whereby Tully and Demosthenes acquired that amazing influence and success in their own age and nation, and that immortal fame through all nations and ages. And it is with great advantage these rules may be perused and learned. But a happy genius, a lively imagination, and warm passions, together with a due degree of knowledge and skill in the subject to be debated, and a perpetual perusal of the writings of the best orators, and hearing the best speakers, will do more to make an orator, than all the rules of art in the world, without these natural talents, and this careful imitation of the most approved and happiest orators.

XXXIV. Now you will presently suppose that pleaders at the bar have great need of this art of rhetoric; but it has been a just doubt, whether pleading in our British courts of justice, before a skilful judge, should admit of any other aid from rhetoric than that which teaches to open a cause clearly, and spread it in the most perspicuous, complete, and impartial manner, before the eyes of him who judges: for impartial justice being the thing which is sought, there should be no artifices used, no eloquence or power of language employed to persuade the will or work upon the passions, lest the decisive sentence of the judge should be biased or warped into injustice. For this reason Mr. Locke would banish all pleaders in the law for fees out of his government of Carolina, in his posthumous works, though that great man might possibly be too severe in so universal a censure of the profession.

XXXV. But the case is very different with regard to divines: the eloquence of the pulpit, beyond all controversy, has a much larger extent.

Their business is not to plead a cause of right and wrong

before a wise and skilful judge, but to address all the ranks of mankind, the high and low, the wise and the unwise, the sober and the vicious, and persuade them all to pursue and persevere in virtue with regard to themselves, in justice and goodness with regard to their neighbours, and piety towards God. These are affairs of everlasting importance, and most of the persons to whom these addresses are made are not wise and skilful judges, but are influenced and drawn to the contrary side by their own sinful appetites and passions, and bribed or biased by the corrupt customs of the world.

There is therefore a necessity not only of a clear and faithful representation of things to men, in order to convince their reason and judgment, but of all the skill and force of persuasion addressed to the will and the passions. So Tully addressed the whole senate of Rome, and Demosthenes the Athenian people, among whom were capacities and inclinations of infinite variety; and therefore they made use of all the lightning and thunder, all the entreaties and terrors, all the soothing elegancies and the flowery beauties of language, which their art could furnish them with. Divines in the pulpit have much the same sort of hearers, and therefore they should imitate those ancient examples. The understanding indeed ought to be first convinced by the plainest and strongest force of reasoning; but when this is done, all the powerful motives should be used which have any just influence upon human nature; all the springs of passion should be touched, to awaken the stupid and the thoughtless into consideration, to penetrate and melt the hardest heart, to persuade the unwilling, to excite the lazy, to reclaim the obstinate, and reform the vicious part of mankind, as well as to encourage those who are humble and pious, and to support their practice and their hope. The tribes of men are sunk into so fatal a degeneracy and dreadful distance from God, and from all that is holy and happy, that all the eloquence which a preacher is master of should be employed in order to recover the world from its shameful ruin and wretchedness by the Gospel of our blessed Saviour, and restore it to virtue and piety, to God and happiness, by the divine power of this Gospel. O may such glorious masters and sacred oratory never be wanting in the pulpits of Great Britain!

XXXVI. Shall I now speak something of my sentiments concerning poesy?

As for books of poesy, whether in the learned or in the modern languages, they are of great use to be read at hours of leisure by all persons, that make any pretence to good education or learning; and that for several reasons.

1. Because there are many couplets or stanzas written in poetic measures, which contain a variety of morals or rules of practice relating to the common prudentials of mankind, as well as to matters of religion; and the poetic numbers (or rhyme, if there be any) add very considerable force to the memory.

Besides, many an elegant and admirable sentiment or description of things which are found among the poets are well worth committing to memory, and the particular measures of verse greatly assist us in recollecting such excellent passages, which might sometimes raise our conversation from low and grovelling subjects.

2. In heroic verse, but especially in the grander lyrics, there are sometimes such noble elevations of thought and passion as illuminate all things around us, and convey to the soul most exalted and magnificent images and sublime sentiments: these furnish us with glorious springs and mediums to raise and aggrandize our conceptions, to warm our souls, to awaken the better passions, and to elevate them to a divine pitch, and that for devotional purposes. It is the lyric ode which has shown to the world some of the happiest examples of this kind, and I cannot say but this part of poesy has been my favourite amusement above all others.

And for this reason it is that I have never thought the heroic poems, Greek, Latin, or English, which have obtained the highest fame in the world are sufficiently diversified, exalted, or animated, for want of the interspersion of now and then an elegiac or lyric ode. This might have been done with great and beautiful propriety, where the poet has introduced a song at a feast, or the joys of a victory, or soliloquies of divine satisfaction, or the pensive and despairing agonies of distressing sorrows. Why should that which is called the most glorious form of poesy be bound down and confined to such a long and endless uniformity of measures, when it should kindle or melt the soul, swell or sink into all the various and transporting chances which human nature is capable of?

Cowley, in his unfinished fragment of the Davideis, has shown this way to improvement; and whatever blemishes may be found in other parts of that heroic essay, this beauty and glory of it ought to be preserved for imitation. I am well assured that if Homer and Virgil had happened to practise it, it would have been renowned and glorified by every critic. I am greatly mistaken if this wise mixture of numbers would not be a further reach of perfection than they have ever attained to without it: let it be remembered, that it is not nature, and strict reason, but a weak and awful reverence of antiquity, and the vogue of fallible men, that has established these Greek and Roman writings as absolute and complete patterns. In several ages there have been some men of learning who have very justly disputed this glory, and have pointed to many of their mistakes.

3. But still there is another end of reading poesy, and perhaps the most considerable advantage to be obtained from it by the bulk of mankind, and that is, to furnish our tongues with the richest and the most polite variety of phrases and words upon all occasions of life or religion. He that writes well in verse will often find a necessity to send his thoughts in search through all the treasure of words that express any one idea in the same language, that so he may comport with the measures or the rhyme of the verse which he writes, or with his own most beautiful and vivid sentiments of the thing he describes. Now by much reading of this kind we shall insensibly acquire the habit and skill of diversifying our ideas in the most proper and beautiful language, whether we write or speak of the things of God or men.

It is a pity that some of these harmonious writers have ever indulged any thing uncleanly or impure to defile their paper and abuse the ears of their readers, or to offend against the rules of the nicest virtue and politeness: but still amongst the writings of Mr. Dryden, and Mr. Pope, and Dr. Young, as well as others, there is a sufficient choice in our own language, wherein we shall not find any indecency to shock the most modest tongue or ear.

Perhaps there has hardly been a writer in any nation, and I may dare to affirm there is none in ours, has a richer and happier talent of painting to the life, or has ever discovered such a large and inexhausted variety of description, as the celebrated Mr. Pope. If you read his translation of Homer's Iliad, you will find almost all the terms or phrases in our tongue that are needful to express any thing that is grand or magnificent; but if you peruse his Odyssey, which descends much more into common life, there is scarce any useful subject of discourse or thought, or any ordinary occurrence, which he has not cultivated and dressed in the most proper language; and yet still he has ennobled and enlivened even the lower subjects with the brightest and most agreeable ornaments.

I should add here also, that if the same author had more frequently employed his pen on divine themes, his short poem on the Messiah, and some part of his letters between Abelard and Eloisa, with that ode on the Dying Christian, &c. sufficiently assure us that his pen would have honourably imitated some of the tender scenes of penitential sorrow, as well as the sublimer odes of the Hebrew Psalmist, and perhaps discovered to us, in a better manner than any other translation has done, how great a poet sat upon the throne of Israel.

After all that I have said, there is yet a further use of reading poesy; and that is, when the mind has been fatigued with studies of a more laborious kind, or when it is any ways unfit for the pursuit of more difficult subjects, it may be as it were unbent, and repose itself awhile on the flowery meadows where the muses dwell. It is a very sensible relief to the soul, when it is overtired, to amuse itself with the numbers and the beautiful sentiments of the poets; and in a little time this agreeable amusement may recover the languid spirits to activity and more important service.

XXXVII. All this I propose to the world as my best observations about reading of verse. But if the question were offered to me, Shall a student of a bright genius never divert himself with writing poesy? I would answer, Yes, when he cannot possibly help it; a lower genius, in mature years, would heartily wish that he had spent much more time in reading the best authors of this kind, and employed much fewer hours in writing. But it must be confessed or supposed at least, that there may be seasons when it is hardly possible for a poetic soul to restrain the fancy or quench the flame, when it is hard to suppress the exuberant flow of lofty sentiments, and prevent the imagination from this sort of style or language: and that is the only season I think wherein this inclination should be indulged, especially by persons who have devoted themselves to professions of a different kind; and one reason is, because what they write in that hour is more likely to carry in it some appearance above nature, some happy imitation of the dictates of the muse.*

XXXVIII. There are other things besides history, grammar and languages, rhetoric and poesy, which had been included under the name of philological knowledge; such as an acquaintance with the notions, customs, manners, tempers, polity, &c. of the various nations of the earth, or the distinct sects and tribes of mankind. This is necessary in order to understand history the better; and every man who is a lawyer or a gentleman ought to obtain some acquaintance with these things, without which he can never read history to any great advantage, nor can he maintain his own station and character in life with honour and dignity, without some insight into them.

XXXIX. Students in divinity ought to seek a larger acquaintance with the Jewish laws, polity, customs, &c.

*The muse, in the ancient heathen sense, is supposed to be a goddess; but in the philosophic sense, it can mean no more than a bright genius, with a warm and strong imagination elevated to an uncommon degree.

in order to understand many passages of the Old Testament and the New, and to vindicate the sacred writers from the reproaches of infidels. An acquaintance also with many of the Roman and Grecian affairs is needful to explain several texts of Scripture in the New Testament, to lead sincere inquirers into the true and genuine sense of the evangelists and apostles, and to guard their writings from the unreasonable cavils of men.

XL. The art of criticism is reckoned by some as a distinct part of philology; but it is in truth nothing else than a more exact or accurate knowledge or skill in the other parts of it, and a readiness to apply that knowledge upon all occasions, in order to judge well of what relates to these subjects, to explain what is obscure in the authors which we read, to supply what is defective, and amend what is erroneous in manuscripts or ancient copies, to correct the mistakes of authors and editors in the sense of the words, to reconcile the controversies of the learned, and by this means to spread a juster knowledge of these things among the inquisitive part of mankind.

Every man who pretends to the learned professions, if he doth not arise to be a critic himself in philological matters, he should be frequently conversing with those books, whether dictionaries, paraphrasts, commentators, or other critics, which may relieve any difficulties he meets with, and give him a more exact acquaintance with those studies which he pursues.

And whensoever any person is arrived to such a degree of knowledge in these things as to furnish him well for the practice of criticism, let him take great care that pride and vanity, contempt of others, with inward wrath and insolence, do not mingle themselves with his remarks and censures. Let him remember the common frailties of human nature, and the mistakes to which the wisest man is sometimes liable, that he may practise this art with due modesty and candour.

THE

IMPROVEMENT OF THE MIND.

PART II.

INTRODUCTION.

The chief design of the former part of this book is to lead us into proper methods for the improvement of our own knowledge. Let us now consider what are the best means of improving the minds of others, and of communicating to them the knowledge which we have acquired. If the treasures of the mind should be hoarded up and concealed, they would profit none besides the possessor; and even his advantage by the possession would be poor and narrow in comparison of what the same treasures would yield, both to himself and to the world, by a free communication and diffusion of them. Large quantities of knowledge acquired and reserved by one man, like heaps of gold and silver, would contract a sort of rust and disagreeable aspect by lying in everlasting secrecy and silence; but they are burnished and glitter by perpetual circulation through the tribes of mankind.

The two chief ways of conveying knowledge to others are that of verbal instruction to our disciples, or by writing and publishing our thoughts to the world.

Here therefore I shall propose some observations which relate to the conveyance of knowledge to others, by regular lectures of verbal instruction, or by conversation: I shall represent several of the chief prejudices of which learners are in danger, with directions to guard against them; and then mention some of the easiest and most effectual ways of convincing persons of their mistakes, and of dealing with their understanding when they labour under the power of prejudice. I shall afterwards add, by way of appendix, an essay, written many years ago, on the subject of Education, when I designed a more complete treatise of it.

CHAPTER I.

METHODS OF TEACHING AND READING LECTURES.

He that has learned any thing thoroughly, in a clear and methodical manner, and has attained a distinct perception, and an ample survey of the whole subject, is generally best prepared to teach the same subject in a clear and easy method: for having acquired a large and distinct idea of it himself, and made it familiar to him by frequent meditation, reading, and occasional discourse, he is supposed to see it on all sides, to grasp it, with all its appendices and relations, in one survey, and is better able to represent it to the learner in all its views, with all its properties, relations, and consequences. He knows which view or side of the subject to hold out first to his disciple, and how to propose to his understanding that part of it which is easiest to apprehend; and also knows how to set it in such a light as is most likely to allure and to assist his further inquiry.

But it is not every one who is a great scholar that always becomes the happiest teacher, even though he may have a clear conception, and a methodical as well as an extensive survey of the branches of any science. He must also be well acquainted with words, as well as ideas, in a proper variety, that when his disciple does not take in the ideas of one form of expression, he may change the phrase into several forms, till at last he hits the understanding of his scholar, and enlightens it in the just idea of truth.

Besides this, a tutor should be a person of a happy and condescending temper, who has patience to bear with a slowness of perception or want of sagacity in some learners. He should also have much candour of soul, to pass a gentle censure on their impertinences, and to pity them in their mistakes, and use every mild and engaging method for insinuating knowledge into those who are willing and diligent in seeking truth, as well as reclaiming those who are wandering into error.

But of this I have spoken somewhat already in a

chapter of the former part, and shall have occasion to express somewhat more of it shortly.

A very pretty and useful way to lead a person into any particular truth is, by questions and answers, which is the Socratical method of disputation, and therefore I refer the reader to that chapter or section which treats of it. On this account dialogues are used as a polite and pleasant mode of leading gentlemen and ladies into some of the sciences, who seek not the most accurate and methodical measure of learning.

But the most useful, and perhaps the most excellent way of instructing students in any of the sciences, is by reading lectures, as tutors in the academy do to their pupils.

The first work is to choose a book well written, which contains a short scheme or abstract of that science, or at least it should not be a very copious and diffusive treatise. Or if the tutor knows not any such book already written, he should draw up an abstract of that science himself, containing the most substantial and important parts of it, disposed in such a method as he best approves.

Let a chapter or section of this be read daily by the learner, on which the tutor should paraphrase in this manner, namely,—

He should explain both words and ideas more largely; and especially what is dark and difficult should be opened and illustrated, partly by various forms of speech, and partly by apt similitudes and examples. Where the sense of the author is dubious, it must also be fixed and determined.

Where the arguments are strong and cogent, they should be enforced by some further paraphrase, and the truth of the inferences should be made plainly to appear. Where the arguments are weak and insufficient, they should be either confirmed or rejected as useless; and new arguments, if need be, should be added to support that doctrine.

What is treated very concisely in the author should be amplified; and where several things are laid closely together, they must be taken to pieces and opened by parts.

Where the tutor differs from the author which he reads, he should gently point out and confute his mistakes.

Where the method and order of the book is just and happy, it should be pursued and commended: where it is defective and irregular, it should be corrected.

The most necessary, the most remarkable and useful parts of that treatise, or of that science, should be peculiarly recommended to the learners, and pressed upon them that they would retain it in memory; and what is more necessary or superfluous should be distinguished, lest the learner should spend too much time in the more needless parts of a science.

The various ends, uses, and services of that science, or of any part of it, should also be declared and exemplified, as far as the tutor hath opportunity and furniture to do it; particularly in mathematics and natural philosophy.

And if there be any thing remarkably beautiful or defective in the style of the writer, it is proper for the tutor to make a just remark upon it.

While he is reading and explaining any particular treatise to his pupils, he may compare the different editions of the same book, or different writers upon the same subject: he should inform them where that subject is treated by other authors which they may peruse, and lead his disciples thereby to a further elucidation, confirmation, or improvement of that theme of discourse in which he is instructing them.

It is alluring and agreeable to the learner also, now and then, to be entertained with some historical remarks on any occurrences or useful stories which the tutor has met with, relating to the several parts of such a science; provided he does not put off his pupils merely with such stories, and neglect to give them a solid and rational information of the theme in hand. Teachers should endeavour, as far as possible, to join profit and pleasure together, and mingle delight with their instructions; but at the same time they must take heed that they do not merely amuse the ears and gratify the fancy of their disciples without enriching their minds.

In reading lectures of instruction, let the teacher be very solicitous that the learners take up his meaning; and therefore he should frequently inquire whether he expresses himself intelligibly? whether they understand his sense, and take in all his ideas as he endeavours to convey them in his own forms of speech?

It is necessary that he who instructs others should use the most proper style for the conveyance of his ideas easily into the minds of those who hear him; and though in teaching the sciences, a person is not confined to the same rules by which we must govern our language in conversation, for he must necessarily make use of many terms of art and hard words, yet he should never use them merely to show his learning, nor affect sounding language without necessity, a caution which we shall further inculcate anon.

I think it very convenient and proper, if not absolutely necessary, that when a tutor reads a following lecture to his pupils, he should run over the foregoing lecture in questions proposed to them, and by this means acquaint himself with their daily proficiency.* It is in vain for the learner to object, Surely we are not schoolboys, to say our lessons again: we came to be taught, not to be catechised and examined. But, alas! how is it possible for a teacher to proceed in his instructions, if he knows not how far the learner takes in and remembers what he has been taught?

Besides, I must generally believe it is sloth or idleness, it is real ignorance, incapacity, or unreasonable pride, that makes a learner refuse to give his teacher an account how far he has profited by his last instructions. For want of this constant examination young gentlemen have spent some idle and useless years, even under

* This precaution, though never to be neglected, is of especial importance when a pupil is entering on any new branch of learning, where it is absolutely necessary that the fundamental definitions and principles should not only be clearly understood, but rendered very familiar to the mind; and probably most tutors have found young persons sadly bewildered as they have gone on in their lectures, for want of a little more patience and care in this respect.

daily labours and inspections of a learned teacher; and they have returned from the academy without the gain of any one science, and even with the shameful loss of their classical learning, that is, the knowledge of Greek and Latin, which they had learned in the grammar-school.

Let the teacher always accommodate himself to the genius, temper, and capacity of his disciples, and practise various methods of prudence to allure, persuade, and assist every one of them in their pursuit of knowledge.

Where the scholar has less capacity, let the teacher enlarge his illustrations; let him search and find out where the learner sticks, what is the difficulty, and thus let him help the labouring intellect.

Where the learner manifests a forward genius and a sprightly curiosity by frequent inquiries, let the teacher oblige such an inquisitive soul by satisfying those questions as far as may be done with decency and conveniency; and where these inquiries are unseasonable, let him not silence the young inquirer with a magisterial rebuff, but with much candour and gentleness postpone those questions, and refer them to a proper hour.

Curiosity is a useful spring of knowledge: it should be encouraged in children, and awakened by frequent and familiar methods of talking with them. It should be indulged in youth, but not without a prudent moderation. In those who have too much, it should be limited by a wise and gentle restraint or delay, lest by wandering after every thing, they learn nothing to perfection. In those who have too little, it should be excited, lest they grow stupid, narrow-spirited, self-satisfied, and never attain a treasure of ideas, or an amplitude of understanding.

Let not the teacher demand or expect things too sublime and difficult from the humble, modest, and fearful disciple: and where such a one gives a just and happy answer, even to plain and easy questions, let him have words of commendation and love ready for him. Let him encourage every spark of kindling light, till it grow up to bright evidence and confirmed knowledge.

When he finds a lad pert, positive, and presuming, let the tutor take every just occasion to show him his error; let him set the absurdity in complete light before him, and convince him by a full demonstration of his mistake, till he sees and feels it, and learns to be modest and humble.

A teacher should not only observe the different spirit and humor among his scholars, but he should watch the various efforts of their reason and growth of their understanding. He should practise in his young nursery of learning as a skilful gardener does in his vegetable dominions, and apply prudent methods of cultivation to every plant. Let him with a discreet and gentle hand nip or prune the irregular shoots; let him guard and encourage the tender buddings of the understanding, till they be raised to a blossom, and let him kindly cherish the younger fruits.

The tutor should take every occasion to instil knowledge into his disciples, and make use of every occurrence of life to raise some profitable conversation upon it; he should frequently inquire something of his disciples that may set their young reason to work, and teach them how to form inferences, and to draw one proposition out of another.

Reason being that faculty of the mind which he has to deal with in his pupils, let him endeavour by all proper and familiar methods to call it into exercise, and to enlarge the powers of it. He should take frequent opportunities to show them when an idea is clear or confused, when the proposition is evident or doubtful, and when an argument is feeble or strong. And by this means their minds will be so formed, that whatsoever he proposes with evidence and strength of reason they will readily receive.

When any uncommon appearances arise in the natural, moral, or political world, he should invite and instruct them to make their remarks on it, and give them the best reflections of his own for the improvement of their minds.

He should by all means make it appear that he loves

his pupils, and that he seeks nothing so much as their increase of knowledge, and their growth in all valuable acquirements; this will engage their affection to his person, and procure a just attention to his lectures.

And indeed there is but little hope that a teacher should obtain any success in his instructions, unless those that hear him have some good degree of esteem and respect for his person and character. And here I cannot but take notice by the way, that it is a matter of infinite and unspeakable injury to the people of any town or parish where the minister lies under contempt. If he has procured it by his own conduct he is doubly criminal, because of the injury he does to the souls of them that hear him: but if this contempt and reproach be cast upon him by the wicked, malicious, and unjust censures of men, they must bear all the ill consequences of receiving no good by his labours, and will be accountable hereafter to the great and divine Judge of all.

It would be very necessary to add in this place (if tutors were not well apprized of it before) that since learners are obliged to seek a divine blessing on their studies by fervent prayer to the God of all wisdom, their tutors should go before them in this pious practice, and make daily addresses to Heaven for the success of their instructions.

CHAPTER II.

OF AN INSTRUCTIVE STYLE.

The most necessary and most useful character of a style fit for instruction is that it be plain, perspicuous, and easy. And here I shall first point out all those errors in a style which diminish or destroy the perspicuity of it, and then mention a few directions how to obtain a perspicuous and easy style.

The errors of style, which must be avoided by teachers, are these that follow:

1. The use of many foreign words, which are not sufficiently naturalized and mingled with the language which we speak or write. It is true, that in teaching the sciences in English, we must sometimes use words borrowed from the Greek and Latin; for we have not in English names for a variety of subjects which belong to learning; but when a man affects, upon all occasions, to bring in long-sounding words from the ancient languages, without necessity, and mingles French and other outlandish terms and phrases, where plain English would serve as well, he betrays a vain and foolish genius, unbecoming a teacher.

2. Avoid a fantastic learned style, borrowed from the various sciences, where the subject and matter do not require the use of them. Do not affect terms of art on every occasion, nor seek to show your learning by sounding words and dark phrases; this is properly called pedantry.

Young preachers, just come from the schools, are often tempted to fill their sermons with logical and metaphysical terms in explaining their text, and feed their hearers with sonorous words of vanity. This scholastic language perhaps may flatter their own ambition, and raise a wonderment at their learning among the staring multitude, without any manner of influence toward the instruction of the ignorant, or the reformation of the immoral or impious: these terms of art are but the tools of an artificer, by which his work is wrought in private: but the tools ought not to appear in the finished workmanship.

There are some persons so fond of geometry, that they bring in lines and circles, tangents and parabolas, theorems, problems, and postulates, upon all occasions. Others who have dealt in astronomy, borrow even their nouns and their verbs in their common discourse from the stars and planets. Instead of saying Jacob had twelve sons, they tell you Jacob had as many sons as there are signs in the zodiac. If they describe an inconstant person, they make a planet of him, and set him forth in all his appearances, direct, retrograde, and stationary. If a candle be set behind a screen, they call it eclipsed; and tell you fine stories of the orbit and the revolutions, the radii and the limb or circumference of a cart-wheel.

Others again dress up their sense in chymical language. Extracts and oils, salts and essences, exalt and invigorate their discourses: a great wit with them is sublimated spirit, and a blockhead is a *caput mortuum*. A certain doctor in his bill swells in his own idea, when he tells the town that he has been counsellor to the counsellors of several kings and princes; that he has arrived at the knowledge of the green, black, and golden dragon, known only to magicians and hermetic philosophers. It would be well if the quacks alone had a patent for this language.

3. There are some fine affected words that are used only at court; and some peculiar phrases that are sounding or gaudy, and belong only to the theatre; these should not come into the lectures of instruction; the language of poets has too much of metaphor in it to lead mankind into clear and distinct ideas of things: the business of poesy is to strike the soul with a glaring light, and to urge the passions into a flame by splendid shows, by strong images, and a pathetic vehemence of style: but it is another sort of speech that is best suited to lead the calm inquirer into just conceptions of things.

4. There is a mean vulgar style, borrowed from the lower ranks of mankind, the basest characters, and meanest affairs of life: this is also to be avoided; for it should be supposed, that persons of liberal education have not been bred up within the hearing of such language, and consequently they cannot understand it; besides that it would create very offensive ideas, should we borrow even similes for illustration from the scullery, the dunghill, and the jakes.

5. An obscure and mysterious manner of expression and cloudy language is to be avoided. Some persons have been led by education, or by some foolish prejudices, into a dark and unintelligible way of thinking and speaking; and this continues with them all their lives, and clouds and confounds their ideas: perhaps some of these may have been blessed with a great and compre-

hensive genius, with sublime natural parts, and a torrent of ideas flowing in upon them; yet for want of clearness in the manner of their conception and language, they sometimes drown their own subject of discourse, and overwhelm their argument in darkness and perplexity: such preachers as have read much of the mystical divinity of the papists, and imitated their manner of expression, have many times buried a fine understanding under the obscurity of such a style.

6. A long and tedious style is very improper for a teacher, for this also lessens the perspicuity of it. Some learned writers are never satisfied unless they fill up every sentence with a great number of ideas and sentiments; they swell their propositions to an enormous size by explications, exceptions, and precautions, lest they should be mistaken, and crowd them all into the same period: they involve and darken their discourse by many parentheses, and prolong their sentences to a tiresome extent, beyond the reach of a common comprehension: such sort of writers or speakers may be rich in knowledge, but they are seldom fit to communicate it. He that would gain a happy talent for the instruction of others must know how to disentangle and divide his thoughts, if too many of them are ready to crowd into one paragraph; and let him rather speak three sentences distinctly and perspicuously, which the hearer receives at once with his ears and his soul, than crowd all the thoughts into one sentence, which the hearer has forgot before he can understand it.

But this leads me to the next thing I proposed, which was to mention some methods whereby such a perspicuity of style may be obtained as is proper for instruction.

1. Accustom yourself to read those authors who think and write with great clearness and evidence, such as convey their ideas into your understanding as fast as your eye or tongue can run over their sentences: this will imprint upon the mind a habit of imitation: we shall learn the style with which we are very conversant, and practise it with ease and success.

2. Get a distinct and comprehensive knowledge of

the subject which you treat of, survey it on all sides, and make yourself perfect master of it; then you will have all the sentiments that relate to it in your view and under your command; and your tongue will very easily clothe those ideas with words which your mind has first made so familiar and easy to itself.

> Scribendi recte sapere est et principium et fons:
> Verbaque provisam rem non invita sequentur.
>
> *Hor. de Art Poetica.*

> Good teaching from good knowledge springs;
> Words will make haste to follow things.

3. Be well skilled in the language which you speak; acquaint yourself with all the idioms and special phrases of it, which are necessary to convey the needful ideas on the subject of which you treat in the most various and most easy manner to the understanding of the hearer: the variation of a phrase in several forms is of admirable use to instruct; it is like turning all sides of the subject to view; and if the learner happen not to take in the ideas in one form of speech, probably another may be successful for that end.

Upon this account I have always thought it a useful manner of instruction, which is used in some Latin schools, which they call variation. Take some plain sentence in the English tongue, and turn it into many forms in Latin; as for instance, A wolf let into the sheepfold will devour the sheep: If you let a wolf into the fold, the sheep will be devoured: The wolf will devour the sheep, if the sheepfold be left open: If the fold be not shut carefully, the wolf will devour the sheep: The sheep will be devoured by the wolf, if it find the way into the fold open: There is no defence of the sheep from the wolf, unless it be kept out of the fold: A slaughter will be made among the sheep, if the wolf can get into the fold. Thus, by turning the active voice of verbs into the passive, and the nominative case of nouns into the accusative, and altering the connexion of short sentences by different adverbs or conjunctions, and by ablative cases with a preposition brought instead of the nominative, or by particles sometimes put instead of the verbs, the negation of the contrary instead of the assertion of the thing first proposed, a great variety of forms of speech will be created which shall express the same sense.

4. Acquire a variety of words, a *copia verborum.* Let your memory be rich in synonymous terms, or words expressing the same thing: this will not only attain the same happy effect with the variation of phrases in the foregoing direction, but it will add a beauty also to your style, by securing you from an appearance of tautology, or repeating the same words too often, which sometimes may disgust the ear of the learner.

5. Learn the art of shortening your sentences by dividing a long complicated period into two or three small ones. When others connect and join two or three sentences in one by relative pronouns, as, which, whereof, wherein, whereto, &c. and by parentheses frequently inserted, do you rather divide them into distinct periods; or at least, if they must be united, let it be done rather by conjunctions and copulatives, that they may appear like distinct sentences, and give less confusion to the hearer or reader.

I know no method so effectually to learn what I mean, as to take now and then some page of an author, who is guilty of such a long involved parenthetical style, and translate it into plainer English, by dividing the ideas or the sentences asunder, and multiplying the periods, till the language become smooth and easy, and intelligible at first reading.

6. Talk frequently to young and ignorant persons upon subjects which are new and unknown to them, and be diligent to inquire whether they understand you or no: this will put you upon changing your phrases and forms of speech in a variety, till you can hit their capacity, and convey your ideas into their understanding.

CHAPTER III.

OF CONVINCING OTHER PERSONS OF ANY TRUTH, OR DELIVERING THEM FROM ERRORS AND MISTAKES.

When we are arrived at a just and rational establishment in an opinion, whether it relate to religion or common life, we are naturally desirous of bringing all the world into our sentiments; and this proceeds from the affectation and pride of superior influence upon the judgment of our fellow creatures, much more frequently than it does from a sense of duty, or a love of truth; so vicious and corrupt is human nature. Yet there is such a thing to be found as an honest and sincere delight in propagating truth, arising from a dutiful regard to the honours of our Maker, and a hearty love to mankind. Now, if we would be successful in our attempts to convince men of their errors, and promote the truth, let us divest ourselves, as far as possible, of that pride and affectation which I mentioned before; and seek to acquire that disinterested love to men, and zeal for the truth, which will naturally lead us into the best methods to promote it.

And here the following directions may be useful:

1. If you would convince a person of his mistake, choose a proper place, a happy hour, and the fittest concurrent circumstance for this purpose. Do not unseasonably set upon him when he is engaged in the midst of other affairs, but when his soul is at liberty and at leisure to hear and attend. Accost him not upon that subject when his spirit is ruffled or discomposed with any occurrences of life, and especially when he has heated his passions in the defence of a contrary opinion; but rather seize some golden opportunity, when some occurrences of life may cast a favourable aspect upon the truth of which you would convince him, or which may throw some dark and unhappy colour of consequences upon that error from which you would fain deliver him. There are in life some *mollissima tempora fandi*, some very agreeable moments of addressing a person, which, if rightly managed, may render your attempts

much more successful, and his conviction easy and pleasant.

2. Make it appear, by your whole conduct to the person you would teach, that you mean him well; that your design is not to triumph over his opinion, nor to expose his ignorance, or his incapacity of defending what he asserts. Let him see that it is not your aim to advance your own character as a disputant; nor to set yourself up for an instructor of mankind; but that you love him, and seek his true interest; and do not only assure him of this in words, when you are entering on an argument with him, but let the whole of your conduct to him at all times demonstrate your real friendship for him. Truth and argument come with particular force from the mouth of one whom we trust and love.

3. The softest and gentlest address to the erroneous is the best way to convince them of their mistake. Sometimes it is necessary to represent to your opponent that he is not far from the truth, and that you would fain draw him a little nearer to it. Commend and establish whatever he says that is just and true, as our blessed Saviour treated the young scribe, when he answered well concerning the two great commandments, "Thou art not far," says our Lord, "from the kingdom of heaven," Mark, xii. 34. Imitate the mildness and conduct of the blessed Jesus.

Come as near your opponent as you can in all your propositions, and yield to him as much as you dare in a consistence with truth and justice.

It is a very great and fatal mistake in persons who attempt to convince and reconcile others to their party, when they make the difference appear as wide as possible; this is shocking to any person who is to be convinced; he will choose rather to keep and maintain his own opinions, if he cannot come into yours without renouncing and abandoning every thing that he believed before. Human nature must be flattered a little as well as reasoned with, that so the argument may be able to come at his understanding, which otherwise will be thrust off at a distance. If you charge a man with nonsense and absurdities, with heresy and self-contradiction, you take a very wrong step toward convincing him.

Always remember that error is not to be rooted out of the mind of man by reproaches and railing, by flashes of wit and biting jests, by loud exclamations of sharp ridicule: long declamations, and triumph over our neighbour's mistake, will not prove the way to convince him; these are signs either of a bad cause, or a want of arguments or capacity for the defence of a good one.

4. Set therefore a constant watch over yourself, lest you grow warm in dispute before you are aware. The passions never clear the understanding, but raise darkness, clouds, and confusion in the soul: human nature is like water which has mud at the bottom of it, it may be clear when it is calm and undisturbed, and the ideas, like pebbles, appear bright at the bottom; but when once it is stirred and moved by passion, the mud rises uppermost, and spreads confusion and darkness over all the ideas: you cannot set things in so just and so clear a light before the eyes of your neighbour, while your own conceptions are clouded with heat and passion.

Besides, when your own spirits are a little disturbed, and your wrath is awakened, this naturally kindles the same fire in your correspondent, and prevents him from taking in your ideas, were they ever so clear; for his passions are engaged all on a sudden for the defence of his own mistakes, and they combat as fiercely as yours do, which perhaps may be awakened on the side of truth.

To provoke a person whom you would convince, not only arouses his anger, and sets it against your doctrine, but it directs its resentment against your person, as well as against all your instructions and arguments. You must treat an opponent like a friend, if you would persuade him to learn any thing from you; and this is one great reason why there is so little success on either side between two disputants, or controversial writers, because they are so ready to interest their passions in the subject of contest, and thereby to prevent the mutual light that might be given and received on either side: ambition, indignation, and a professed zeal, reign on both sides: victory is the point designed, while truth is pretended; and truth oftentimes perishes in the fray, or retires from the field of battle: the combatants end just where they began, their understandings hold fast the same opinions, perhaps with this disadvantage, that they are a little more obstinate and rooted in them, without fresh reason; and they generally come off with the loss of temper and charity.

5. Neither attempt nor hope to convince a person of his mistake by any penal methods or severe usage. There is no light brought into the mind by all the fire and sword, and bloody persecutions, that were ever introduced into the world. One would think both the princes, the priests, and the people, the learned and the unlearned, the great and the mean, should have all by this time seen the folly and madness of seeking to propagate the truth by the laws of cruelty: we compel a beast to the yoke by blows, because the ox and the ass have no understanding: but intellectual powers are not to be fettered and compelled at this rate. Men cannot believe what they will, nor change their religion and their sentiments as they please: they may be made hypocrites by the forms of severity, and constrained to profess what they do not believe; they may be forced to comply with external practices and ceremonies contrary to their own consciences; but this can never please God, nor profit men.

6. In order to convince another, you should always make choice of those arguments that are best suited to his understanding and capacity, his genius and temper, his state, station, and circumstances. If I were to persuade a ploughman of the truth of any form of church government, it should not be attempted by the use of Greek and Latin fathers; but from the word of God, the light of nature, and the common reason of things.

7. Arguments should always be proposed in such a manner as may lead the mind onward to perceive the truth in a clear and agreeable light, as well as to constrain the assent by the power of reasoning. Clear ideas, in many cases, are as useful towards conviction as a well formed and unanswerable syllogism.

8. Allow the person you desire to instruct a reasonable

time to enter into the force of your arguments. When you have declared your own sentiments in the brightest manner of illustration, and enforced them with the most convincing arguments, you are not to suppose that your friend should be immediately convinced, and receive the truth: habitude in a particular way of thinking, as well as in most other things, obtains the force of nature; and you cannot expect to wean a man from his accustomed errors but by slow degrees, and by his own assistance; entreat him therefore not to judge on the sudden, nor determine against you at once; but that he would please to review your scheme, reflect upon your arguments with all the impartiality he is capable of, and take time to think these over again at large; at least, that he would be disposed to hear you speak yet further on this subject without pain or aversion.

Address him therefore in an obliging manner, and say, I am not so fond as to think I have placed the subject in such lights as to throw you on a sudden into a new track of thinking, or to make you immediately lay aside your present opinions or designs; all that I hope is, that some hint or other which I have given is capable of being improved by you to your own conviction, or possibly it may lead you to such a train of reasoning, as in time to effect a change in your thoughts. Which hint leads me to add,—

9. Labour as much as possible to make the person you would teach his own instructor. Human nature may be allured, by a secret pleasure and pride in its own reasoning, to seem to find out by itself the very thing that you would teach; and there are some persons that have so much of this natural bias toward self rooted in them, that they can never be convinced of a mistake by the plainest and strongest arguments to the contrary, though the demonstration glare in their faces; but they may be tempted, by such gentle insinuations, to follow a track of thought which you propose, till they have wound themselves out of their own error, and led themselves hereby into your own opinion, if you do but let it appear that they are under their own guidance rather than yours. And perhaps there is nothing which

shows more dexterity of address than this secret influence over the minds of others, which they do not discern even while they follow it.

10. If you can gain the main point in question, be not very solicitous about the nicety with which it shall be expressed. Mankind is so vain a thing, that it is not willing to derive from another; and though it cannot have every thing from itself, yet it would seem at least to mingle something of its own with what it derives elsewhere: therefore, when you have set your sentiment in the fullest light, and proved it in the most effectual manner, an opponent will bring in some frivolous and useless distinction, on purpose to change the form of words in the question, and acknowledge that he receives your propositions in such a sense, and in such a manner of expression, though he cannot receive it in your terms and phrases. Vanillus will confess he is now convinced, that a man who behaves well in the state ought not to be punished for his religion, but yet he will not consent to allow a universal toleration of all religions which do not injure the state, which is the proposition I had been proving. Well, let Vanillus, therefore, use his own language; I am glad he is convinced of the truth; he shall have leave to dress it in his own way.

To these directions I shall add two remarks in the conclusion of this chapter, which would not so properly fall under the preceding directions.

I. Remark.—When you have laboured to instruct a person in some controverted truth, and yet he retains some prejudice against it, so that he doth not yield to the convincing force of your arguments, you may sometimes have happy success in convincing him of that truth, by setting him to read a weak author who writes against it: a young reader will find such pleasure in being able to answer the arguments of the opposer, that he will drop his former prejudices against the truth, and yield to the power and evidence of your reason. I confess this looks like setting up one prejudice to overthrow another; but where prejudices cannot be fairly removed by the dint of reason, the wisest and best of teachers will sometimes find it necessary to make a way for reason and truth to take place, by this contrast of prejudices.

II. Remark.—When our design is to convince a whole family or community of persons of any mistake, and to lead them into any truth, we may justly suppose there are various reigning prejudices among them; and therefore it is not safe to attempt, nor so easy to effect it, by addressing the whole number at once. Such a method has been often found to raise a sudden alarm, and has produced a violent opposition even to the most fair, pious, and useful proposal; so that he who made the motion could never carry his point.

We must therefore first make as sure as we can of the most intelligent and learned, at least the most leading persons amongst them, by addressing them apart prudently, and offering proper reasons, till they are convinced and engaged on the side of truth; and these may with more success apply themselves to others of the same community: yet the original proposer should not neglect to make a distinct application to all the rest, so far as circumstances admit.

Where a thing is to be determined by a number of votes, he should labour to secure a good majority; and then take care that the most proper persons should move and argue the matter in public, lest it be quashed in the very first proposal by some prejudice against the proposer.

So unhappily are our circumstances situated in this world, that if truth, and justice, and goodness, could put on human forms, and descend from heaven to propose the most divine and useful doctrines, and bring with them the clearest evidence, and publish them at once to a multitude whose prejudices are engaged against them, the proposal would be vain and fruitless, and would neither convince nor persuade; so necessary it is to join art and dexterity, together with the force of reason, to convince mankind of truth, unless we came furnished with miracles or omnipotence to create a conviction.*

CHAPTER IV.

OF AUTHORITY. OF THE ABUSE OF IT: AND OF ITS REAL AND PROPER USE AND SERVICE.

The influence which other persons have upon our opinions is usually called authority. The power of it is so great and widely extensive, that there is scarce any person in the world entirely free from the impressions of it, even after their utmost watchfulness and care to avoid it. Our parents and tutors, yea, our very nurses, determine a multitude of our sentiments; our friends our neighbours, the custom of the country where we dwell, and the established opinions of mankind, form our belief: the great, the wise, the pious, the learned, and the ancient, the king, the priest, and the philosopher, are characters of mighty efficacy to persuade us to receive what they dictate. These may be ranked under different heads of prejudice, but they are all of a kindred nature, and may be reduced to this one spring or head of authority.

I have treated of these particularly in Logic, Part II. Chapter III. Section 4; yet, a few other remarks occurring among my papers, I thought it not improper to let them find a place here.

Cicero was well acquainted with the unhappy influences of authority, and complains of it in his first book *De Naturâ Deorum:* "In disputes and controversies (says he) it is not so much the authors or patrons of any opinion, as the weight and force of argument, which should influence the mind. The authority of those who

* The conduct of Christ and his apostles, armed as they were with supernatural powers, in the gradual openings of truths, against which the minds of their disciples were strongly prejudiced, may not only secure such an address from the imputation of dishonest craft, but may demonstrate the expediency, and in some cases the necessity, of attending to it.

teach is a frequent hinderance to those who learn, because they utterly neglect to exercise their own judgment, taking for granted whatsoever others whom they reverence have judged for them. I can by no means approve what we learn from the Pythagoreans, that if any thing asserted in disputation was questioned, they were wont to answer, *Ipse dixit*, that is, He himself said so, meaning Pythagoras. So far did prejudice prevail, that authority without reason was sufficient to determine disputes, and to establish truth."

All human authority, though it be never so ancient, though it hath had universal sovereignty, and swayed all the learned and the vulgar world for some thousands of years, yet has no certain and undoubted claim to truth: nor is it any violation of good manners to enter a caveat with due decency against its pretended dominion. What is there among all the sciences that has been longer established and more universally received ever since the days of Aristotle, and perhaps for ages before he lived, than this, that all heavy bodies whatsoever tend toward the centre of the earth? But Sir Isaac Newton has found, that those bulky and weighty bodies, the earth and all the planets, tend toward the centre of the sun, whereby the authority of near three thousand years or more is not only called in question, but actually refuted and renounced.

Again: Was ever any thing more universally agreed among the nation of poets and critics, than that Homer and Virgil are inimitable writers of heroic poems? and whoever presumed to attack their writings, or their reputation, was either condemned for his malice or derided for his folly. These ancient authors have been supposed to derive peculiar advantages to aggrandize their verses from the heathen theology, and that variety of appearances in which they could represent their gods, and mingle them with the affairs of men. Yet within these few years Sir Richard Blackmore (whose prefaces are universally esteemed superior in their kind to any of his poems) has ventured to pronounce some noble truths in that excellent preface to his poem called Alfred, and has bravely demonstrated there, beyond all possible exception, that both Virgil and Homer are often guilty of very gross blunders, indecencies, and shameful improprieties; and that they were so far from deriving any advantage from the rabble of heathen gods, that their theology almost unavoidably exposed them to many of those blunders; and that it is not possible upon the foot of gentile superstition to write a perfect epic poem: whereas the sacred religion of the Bible would furnish a poem with much more just and glorious scenes, and a nobler machinery.

Mr. Dennis also had made it appear in his essays some years before, that there were no images so sublime in the brightest of the heathen writers as those with which we are furnished in the poetic parts of the Holy Scripture; and Rapin, the French critic, dared to profess the same sentiments, notwithstanding the world of poets and critics had so universally and unanimously exalted the heathen writers to the sovereignty for so many ages. If we would find out the truth in many cases, we must dare to deviate from the long-beaten track, and venture to think with a just and unbiassed liberty.

Though it be necessary to guard against the evil influences of authority, and the prejudices derived thence, because it has introduced thousands of errors and mischiefs into the world, yet there are three eminent and remarkable cases wherein authority or the sentiments of other persons must or will determine the judgment and practice of mankind.

I. Parents are appointed to judge for their children in their younger years, and instruct them what they should believe, and what they should practise in civil and religious life. This is a dictate of nature, and doubtless it would have been so in a state of innocence. It is impossible that children should be capable of judging for themselves before their minds are furnished with a competent number of ideas, before they are acquainted with any principles and rules of just judgment, and before their reason is grown up to any degrees of maturity and proper exercises upon such subjects.

I will not say that a child ought to believe nonsense

and impossibility because his father bids him; for so far as the impossibility appears he cannot believe it: nor will I say he ought to assent to all the false opinions of his parents, or to practise idolatry and murder, or mischief, at their command; yet a child knows not any better way to find out what he should believe, and what be should practise, before he can possibly judge for himself, than to run to his parents and receive their sentiments and their directions.

You will say this is hard indeed, that the child of a heathen idolator, or a cruel cannibal, is laid under a sort of necessity by nature of sinning against the light of nature; I grant it is hard indeed, but it is only owing to our original fall and apostasy: the law of nature continues as it was in innocence, namely, That a parent should judge for his child; but if the parent judges ill, the child is greatly exposed by it, through that universal disorder that is brought into the world by the sin of Adam our common father; and from the equity and goodness of God, we may reasonably infer, that the great Judge of all will do right: he will balance the ignorance and incapacity of the child with the criminal nature of the offence in those puerile instances, and will not punish beyond just demerit.

Besides, what could God, as a Creator, do better for children in their minority, than to commit them to the care and instruction of parents? None are supposed to be so much concerned for the happiness of children as their parents are; therefore it is the safest step to happiness, according to the original law of creation, to follow their directions, their parents' reason acting for them before they had reason of their own in proper exercise; nor indeed is there any better general rule in our fallen state by which children are capable of being governed, though in many particular cases it may lead them far astray from virtue and happiness.

If children by Providence be cast under some happier instructions, contrary to their parents' erroneous opinions, I cannot say it is the duty of such children to follow error when they discern it to be error, because their father believes it: what I said before is to be interpreted only of those that are under the immediate care and education of their parents, and not yet arrived at years capable of examination. I know not how these can be freed from receiving the dictates of parental authority in their youngest years, except by immediate or divine inspiration.

It is hard to say at what exact time of life the child is exempted from the sovereignty of parental dictates. Perhaps it is much juster to suppose that this sovereignty diminishes by degrees, as the child grows in understanding and capacity, and is more and more capable of exerting his own intellectual powers, than to limit this matter by months and years.

When childhood and youth are so far expired that the reasoning faculties are grown up to any just measures of maturity, it is certain that persons ought to begin to inquire into the reasons of their own faith and practice in all the affairs of life and religion: but as reason does not arrive at this power and self-sufficiency in any single moment of time, so there is no single moment when a child should at once cast off all his former beliefs and practices; but by degrees, and in slow succession, he should examine them, as opportunity and advantage offer, and either confirm, or doubt of, or change them, according to the leading of conscience and reason, with all its advantages of information.

When we are arrived at manly age, there is no person on earth, no set or society of men whatsoever, that have power and authority given them by God, the creator and governor of the world, absolutely to dictate to others their opinions or practices in moral and religious life. God has given every man reason to judge for himself, in higher or lower degrees. Where less is given, less will be required. But we are justly chargeable with criminal sloth and misimprovement of the talents with which our Creator has intrusted us, if we take all things for granted which others assert, and believe and practise all things which they dictate without due examination.

II. Another case wherein authority must govern our assent is in many matters of fact. Here we may and ought to be determined by the declarations or narratives of other men; though I confess this is usually called testimony rather than authority. It is upon this foot that every son or daughter among mankind are required to believe that such and such persons are their parents, for they can never be informed of it but by the dictates of others. It is by testimony that we are to believe the laws of our country, and to pay all proper deference to the prince and to magistrates in subordinate degrees of authority, though we did not actually see them chosen, crowned, or invested with their title and character. It is by testimony that we are necessitated to believe there is such a city as Canterbury or York, though perhaps we have never been at either; that there are such persons as papists at Paris and Rome, and that there are many sottish and cruel tenets in their religion. It is by testimony that we believe that Christianity, and the books of the Bible, have been faithfully delivered down to us through many generations; that there was such a person as Christ our Saviour, that he wrought miracles, and died on the cross, that he rose again and ascended to heaven.

The authority or testimony of men, if they are wise and honest, if they had full opportunities and capacities of knowing the truth, and are free from all suspicion of deceit in relating it, ought to sway our assent; especially when multitudes concur in the same testimony, and when there are many other attending circumstances which raise the proposition which they dictate to the degree of moral certainty.

But in this very case, even in matters of fact and affairs of history, we should not too easily give into all the dictates of tradition, and the pompous pretences to the testimony of men, till we have fairly examined the several things which are necessary to make up credible testimony, and to lay a just foundation for our belief. There are and have been so many falsehoods imposed upon mankind with specious pretences of eye and ear witnesses, that should make us wisely cautious and justly suspicious of reports, where the concurrent signs of truth do not fairly appear, and especially where the matter is of considerable importance. And the less probable the fact testified is in itself, the greater evidence justly we may demand of the veracity of that testimony on which it claims to be admitted.

III. The last case wherein authority must govern us is when we are called to believe what persons under inspiration have dictated to us. This is not properly the authority of men, but of God himself; and we are obliged to believe what that authority asserts, though our reason at present may not be able, any other way, to discover the certainty or evidence of the proposition; it is enough if our faculty of reason, in its best exercise, can discover the divine authority which has proposed it. Where doctrines of divine revelation are plainly published, together with sufficient proofs of their revelation, all mankind are bound to receive them, though they cannot perfectly understand them, for we know that God is true, and cannot dictate falsehood.

But if these pretended dictates are directly contrary to the natural faculties of understanding and reason which God has given us, we may be well assured these dictates were never revealed to us by God himself. When persons are really influenced by authority to believe pretended mysteries in plain opposition to reason, and yet pretend reason for what they believe, this is but a vain amusement.

There is no reason whatsoever that can prove or establish any authority so firmly, as to give it power to dictate in matters of belief what is contrary to all the dictates of our reasonable nature. God himself has never given any such revelations: and I think it may be said with reverence, he neither can nor will do it, unless he change our faculties from what they are at present. To tell us we must believe a proposition which is plainly contrary to reason, is to tell us that we must believe two ideas are joined, while (if we attend to reason) we plainly see and know them to be disjoined.

What could ever have established the nonsense of transubstantiation in the world, if men had been fixed in this great truth, That God gives no revelation contradictory to our own reason? Things may be above our reason, that is, reason may have but obscure ideas of them, or reason may not see the connexion of those ideas, or may not know at present the certain and exact manner of reconciling such propositions, either with one another or with other rational truths, as I have explained in some of my logical papers: but when they stand directly and plainly against all sense and reason, as transubstantiation does, no divine authority can be pretended to enforce their belief, and human authority is impudent to pretend to it. Yet this human authority, in the popish countries, has prevailed over millions of souls, because they have abandoned their reason; they have given up the glory of human nature, to be trampled upon by knaves, and so reduced themselves to the condition of brutes.

It is by this amusement of authority (says a certain author) that a horse is taught to obey the words of command, a dog to fetch and carry, and a man to believe inconsistencies and impossibilities. Whips and dungeons, fire and the gibbet, and the solemn terrors of eternal misery after this life, will persuade weak minds to believe against their senses, and in direct contradiction to all their reasoning powers. A parrot is taught to tell lies with much more ease and more gentle usage: but none of all these creatures would serve their masters at the expense of their liberty, had they but knowledge and the just use of reason.

I have mentioned three classes wherein mankind must or will be determined in their sentiments, by authority; that is the case of children in their minority, in regard of the commands of their parents; the case of all men, with regard to universal, and complete, and sufficient testimony of matter of fact; and the case of every person, with regard to the authority of divine revelation, and of men divinely inspired; and under each of these I have given some such limitations and cautions as were necessary. I proceed now to mention some other cases wherein we ought to pay a great deference to the authority and sentiments of others, though we are not absolutely concluded and determined by their opinions.

I. When we begin to pass out of our minority, and to judge for ourselves in matters of civil and religious life, we ought to pay very great deference to the sentiments of our parents, who in the time of our minority were our natural guides and directors in these matters. So in matters of science, an ignorant and unexperienced youth should pay great deference to the opinions of his instructors; and though he may justly suspend his judgment in matters which his tutors dictate till he perceives sufficient evidence for them, yet neither parents nor tutors should be directly opposed without great and most evident reasons, such as constrain the understanding or conscience of those concerned.

II. Persons of years and long experience in human affairs, when they give advice in matters of prudence or civil conduct, ought to have a considerable deference paid to their authority by those that are young and have not seen the world, for it is more probable that the elder persons are in the right.

III. In the affairs of practical godliness there should be much deference paid to persons of long standing in virtue and piety. I confess, in the particular forms and ceremonies of religion, there may be as much bigotry and superstition among the old as the young; but in questions of inward religion, and pure devotion or virtue, a man who has been long engaged in the sincere practice of these things, is justly presumed to know more than a youth with all his ungoverned passions, appetites, and prejudices about him.

IV. Men in their several professions and arts in which they have been educated, and in which they have employed themselves all their days, must be supposed to have a greater knowledge and skill than others; and therefore there is due respect to be paid to their judgments in those matters.

V. In matters of fact, where there is not sufficient testimony to constrain our assent, yet there ought to be due deference paid to the narratives of persons wise and sober, according to the degrees of their honesty, skill, and opportunity, to acquaint themselves therewith.

I confess, in many of these cases, where the proposition is a mere matter of speculation, and doth not necessarily draw practice along with it, we may delay our assent till better evidence appear; but where the matter is of a practical nature, and requires us to act one way or another, we ought to pay much deference to authority or testimony, and follow such probabilities where we have no certainty; for this is the best light we have; and surely it is better to follow such sort of guidance, where we can have no better, than to wander and fluctuate in absolute uncertainty. It is not reasonable to put out our candle, and sit still in the dark, because we have not the light of sun-beams.

CHAPTER V.

OF TREATING AND MANAGING THE PREJUDICES OF MEN.*

If we had nothing but the reason of men to deal with, and that reason were pure and uncorrupted, it would then be a matter of no great skill or labour to convince another person of common mistakes, or to persuade him to assent to plain and obvious truths. But alas! mankind stands wrapped round in errors, and entrenched in prejudices; and every one of their opinions is supported and guarded by something else besides reason. A young bright genius, who has furnished himself with a variety of truths and strong arguments, but is yet unacquainted with the world, goes forth from the schools, like a knight-errant, presuming bravely to vanquish the follies of men, and to scatter light and truth through all his acquaintance: but he meets with huge giants and enchanted castles, strong prepossessions of mind, habits, customs, education, authority, interest, together with all the various passions of men, armed and obstinate to defend their old opinions; and he is strangely disappointed in his generous attempts. He finds now that he must

* For the nature and causes of prejudices, and for the preventing or curing of them in ourselves, see the Doctor's excellent system of Logic, Part ii. Chapter iii. Of the springs of false judgment, or the doctrine of prejudices.

not trust merely to the sharpness of his steel, and to the strength of his arm, but he must manage the weapons of his reason with much dexterity and artifice, with skill and address, or he shall never be able to subdue errors, and to convince mankind.

Where prejudices are strong, there are these several methods to be practised in order to convince persons of their mistakes, and make a way for truth to enter into their minds.

I. By avoiding the power and influence of the prejudice without any direct attack upon it: and this is done by choosing all the slow, soft, and distant methods of proposing your own sentiments and your arguments for them, and by degrees leading the person step by step into those truths which his prejudices would not bear if they were proposed all at once.

Perhaps your neighbour is under the influence of superstition and bigotry in the simplicity of his soul: you must not immediately run upon him with violence, and show him the absurdity or folly of his own opinions, though you might be able to set them in a glaring light; but you must rather begin at a distance, and establish his assent to some familiar and easy propositions which have a tendency to refute his mistakes, and to confirm the truth; and then silently observe what impression this makes upon him, and proceed by slow degrees as he is able to bear, and you must carry on the work, perhaps at distant seasons of conversation: the tender or diseased eye cannot bear a deluge of light at once.

Therefore we are not to consider our arguments merely according to our own notions of their force, and from thence expect the immediate conviction of others; but we should regard how they are likely to be received by the persons we converse with; and thus manage our reasoning, as the nurse gives a child drink by slow degrees, lest the infant should be choked, or return it all back again, if poured in too hastily. If your wine be ever so good, and you are ever so liberal in bestowing it on your neighbour, yet if his bottle, into which you attempt to pour it with freedom, has a narrow mouth, you will sooner overset the bottle than fill it with wine.

Overhastiness and vehemence in arguing is oftentimes the effect of pride; it blunts the poignancy of the argument, breaks its force, and disappoints the end. If you were to convince a person of the falsehood of the doctrine of transubstantiation, and you take up the consecrated bread before him, and say—"You may see, and taste, and feel, this is nothing but bread; therefore while you assert that God commands you to believe it is not bread; you most wickedly accuse God of commanding you to tell a lie." This sort of language would only raise the indignation of the person against you, instead of making any impressions upon him. He will not so much as think at all on the arguments you have brought, but he rages at you as a profane wretch, setting up your sense and reason above sacred authority; so that though what you affirm is a truth of great evidence, yet you lose the benefit of your whole argument by an ill management, and the unseasonable use of it.

II. We may expressly allow and indulge those prejudices for a season which seem to stand against the truth, and endeavour to introduce the truth by degrees, while those prejudices are expressly allowed, till by degrees the advanced truth may of itself wear out the prejudice. Thus God himself dealt with his own people the Jews after the resurrection of Christ; for though from the following days of Pentecost, when the Gospel was proclaimed and confirmed at Jerusalem, the Jewish ceremonies began to be void and ineffectual for any divine purpose, yet the Jews who received Christ the Messiah were permitted to circumcise their children, and to practise many Levitical forms, till that constitution, which then waxed old, should in time vanish away.

Where the prejudices of mankind cannot be conquered at once, but they will rise up in arms against the evidence of truth, there we must make some allowances, and yield to them for the present, as far as we can safely do it without real injury to truth: and if we would have any success in our endeavours to convince the world, we must practise this complaisance for the benefit of mankind.

Take a student who has deeply imbibed the principles of the Peripatetics, and imagines certain immaterial beings called substantial forms to inhabit every herb, flower, mineral, metal, fire, water, &c. and to be the spring of all its properties and operations; or take a Platonist, who believes an *anima mundi*, a universal soul of the world to pervade all bodies, to act in and by them according to their nature, and indeed to give them their nature and their special powers; perhaps it may be very hard to convince these persons by argument, and constrain them to yield up these fancies. Well then, let the one believe his universal soul, and the other go on with his notion of substantial forms, and at the same time teach them how by certain original laws of motion, and the various sizes, shapes, and situations of the parts of matter, allowing a continued divine concourse in and with all, the several appearances in nature may be solved, and the variety of effects produced, according to the corpuscular philosophy improved by Descartes, Mr. Boyle, and Sir Isaac Newton; and when they have attained a degree of skill in this science, they will see these airy notions of theirs, these imaginary powers, to be so useless and unnecessary, that they will drop them of their own accord: the Peripatetic forms will vanish from the mind like a dream, and the Platonic soul of the world will expire.

Or suppose a young philosopher, under a powerful persuasion that there is nothing but what has three dimensions, length, breadth, and thickness, and consequently that every finite being has a figure or shape (for shape is but the term and boundary of dimension:) suppose this person, through the long prejudices of sense and imagination, cannot be easily brought to conceive of a spirit or a thinking being without shape and dimensions; let him then continue to conceive a spirit with dimensions; but be sure in all his conceptions to retain the idea of cogitation, or a power of thinking, and thus proceed to philosophize upon the subject. Perhaps in a little time he will find that length, breadth, and shape have no share in any of the actions of a spirit, and that he can manifest all the properties and relations of such a being, with all its operations of sensation, volition,

&c. to be as well performed without the use of this supposed shape or these dimensions; and that all these operations and these attributes may be ascribed to a spirit considered merely as a power of thinking. And when he further conceives that God, the infinite Spirit, is an almighty, self-consistent, thinking power, without shape and dimensions of length, breadth, and depth, he may then suppose the human spirit may be an inferior self-subsisting power of thought; and he may be inclined to drop the ideas of dimension and figure by degrees, when he sees and is convinced they do nothing toward thinking, nor are they necessary to assist or explain the operations or properties of a spirit.

I may give another instance of the same practice, where there is a prejudicate fondness of particular words and phrases. Suppose a man is educated in an unhappy form of speech, whereby he explains some great doctrine of the gospel, and by the means of this phrase he has imbibed a very false idea of that doctrine: yet he is so bigoted to his form of words, that he imagines if those words are omitted, the doctrine is lost. Now if I cannot possibly persuade him to part with his improper terms, I will indulge them a little, and try to explain them in a scriptural sense, rather than let him go on in his mistaken ideas.

Credonius believes that Christ descended into hell: I think the word *hell*, as now commonly understood, is very improper here; but since the bulk of Christians, and Credonius amongst them, will by no means part with the word out of their English creed, I will explain the word *hell* to signify *the state of the dead*, or *the separate state of souls;* and thus lead my friend into more just ideas of the truth, namely, that the soul of Christ existed three days in the state of separation from his body, or was in the invisible world, which might be originally called *hell* in English, as well as *hades* in Greek.

Anilla has been bred a pap st all her days, and though she does not know much of religion, yet she resolves never to part from the Roman catholic faith, and is obstinately bent against a change. Now I cannot think it unlawful to teach her the true Christian, that is, the protestant religion, out of the Epistle to the Romans, and show her that the same doctrine is contained in the catholic epistles of St. Peter, James, and Jude: and thus let her live and die a good Christian in the belief of the religion I teach her out of the New Testament, while she imagines she is a Roman catholic still, because she finds the doctrines she is taught in the catholic epistles and in that to the Romans.

I grant it is most proper there should be different words (as far as possible) applied to different ideas; and this rule should never be dispensed with, if we had to do only with the reason of mankind; but their various prejudices and zeal for some party phrases sometimes make it necessary that we should lead them into truth under the covert of their own beloved forms of speech, rather than permit them to live and die obstinate and unconvincible in any dangerous mistake: whereas an attempt to deprive them of their old established words would raise such a tumult within them, as to render their conviction hopeless.

III. Sometimes we may make use of the very prejudices under which a person labours in order to convince him of some particular truth, and argue with him upon his own professed principles as though they were true. This is called *argumentum ad hominem*, and is another way of dealing with the prejudices of men.

Suppose a Jew lies sick of a fever, and is forbid flesh by his physician; but hearing that rabbits were provided for the dinner of the family, desired earnestly to eat of them; and suppose he became impatient because his physician did not permit him, and he insisted upon it that it could do him no hurt. Surely rather than let him persist in that fancy and that desire, to the danger of his life, I would tell him that those animals were strangled, which sort of food was forbidden by the Jewish law, though I myself may believe that law is now abolished.

In the same manner was Tenerilla persuaded to let Damon her husband prosecute a thief who broke open their house on a Sunday. At first she abhorred the thoughts of it, and refused it utterly, because, if the thief were condemned, according to the English law he must be hanged, whereas (said she) the law of God, in the writings of Moses, doth not appoint death to be the punishment of such criminals, but tells us, that a thief should be sold for his theft.—Exod. xxii. 3. But when Damon could no otherwise convince her that the thief ought to be prosecuted, he put her in mind that the theft was committed on Sunday morning: now the same law of Moses requires that the sabbath-breaker shall surely be put to death.—Exod. xxxi. 15; Numb. xv. 35. This argument prevailed with Tonerilla, and she consented to the prosecution.

Encrates used the same means of conviction when he saw a Mahometan drink wine to excess, and heard him maintain the lawfulness and pleasure of drunkenness; Encrates reminded him that his own prophet Mahomet had utterly forbidden all wine to his followers, and the good man restrained his vicious appetite by this superstition, when he could no otherwise convince him that drunkenness was unlawful, nor withhold him from excess.

When we find any person obstinately persisting in a mistake in opposition to all reason, especially if the mistake be very injurious or pernicious, and we know this person will hearken to the sentiment or authority of some favourite name, it is needful sometimes to use the opinion and authority of that favourite person, since that is likely to be regarded much more than reason. I confess I am almost ashamed to speak of using any influence of authority while I would teach the art of reasoning. But in some cases it is better that poor, silly, perverse, obstinate creatures should be persuaded to judge and act aright, by a veneration for the sense of others, than to be left to wander in pernicious errors, and continue deaf to all argument, and blind to all evidence. They are but children of a larger size; and since they persist all their lives in their minority, and reject all true reasoning, surely we may try to persuade them to practise what is for their own interest by such childish reasons as they will hearken to: we may overawe them from pursuing their own ruin by the terrors of a solemn shadow, or allure them by a sugar-plum to their own happiness.

But after all, we must conclude that wheresoever it can be done, it is best to remove and root out those prejudices which obstruct the entrance of truth into the mind, rather than to palliate, humour, or indulge them; and sometimes this must necessarily be done before you can make a person part with some beloved error, and lead him into better sentiments.

Suppose you would convince a gamester that gaming is not a lawful calling or business of life to maintain one's self by it, and you make use of this argument, namely, "That which doth not admit us to ask the blessing of God that we may get gain by it, cannot be a lawful employment; but we cannot ask the blessing of God on gaming, therefore," &c. The minor is proved thus: "We cannot pray that our neighbour may lose; this is contrary to the rule of seeking our neighbour's welfare, and loving him as ourselves; this is wishing mischief to our neighbour. But in gaming we can gain but just so much as our neighbour loses: therefore in gaming we cannot pray for the blessing of God that we may gain by it."

Perhaps the gamester shrugs and winces, turns and twists the argument every way, but he cannot fairly answer it, yet he will patch up an answer to satisfy himself, and will never yield to the conviction, because he feels so much of the sweet influence of gaming, either toward the gratification of his avarice, or the support of his expenses. Thus he is under a strong prejudice in favour of it, and is not easily convinced.

Your first work therefore must be to lead him by degrees to separate the thoughts of his own interest from the argument, and show him that our own temporal interests, our livelihood, or our loss, hath nothing to do to determine this point in opposition to the plain reason of things, and that he ought to put that consideration quite out of the question, if he would be honest and sincere in his search after truth or duty; and that he must be contented to hearken to the voice of reason and truth, even though it should run counter to his secular interest. When this is done, then an argument may carry some weight or force with it towards his conviction.

In like manner if the question were, whether Matrissa ought to expose herself and her other children to poverty and misery in order to support the extravagances of a favourite son? Perhaps the mother can hear no argument against it; she feels no conviction in the most cogent reasonings, so close do her fond prejudices stick to her heart. The first business here is to remove this prejudice. Ask her therefore, Whether it is not a parent's duty to love all her children so as to provide for their welfare? Whether duty to God and her family ought not to regulate her love to a favourite? Whether her neighbour Floris did well in dressing up her daughters with expensive gaudery, and neglecting the education of her son till she saw his ruin? Perhaps by this method she may be brought to see that peculiar fondness for one child should have no weight or force in determining the judgment in opposition to plain duty: and she may then give herself up to conviction in her own case, and to the evidence of truth, and thus correct her mistaken practice.

Suppose you would convert Rominda from popery, and you set all the errors, absurdities, and superstitions of that church before her in the most glaring evidence: she holds them fast still, and cannot part with them, for she hath a most sacred reverence for the faith and the church of her ancestors, and cannot imagine that they were in the wrong. The first labour must be therefore to convince her that our ancestors were fallible creatures; that we may part with their faith without any dishonour done to them; that all persons must choose their religion for themselves; that we must answer for ourselves in the great day of judgment, and not we for our parents, nor they for us; that Christianity itself had never been received by her ancestors in this nation, if they had persisted always in the religion of their parents, for they were all heathens. And when she has by these methods of reasoning been persuaded that she is not bound always to cleave to the religion of her parents, she may then receive an easier conviction of the errors of Rome.*

CHAPTER VI.

OF INSTRUCTION BY PREACHING.

SECTION I.

Wisdom better than Learning in the Pulpit.

TYRO is a young preacher just come from the schools of logic and divinity, and advanced to the pulpit; he was counted a smart youngster in the academy for analysing a proposition, and is full even to the brim with the terms of his art in learning. When he has read his text, after a short flourish of introduction, he tells you in how many senses the chief word is taken, first among Greek heathen writers, and then in the New Testament; he cites all the chapters and verses exactly, and endeavours to make you understand many a text before he comes to let you know fully what he means by his own.

He finds these things at large in the critics which he has consulted, where this sort of work is necessary and beautiful, and therefore he imagines it will become his sermon well. Then he informs you very learnedly of the various false expositions which have been given by divines and commentators on this part of scripture, and

* But perhaps of all these different methods of curing prejudices none can be practised with greater pleasure to a wise and good man, or with greater success, where success is most desirable, than attempting to turn the attention of well meaning people from some point in which prejudice prevails, to some other of greater importance, and fixing their thoughts and heart on some great truth which they allow, and which leads into consequences contrary to some other notion which they espouse and retain. By this means they may be led to forget their errors while attentive to opposite truth, and in proportion to the degree in which their minds open, and their tempers grow more generous and virtuous, may be induced to resign it. And surely nothing can give a benevolent mind more satisfaction than to improve his neighbour in knowledge and in goodness at the same time.

it may be the reasons of each of them too; and he refutes them with much zeal and contempt. Having thus cleared his way, he fixes upon the exposition which his judgment best approves, and dwells, generally, five or ten minutes upon the arguments to confirm it: and this he does not only in texts of darkness and difficulty, but even when scarce a child could doubt of his meaning.

This grammatical exercise being performed, he applies himself to his logic. The text is divided and subdivided into many little pieces; he points you precisely to the subject and predicate, brings you acquainted with the agent and the object, shows you all the properties and the accidents which attend it, and would fain make you understand the matter and form of it as well as he does himself. When he has thus done, two-thirds of the hour is spent, and his hearers are quite tired; then he begins to draw near to his doctrine or grand theme of discourse, and having told the audience with great formality and exactness in what method he shall manage it, he names you one or two particulars under the first general head; and by this time finds it necessary to add, "He intended indeed to have been larger in the illustration of his subject, and he should have given you some reasons for the doctrine, but he is sorry that he is prevented: and then he designed also to have brought it down to the conscience of every man by a warm address, but his time being gone he must break off." He hurries over a hint or two which should have been wrought up into exhortation or instruction, but all in great haste, and thus concludes his work. The obstinate and careless sinner goes away unawakened, unconvinced; and the mourning soul departs uncomforted: the unbeliever is not led to faith in the gospel, nor the immoral wretch to hate or forsake his iniquities: the hypocrite and the man of sincerity are both unedified, because the preacher had not time. In short, he hath finished his work, and hath done nothing.

When I hear this man preach it brings to my remembrance the account which I have heard concerning the Czar of Muscovy, the first time his army besieged a town in Livonia: he was then just come from his travels in Great Britain, where he and his ministers of state had learned the mathematics of an old acquaintance of mine: the Czar took great care to begin the siege in form; he drew all the lines of circumvallation and contravallation according to the rules of art; but he was so tedious and so exact in these mathematical performances, that the season was spent, he was forced to break up the siege, and retire without any execution done upon the town.

Ergates is another sort of preacher, a workman that need not be ashamed: he had in his younger days but few of these learned vanities, and age and experience have now worn them all off. He preaches like a man who watches for our souls, as one that must give an account; he passes over lesser matters with speed, and pursues his great design, namely, to save himself and them that hear him, 1 Tim. iv. 16, and by following this advice of St. Paul, he happily complies with that great and natural rule of Horace, always to make haste towards the most valuable end:—

Semper ad eventum festinat.—

He never affects to choose a very obscure text, lest he should waste too much of the hour in explaining the literal sense of it: he reserves all those obscurities till they come in course at his seasons of public exposition. For it is his opinion, that preaching the gospel for the salvation of men carries in it a little different idea from a learned and critical exposition of the difficult texts of scripture.

He knows well how to use his logic in his compositions; but he calls no part of the words by its logical name, if there be any vulgar name that answers it: reading and meditation have furnished him with extensive views of his subject, and his own good sense hath taught him to give sufficient reasons for every thing he asserts; but he never uses one of them till a proof is needful. He is acquainted with the mistaken glosses of expositors, but he thinks it needless to acquaint his hearers with them, unless there be evident danger that they might run into the same mistake. He understands very well what his subject is not, as well as what it is; but when he would explain it to you he never says, first, negatively, unless some remarkable error is at hand, and which his hearers may easily fall into, for want of such a caution.

Thus, in five or ten minutes at the most, he makes his way plain to the proposition or theme on which he designs to discourse; and being so wise as to know well what to say and what to leave out, he proportions every part of his work to his time; he enlarges a little upon the subject by way of illustration, till the truth becomes evident and intelligible to the weakest of his hearers; then he confirms the point with a few convincing arguments where the matter requires it, and makes haste to turn the doctrine into use and improvement. Thus the ignorant are instructed, and the growing Christians are established and improved: the stupid sinner is loudly awakened, and the mourning soul receives consolation: the unbeliever is led to trust in Christ and his Gospel, and the impenitent and immoral are convinced and softened, are melted and reformed. The inward voice of the holy Spirit joins with the voice of the minister; the good man and the hypocrite have their proper portions assigned them; and the work of the Lord prospers in his hand.

This is the usual course and manner of his ministry; this method being natural, plain, and easy, he casts many of his discourses into this form; but he is no slave to forms and methods of any kind; he makes the nature of his subject, and the necessity of his hearers, the great rule to direct him in what method he shall choose in every sermon, that he may the better enlighten, convince, and persuade. Ergates well knows that where the subject itself is entirely practical, he has no need of the formality of long uses and exhortations: he knows that practice is the chief design of doctrine; therefore he bestows most of his labour upon this part of his office, and intermingles much of the pathetic under every particular. Yet he wisely observes the special dangers of his flock, and the errors of the times he lives in, and now and then (though very seldom) he thinks it necessary to spend almost a whole discourse in mere doctrinal articles.—Upon such an occasion he thinks it proper to take up a little larger part of his hour in explaining and confirming the sense of his text, and brings it down to the understanding of a child.

At another time perhaps he particularly designs to entertain the few learned and polite among his auditors, and that with this view, that he may ingratiate his discourses with their ears, and may so far gratify their curiosity in this part of his sermon as to give an easier entrance for the more plain, necessary, and important parts of it into their hearts. Then he aims at, and he reaches the sublime, and furnishes out an entertainment for the finest taste; but he scarce ever finishes his sermon without compassion to the unlearned, and an address that may reach their consciences with words of salvation.

I have observed him sometimes, after a learned discourse, come down from the pulpit as a man ashamed and quite out of countenance: he has blushed, and complained to his intimate friends, lest he should be thought to have preached himself, and not Christ Jesus his Lord: he has been ready to wish he had entertained the audience in a more unlearned manner, and on a more vulgar subject, lest the servants and the labourers and tradesmen there should reap no advantage to their souls, and the important hour of worship should be lost as to their improvement. Well he knows, and keeps it upon his heart, that the middle and the lower ranks of mankind, and people of unlettered character, make up the greater part of the assembly; therefore he is ever seeking how to adapt his thoughts and his language, and far the greater part of all his ministrations, to the instruction and profit of persons of common rank and capacity; it is in the midst of these that he hopes to find his triumph, his joy, and crown, in the last great day, for not many wise, not many noble are called.

There is so much spirit and beauty in his common conversation, that it is sought and desired by the ingenious men of his age; but he carries a severe guard of piety always about him, that tempers the pleasant air of his discourse, even in his brightest and freest hours;

and before he leaves the place (if possible) he will leave something of the savour of heaven there: in the parlour he carries on the design of the pulpit, but in so elegant a manner, that it charms the company, and gives not the least occasion for censure.

His polite acquaintance will sometimes rally him for talking so plainly in his sermons, and sinking his good sense to so low a level: but Ergates is bold to tell the gayest of them,—"Our public business, my friend, is chiefly with the weak and the ignorant; that is, the bulk of mankind: The poor receive the gospel: The mechanics and day-labourers, the women and the children of my assembly have souls to be saved: I will imitate my blessed Redeemer in preaching the gospel to the poor, and learn of St. Paul to become all things to all men, that I may win souls, and lead many sinners to heaven by repentance, faith, and holiness."

Sect. II. *A Branching Sermon.*

I have always thought it a mistake in the preacher to mince his text or his subject too small, by a great number of subdivisions; for it occasions great confusion to the understandings of the unlearned. Where a man divides his matter into more general, less general, special, and more particular heads, he is under a necessity sometimes of saying, firstly or secondly, two or three times together, which the learned may observe; but the greater part of the auditory, not knowing the analysis, cannot so much as take it into their minds, and much less treasure up in their memories, in a just and regular order; and when such hearers are desired to give some account of the sermon, they throw the thirdlies and secondlies into heaps, and make very confused work in a rehearsal, by intermingling the general and the special heads. In writing a large discourse this is much more tolerable,* but in preaching it is less profitable and more intricate and offensive.

* Especially as words may be used to number the generals and figures of different kinds and forms to marshal the primary or secondary ranks of particulars under them.

It is as vain an affectation also to draw out a long rank of particulars in the same sermon under any one general, and run up the number of them to eighteenthly and seven-and-twentiethly. Men that take delight in this sort of work, will cut out all their senses into shreds; and every thing that they can say upon any topic shall make a new particular.

This sort of folly and mistaken conduct appears weekly in Polyramus's lectures, and renders all his discourses lean and insipid. Whether it proceeds from a mere barrenness of thought and native dryness of soul, that he is not able to vary his matter and to amplify beyond the formal topics of analysis; or whether it arises from affectation of such a way of talking, is hard to say: but it is certain that the chief part of his auditory are not overmuch profited or pleased. When I sit under his preaching, I fancy myself brought into the valley of Ezekiel's vision; it was full of bones, and behold, there were very many in the valley, and lo, they were very dry.—Ezek. xxxvii. 1, 2.

It is the variety of enlargement upon a few proper heads that clothes the dry bones with flesh, and animates them with blood and spirits: it is this that colours the discourse, makes it warm and strong, and renders the divine propositions bright and persuasive; it is this brings down the doctrine or the duty to the understanding or conscience of the whole auditory, and commands the natural affections into the interest of the gospel: in short, it is this that, under the influence of the Holy Spirit, gives life and force, beauty and success to a sermon, and provides food for souls. A single rose-bush, or a dwarf-pear, with all their leaves, flowers, and fruit about them, have more beauty and spirit in themselves, and yield more food and pleasure to mankind, than the innumerable branches, boughs, and twigs of a long hedge of thorns. The fruit will feed the hungry, and the flower will refresh the fainting, which is more than can be said of the thickest oak in Bashan, when it has lost its vital juice; it may spread its limbs indeed far and wide, but they are naked, withered, and sapless.

SECT. III. *The Harangue.*

Is it not possible to forsake one extreme without running into a worse? Is there no medium between a sermon made up of sixty dry particulars, and a long loose declamation without any distinction of the parts of it? Must the preacher divide his work by the breaks of a minute-watch, or let it run on incessant to the last word, like the flowing stream of the hour-glass that measures his divinity? Surely Fluvio preaches as though he knew no medium; and having taken a disgust heretofore at one of Polyramus's lectures, he resolved his discourses should have no distinction of particulars in them. His language flows smoothly in a long connexion of periods, and glides over the ear like a rivulet of oil over polished marble, and, like that too, leaves no trace behind it. The attention is detained in a gentle pleasure, and (to say the best thing possible of it) the hearer is soothed into something like divine delight; but he can give the inquiring friend scarce any account of what it was that pleased him. He retains a faint idea of the sweetness, but has forgot the sense.

Tell me, Fluvio, is this the most effectual way to instruct ignorant creatures in the several articles of faith, and the various duties of the Christian life? Will such a long uniform flow of language imprint all the distinct parts of Christian knowledge on the mind in their best form and order! Do you find such a gentle and gliding stream of words most powerful to call up the souls of sinners from their dangerous or fatal lethargy? Will this indolent and moveless species of oratory make a thoughtless wretch attend to matters of infinite moment? Can a long purling sound awaken a sleepy conscience, and give a perishing sinner just notices of his dreadful hazard? Can it furnish his understanding and his memory with all the awful and tremendous topics of our religion, when it scarce ever leaves any distinct impression of one of them on his soul? Can you make the arrow wound where it will not stick? Where all the discourse vanishes from the remembrance, can you suppose the soul to be profited or enriched? When you brush over the closed eyelids with a feather, did you ever find it give light to the blind? Have any of your soft harangues, your continued threads of silken eloquence, ever raised the dead? I fear your whole aim is to talk over the appointed number of minutes upon the subject, or to practise a little upon the gentler passions, without any concern how to give the understanding its due improvement, or to furnish the memory with any lasting treasure, or to make a knowing and a religious Christian.

Ask old Wheatfield, the rich farmer, ask Plowdown, your neighbour, or any of his family, who have sat all their lives under your ministry, what they know of the common truths of religion, or of the special articles of Christianity? Desire them to tell you what the gospel is, or what is salvation? what are their duties toward God, or what they mean by religion? who is Jesus Christ, or what is the meaning of his atonement, or redemption by his blood? Perhaps you will tell me yourself, that you have very seldom entertained them with these subjects. Well, inquire of them then, what is heaven; which is the way to obtain it; or what hope they have of dwelling there? Entreat them to tell you wherein they have profited as to holiness of heart and life, or fitness for death? They will soon make it appear, by their awkward answers, that they understood very little of all your fine discourses, and those of your predecessor; and have made but wretched improvement of forty years attendance at church. They have now and then been pleased perhaps with the music of your voice, as with the sound of a sweet instrument, and they mistook that for devotion; but their heads are dark still, and their hearts earthly; they are mere heathens with a Christian name, and know little more of God than their yokes of oxen. In short, Polyramus's auditors have some confusion in their knowledge, but Fluvio's hearers have scarce any knowledge at all.

But you will tell me your discourses are not all made up of harangue; your design is sometimes to inform the mind by a train of well connected reasonings, and that all your paragraphs, in their long order, prove and support each other; and though you do not distinguish your discourse into particulars, yet you have kept some invisible method all the way; and by some artificial gradations you have brought your sermon down to the concluding sentence.

It may be so sometimes, and I will acknowledge it; but believe me, Fluvio, this artificial and invisible method carries darkness with it instead of light; nor is it by any means a proper way to instruct the vulgar, that is, the bulk of your auditory: their souls are not capable of so wide a stretch, as to take in the whole chain of your long-connected consequences; you talk reason and religion to them in vain, if you do not make the argument so short as to come within their grasp, and give a frequent rest for their thoughts; you must break the bread of life into pieces to feed children with it, and part your discourses into distinct propositions to give the ignorant a plain scheme of any one doctrine, and enable them to comprehend or retain it.

Every day gives us experiments to confirm what I say, and to encourage ministers to divide their sermons into several distinct heads of discourse. Myrtilla, a little creature of nine years old, was at church twice yesterday: in the morning the preacher entertained his audience with a running oration, and the child could give her parents no other account of it, but that he talked smoothly and sweetly about virtue and heaven. It was Ergates' lot to fulfil the service of the afternoon; he is an excellent preacher, both for the wise and for the unwise: in the evening Myrtilla very prettily entertained her mother with a repetition of the most considerable parts of the sermon; for "Here (said she) I can fix my thoughts upon first, secondly, and thirdly; upon the doctrine, the reasons, and the inferences; and I know what I must try to remember, and repeat it when my friends shall ask me; but as for the morning sermon, I could do nothing but hear it, for I could not tell what I should get by heart."

This manner of talking in a loose harangue has not only injured our pupils, but it makes several essays and treatises that are written now-a-days less capable of improving the knowledge or enriching the memory of the reader. I will easily grant, that where the whole discourse reaches not beyond a few pages, there is no necessity for the formal proposal of the several parts before you handle each of them distinctly; nor is there need of such a set method: the unlearned and narrow understanding can take an easy view of the whole, without the author's pointing to the several parts. But where the essay is prolonged to a greater extent, confusion grows upon the reader almost at every page, without some scheme or method of successive heads in the discourse to direct the mind and aid the memory.

If it be answered here, That neither such treatises nor sermons are a mere heap, for there is a just method observed in the composure, and the subjects are ranked in a proper order, it is easy to reply, That this method is so concealed, that a common reader or hearer can never find it; and you must suppose every one that peruses such a book, and much more that attends such a discourse, to have some good knowledge of the art of logic before he can distinguish the various parts and branches, the connexions and transitions of it. To an unlearned eye or ear it appears a mere heap of good things, without any method, form, or order; and if you tell your young friends they should get it into their heads and hearts, they know not how to set about it.

If we inquire how it comes to pass that our modern ingenious writers should affect this manner, I know no juster reason to give for it, than a humorous and wanton contempt of the customs and preaching of our forefathers: a sensible disgust taken at some of their mistakes and ill conduct at first tempted a vain generation into the contrary extreme near sixty years ago; and now, even to this day, it continues too much in fashion, so that the wise, as well as the weak, are ashamed to oppose it, and are borne down with the current.

Our fathers formed their sermons much upon the model of doctrine, reason, and use: and perhaps there is no one method of more universal service, and more easily applicable to most subjects, though it is not necessary or proper in every discourse; but the very names of doctrine and use are become now-a-days such stale and old fashioned things, that a modish preacher is quite ashamed of them; nor can a modish hearer bear the sound of those syllables. A direct and distinct address to the consciences of saints and sinners must not be named or mentioned, though these terms are scriptural, lest it should be hissed out of the church like the garb of a roundhead or a puritan.

Some of our fathers have multiplied their particulars under one single head of discourse, and run up the tale of them to sixteen or seventeen. Culpable indeed, and too numerous! But in opposition to this extreme, we are almost ashamed in our age to say thirdly; and all fourthlies and fifthlies are very unfashionable words.

Our fathers made too great account of the sciences of logic and metaphysics, and the formalities of definition and division, syllogism and method, when they brought them so often into the pulpit; but we hold those arts so much in contempt and defiance, that we had rather talk a whole hour without order, and without edification, than be suspected of using logic or method in our discourses.

Some of our fathers neglected politeness perhaps too much, and indulged a coarseness of style, and a rough or awkward pronunciation; but we have such a value for elegancy, and so nice a taste for what we call polite, that we dare not spoil the cadence of a period to quote a text of Scripture in it, nor disturb the harmony of our sentences to number or to name the heads of our discourse. And for this reason I have heard it hinted, that the name of Christ has been banished out of polite sermons, because it is a monosyllable of so many consonants and so harsh a sound.

But after all, our fathers, with all their defects, and with all their weaknesses, preached the gospel of Christ to the sensible instruction of whole parishes, to the conversion of sinners from the errors of their way, and the salvation of multitudes of souls. But it has been the late complaint of Dr. Edwards, and other worthy sons of the established church, that in too many pulpits now-a-days there are only heard some smooth declamations, while the hearers that were ignorant of the gospel abide still without knowledge, and the profane sinners are profane still. O that divine grace would descend, and reform what is amiss in all the sanctuaries of the nation!*

CHAPTER VII.

OF WRITING BOOKS FOR THE PUBLIC.

In the explication and distinction of words and things by definition and description, in the division of things into their several parts, and in the distribution of things into their several kinds, be sure to observe a just medium. We must not always explain and distinguish, define, divide, and distribute; nor must we always omit it: sometimes it is useless and impertinent, sometimes it is proper and necessary. There is confusion brought into our argument and discourse by too many or by too few of these. One author plunges his reader into the midst of things without due explication of them; another jumbles together, without distinction, all those ideas which have any likeness; a third is fond of explaining every word, and coining distinctions between ideas which have little or no difference; but each of these runs into extremes, for all these practices are equal hinderances to clear, just, and useful knowledge. It is not a long train of rules, but observation and good judgment can teach us when to explain, define, and divide, and when to omit it.

In the beginning of a treatise it is proper and necessary sometimes to premise some præcognita, or general principles, which may serve for an introduction to the

* It appears by the date at the bottom of this paper, in the manuscript, that it was written in the year 1718. The first and perhaps the second section of it may seem now to be grown, in a great measure, out of date; but whether the third is not at least as seasonable now as ever, may deserve serious consideration. The author has, since this was drawn up, delivered his sentiments more fully in the first part of that excellent piece, entitled "An Humble Attempt for the Revival of Religion," &c.

subject in hand, and give light or strength to the following discourse; but it is ridiculous, under a pretence of such introductions or prefaces, to wander to the most remote or distant themes, which have no near or necessary connexion with the thing in hand; this serves for no other purpose but to make a gaudy show of learning. There was a professor of divinity who began an analytical exposition of the Epistle to the Romans with such præcognita as these: first he showed the excellence of man above other creatures, who was able to declare the sense of his mind by arbitrary signs: then he harangued upon the origin of speech; after that he told of the wonderful invention of writing, and inquired into the author of that art which taught us to paint sounds; when he had given us the various opinions of the learned upon this point, and distributed writing into the several kinds, and laid down definitions of them all, at last he came to speak of epistolary writing, and distinguished epistles into familiar, private, public, recommendatory, credential, and what not: thence he descended to speak of the superscription, subscription, &c.; and some lectures were finished before he came to the first verse of St. Paul's Epistle. The auditors, being half starved and tired with expectation, dropped away one by one, so that the professor had scarce any hearer to attend the college or lectures which he had promised on that part of Scripture.

The rules which Horace has given in his Art of Poetry would instruct many a preacher and professor of theology, if they would but attend to them. He informs us that a wise author, such as Homer, who writes a poem of the Trojan war, would not begin a long and far distant story of Jupiter, in the form of a swan, impregnating Leda with a double egg; from one part whereof Helen was hatched, who was married to Menelaus, a Greek general, and then stolen from him by Paris, son of Priam, king of Troy; which awakened the resentment of the Greeks against the Trojans:

Nec gemino bellum Trojanum orditur ab ovo.

But the writer, says he, makes all proper haste to the event of things, and does not drag on slowly, perpetually turning aside from his point, and catching at every incident to prolong his story, as though he wanted matter to furnish out his tale:

Semper ad eventum festinat.

Though I must confess I cannot think Homer has always followed this rule in either of his two famous epic poems; but Horace does not hear what I say. There is also another rule near akin to the former.

As a writer or speaker should not wander from his subject to fetch in foreign matter from afar, so neither should he amass together and drag in all that can be said, even on his appointed theme of discourse; but he should consider what is his chief design, what is the end he hath in view, and then to make every part of his discourse subserve that design. If he keep his great end always in his eye, he will pass hastily over those parts or appendages of his subject which have no evident connexion with his design; or he will entirely omit them, and hasten continually toward his intended mark, employing his time, his study, and labour, chiefly on the part of his subject which is most necessary to attain his present and proper end.

This might be illustrated by a multitude of examples; but an author who would heap them together on such an occasion might be in danger of becoming himself an example of the impertinence he is cautioning others to avoid.

After you have finished any discourse which you design for the public, it would be always best, if other circumstances would permit, to let it sleep some time before you expose it to the world, that so you may have opportunity to review it with the indifference of a stranger, and to make the whole of it pass under a new and just examination: for no man can judge so justly of his own work, while the pleasure of his invention and performance is fresh, and has engaged his self-love too much on the side of what he has newly finished.

If an author would send a discourse into the world which should be most universally approved, he should consult persons of very different genius, sentiment, and party, and endeavour to learn their opinions of it: in the world it will certainly meet with all these. Set it therefore to view among several of your acquaintance first, who may survey the argument on all sides, and one may happen to suggest a correction which is entirely neglected by others; and be sure to yield yourself to the dictates of true criticism and just censure wheresoever you meet with them, nor let a fondness for what you have written blind your eyes against the discovery of your own mistakes.

When an author desires a friend to revise his work, it is too frequent a practice to disallow almost every correction which a judicious friend shall make. He apologizes for this word, and the other expression; he vindicates this sentence, and gives his reasons for another paragraph, and scarcely ever submits to correction; and thus utterly discourages the freedom that a true friend would take in pointing out our mistakes. Such writers, who are so full of themselves, may go on to admire their own incorrect performances, and expose their works and their follies to the world without pity.*

Horace, in his Art of Poetry, talks admirably well on this subject:

Quintilio si quid recitares, Corrige, sodes,
Hoc, aiebat, et hoc: melius te posse negares,
Bis terque expertum frustra, delere jubebat,
Et male tornatos incudi reddere versus.
Si defendere delictum, quam vertere, malles;
Nullum ultra verbum, aut operam insumebat inanem,
Quin sine rivali teque et tua solus amares.

Let good Quintilius all your lines revise,
And he will freely say, Mend this, and this.
Sir, I have often tried, and tried again,
I'm sure I can't do better; 'tis in vain.
Then blot out ev'ry word, or try once more,
And file these ill turn'd verses o'er and o'er.
But if you seem in love with your own thought,
More eager to defend than mend your fault,
He says no more, but lets the fop go on,
And rival-free admire his lovely own. *Creech.*

* To cut off such chicanery, it may perhaps be the most expedient for a person consulted on such an occasion, to note down in a distinct paper, with proper references, the advised alterations, referring it to the author to make such use of them as he, on due deliberation, shall think fit.

If you have not the advantage of friends to survey your writings, then read them over yourself, and all the way consider what will be the sentence and judgment of all the various characters of mankind upon them: think what one of your own party would say, or what would be the sense of an adversary: imagine what a curious or malicious man, what a captious or an envious critic, what a vulgar or a learned reader would object, either to the matter, the manner, or the style; and be sure and think with yourself what you yourself could say against your own writing, if you were of a different opinion or a stranger to the writer: and by these means you will obtain some hints whereby to correct and improve your own work, and to guard it better against the censures of the public, as well as to render it more useful to that part of mankind for whom you chiefly design it.

CHAPTER VIII.

OF WRITING AND READING CONTROVERSIES.

Sect. I. *Of writing Controversies.*

When a person of good sense writes on any controverted subject, he will generally bring the strongest arguments that are usually to be found for the support of his opinion; and when that is done, he will represent the most powerful objections against it in a fair and candid manner, giving them their full force; and at last will put in such an answer to those objections as he thinks will dissipate and dissolve the force of them: and herein the reader will generally find a full view of the controversy, together with the main strength of argument on both sides.

When a good writer has set forth his own opinion at large, and vindicated it with its fairest and strongest proofs, he shall be attacked by some pen on the other side of the question: and if his opponent be a wise and sensible writer, he will show the best reasons why the former opinions cannot be true; that is, he will draw out the objections against them in their fullest array, in order to destroy what he supposes a mistaken opinion; and here we may reasonably suppose that an opponent will draw up his objections against the supposed error in a brighter light, and with stronger evidence than the first writer did, who propounded his opinion, which was contrary to those objections.

If, in the third place, the first writer answers his opponent with care and diligence, and maintains his own point against the objections which were raised in the best manner; the reader may then generally presume, that in these three pieces he has a complete view of the controversy; together with the most solid and powerful arguments on both sides of the debate.

But when a fourth, and fifth, and sixth volume appears in rejoinders and replies, we cannot reasonably expect any great degrees of light to be derived from them, or that much further evidences for truth should be found in them; and it is sufficiently evident, from daily experience, that many mischiefs attend this prolongation of controversies among men of learning, which, for the most part, do injury to the truth, either by turning the attention of the reader quite away from the original point to other matters, or by covering the truth with a multitude of occasional incidents and perplexities, which serve to bewilder rather than guide a faithful inquirer.

Sometimes, in these latter volumes, the writers on both sides will hang upon little words and occasional expressions of their opponent, in order to expose them, which have no necessary connexion with the grand point in view, and which have nothing to do with the debated truth.

Sometimes they will spend many a page in vindicating their own character, or their own little sentences or accidental expressions, from the remarks of their opponent, in which expressions or remarks the original truth has no concern.

And sometimes again you shall find even writers of good sense, who have happened to express themselves in an improper and indefensible manner, led away by the fondness of self-love to justify those expressions, and vindicate those little lapses they were guilty of, rather than they will condescend to correct those little mistakes, or recall those improper expressions. O that we would put off our pride, our self-sufficiency, and our infallibility, when we enter into a debate of truth! But if the writer is guilty of mingling these things with this grand argument, happy will that reader be who has judgment enough to distinguish them, and to neglect every thing that does not belong to the original theme proposed and disputed.

Yet here it may be proper to put in one exception to this general observation or remark, namely, When the second writer attacks only a particular or collateral opinion which was maintained by the first, then the fourth writing may be supposed to contain a necessary part of the complete force of the argument, as well as the second and third, because the first writing only occasionally or collaterally mentioned that sentiment which the second attacks and opposes; and in such a case the second may be esteemed as the first treatise on that controversy. It would take up too much time should we mention instances of this kind which might be pointed to in most of our controversial writers, and it might be invidious to enter into the detail.*

* Upon this it may be remarked farther, that there is a certain spirit of modesty and of benevolence, which never fails to adorn a writer on such occasions, and which generally does him much more service in the judgment of wise and sensible men, than any poignancy of satire with which he might be able to animate his productions; and as this always appears amiable, so it is peculiarly charming when the opponent shows that pertness and petulancy which is so very common on such occasions. When a writer, instead of pursuing with eager resentment the antagonist that has given him such provocation, calmly attends to the main question in debate, with a noble negligence of those little advantages which ill nature and ill manners always give, he acquires a glory far superior to any trophies which wit can raise. And it is highly probable that the solid instruction his pages may contain will give a continuance to his writings far beyond what tracts of peevish controversy are to expect, of which the much greater part are borne away into oblivion by the wind they raise, or burned in their own flame.

Sect. II. *Of reading Controversies.*

When we take a book into our hands wherein any doctrine or opinion is printed in a way of argument, we are too often satisfied and determined beforehand whether it be right or wrong; and if we are on the writer's side, we are generally tempted to take his arguments for solid and substantial. And thus our own former sentiment is established more powerfully, without a sincere search after truth.

If we are on the other side the question, we then take it for granted that there is nothing of force in these arguments, and we are satisfied with a short survey of the book, and are soon persuaded to pronounce mistake, weakness, and insufficiency concerning it. Multitudes of common readers, who are fallen into any error, when they are directed and advised to read a treatise that would set them right, read it with a sort of disgust which they have before entertained; they skim lightly over the arguments, they neglect or despise the force of them, and keep their own conclusion firm in their assent, and thus maintain their error in the midst of light, and grow incapable of conviction.

But if we would indeed act like sincere searchers of the truth, we should survey every argument with a careful and unbiassed mind, whether it agree with our former opinion or no: we should give every reasoning its full force, and weigh it in our sedatest judgment. Now the best way to try what force there is in the arguments which are brought against our own opinions, is to sit down and endeavour to give a solid answer, one by one, to every argument which the author brings to support his own doctrine: and in this attempt, if we find there some arguments which we are not able to answer fairly to our own minds, we should then begin to bethink ourselves whether we have not hitherto been in a mistake, and whether the defender of the contrary sentiments may not be in the right. Such a method as this will effectually forbid us to pronounce at once against those doctrines and those writers which are contrary to our sentiments; and we shall endeavour to find solid arguments to refute their positions, before we entirely establish ourselves in a contrary opinion.

Volatilis had given himself up to the conversation of the freethinkers of our age, upon all subjects; and being pleased with the wit and appearance of argument, in some of our modern deists, had too easily deserted the Christian faith, and gone over to the camp of the infidels. Among other books which were recommended him, to reduce him to the faith of the Gospel, he had Mr. John Reynolds's three Letters to a Deist put into his hand, and was particularly desired to peruse the third of them with the utmost care, as being an unanswerable defence of the truth of Christianity. He took it in hand, and after having given it a short survey, he told his friend he saw nothing in it but the common arguments which we all use to support the religion in which we had been educated; but they wrought no conviction in him; nor did he see sufficient reason to believe that the Gospel of Christ was not a piece of enthusiasm, or a mere imposture.

Upon this, the friend who recommended Mr. Reynolds's three letters to his study, being confident of the force of truth which lay there, entreated Volatilis that he would set himself down with diligence, and try to answer Mr. Reynolds's third letter in vindication of the Gospel; and that he would show under every head how the several steps which were taken in the propagation of the Christian religion might be the natural effects of imposture or enthusiasm, and, consequently, that it deserves no credit amóngst men.

Volatilis undertook the work, and, after he had entered a little way into it, found himself so bewildered, and his arguments to prove the apostles either enthusiasts or impostors so muddled, so perplexed, and so inconclusive, that, by a diligent review of this letter to the deists, at last he acknowledged himself fully convinced that the religion of Jesus was divine: for that Christian author had made it appear it was impossible that that doctrine should have been propagated in the world by simplicity or forty, by fraud or falsehood; and accordingly he resigned his soul up to the gospel of the blessed Jesus.

I fear there have been multitudes of such unbelievers as Volatilis; and he himself has confessed to me, that even his most rational friends would be constrained to yield to the evidence of the Christian doctrine, if they would honestly try the same method.

QUESTIONS

UPON

WATTS'

IMPROVEMENT OF THE MIND.

BY J. S. DENMAN.

INTRODUCTION.

Page.

5—Why are all persons under some obligations to improve their understanding? What will overspread the uncultivated mind? How can knowledge and skill be acquired? What do the various relations of life impose upon all persons?

6—In what have all persons an important concern? What appears to be the necessary duty and interest of all persons? What is the consequence of acting without thought or reason?

CHAPTER I.

7—What does the first chapter contain? What is required by the first rule? What should we review? What would be the result? What should we consider as causes of the frailties and mistakes of the mind? Why should we read works which treat of the doctrine of prejudices,&c.?

8—Why should we realize our own ignorance? What methods are mentioned in the third rule as suited to impress the mind with its imperfect degrees of knowledge?

Page.

9—What would be the consequence of priding ourselves on account of superficial attainments? What is the substance of the fourth rule?

10—What is said, in the fifth rule, of reading? What gives good sense to the reader, and improves his understanding?

11—Should we imagine a life of learning to be one of idleness and ease? What is said of Sobrino, and Languinos?

12—What should incite us to constant industry in the pursuit of knowledge? What is said of the perfection of learning and science? Is it probable that theologians have arrived at a full understanding of all scriptural truths which can be known? What is said of every man who shall aid in the introduction of an age of light and love?

13—What is taught in the eighth rule? What is the effect of judging from a superficial view? Should we form any decided judgment of our own on subjects which we understand very imperfectly? What counsels are given in the ninth rule?

14—What spirit should we constantly guard against? What

Page.
is a dogmatical spirit? What is said of forming unalterable opinions? Mention some of the inconveniences attending a dogmatic spirit.

16—What do frequent changes of opinion indicate? What is said of judging falsely? What of confessing mistakes and renouncing errors? What of humorous conduct and fanciful temper of mind? What is the character of a humorist? What is said of trifling with important things, and sporting with those which are sacred? What of a spirit of ridicule?

17—What is the effect of indulging in any evil habit? Why should we maintain a virtuous and pious frame of spirit? What effect does sensuality and the indulgence of appetite produce upon the mind? Who is in a fair way to wisdom? What is said of piety, and those who abandon religion?

18—What does the fifteenth rule warn us to watch against? What is said of self-sufficiency in the attainment of knowledge? What of those who neglect religion, and depend wholly upon their own reason?

19—What are the teachings of the sixteenth rule? Mention some of the reasons and arguments given in this rule, for uniting industry, study, and devotion, in the pursuit of knowledge and true wisdom.

CHAPTER II.

21—What five methods are mentioned by which the mind is improved in knowledge? What is observation? What

Page.
do we gain by observation from infancy? Mention some facts which we know by observation. When is observation called experience? How do we know we have the power of thinking, fearing, &c.?

22—What does observation include? When is it called experiment? What is said of reading? What of lectures? What of conversation? Is conversation always mutually beneficial?

23—What does meditation include? Mention some of the results of meditation. What furnishes the mind with its first ideas? On what does the foundation of knowledge depend? What is said of the impossibility of being taught by men and books, if we had gained no knowledge, by observation, of external objects, and the operations of our own minds?

24—What is the second advantage mentioned of obtaining knowledge by observation? Why are ideas gained by observation generally clearer and more distinct than those acquired by reading, conversation, &c. Mention the third advantage of acquiring knowledge by observation. What is said of the advantages of reading?

26—Mention some of the advantages of gaining knowledge by means of lectures.

27—What of the advantages of conversation?

28—What is the second advantage mentioned? Third? Fourth? Fifth?

29—Sixth? Seventh?

30—Mention some of the benefits derived from meditation.

CHAPTER III.

Page.

32—What is the subject of this chapter? Does observation, strictly speaking, include any reasonings of the mind? Why are thoughts relating to reason included in the rules for observation? What should be our constant design in life?

33—How can we acquire knowledge by observation, when alone, in darkness and silence? How, when in company? In the country? Whence should we derive instruction?

34—What should we learn from the vicissitudes of individuals and nations? What from the coffin and funeral? The vices and follies of others? Their virtues? Deformity, distress, &c.? What from our natural powers and faculties? From our pains and sorrows? Sins and follies? Why should the laudable curiosity of the young be gratified?

35—What opportunities for observation should be given to the young? What observations should be written down, and for what purpose? What will be the effect of such practice? Should we ever neglect to improve our minds by observation?

36—What is said of the observations of Theobaldino and Puteoli? Why should we guard against passions and prejudices, when making observations? What is said of false judgments, envy, and self-flattery?

37—What is the substance of the fifth rule? Of the sixth? What is said of observations concerning persons? What if the conduct observed is highly culpable? What rule should be observed in conversation?

38—What is the apostolic precept relative to evil speaking? What is a false induction? What is said of general observations which have been drawn from many particulars? What of hastily determining universal principles? What causes scandal to be cast upon a whole nation?

CHAPTER IV.

38—Of what does this chapter treat? What is said of books?

39—What advantage would the young derive from having proper books recommended for their reading? What is said of reading books of importance in a cursory manner? What of the preface and table of contents? How should a good book be read a second time? What is said of passages which contain ideas or truths previously unknown to the reader? Mention a second reason for a superficial survey of a new book?

40—What plan is recommended for several persons reading the same book? What if they are perusing different works on the same subject? What should be our chief object in reading? How should we deal with every author? When yield our assent? What is sufficient evidence to demand our assent to truths of the bible?

41—Whose reason should guide us when reading the productions of uninspired men? What is recommended in the sixth rule? To what, beside reading, may many directions given in this chapter apply?

Page.
What is the substance of the seventh rule?

42—What should we recollect when we have finished any book? What is said of books which have no index? What will compensate for the pains which such method of reading will cost? What of writers who have peculiar excellencies or defects? What benefit will be derived from reading one book in this laborious manner?

43—Will such course of reading improve the reasoning powers? Why do some diligent readers fail to make any advances in true knowledge? To whom is such a reader compared? What is the effect of entering into the sense of all the arguments, and examining all the proofs of the authors read?

44—What is said of Studentio, Plumbinus, and Plumeo? What of those whose reading is designed to fit them for much talk, and little knowledge? What of those of much reading, a retentive memory, and but little meditation? What of reading with a predetermination to believe or disbelieve? To what should the mind always be open?

45—What caution is given in the twelfth rule? What books should we read with freedom of thought after our principles are well established? How should we read works which defend our sentiments? Those that oppose them?

46—To what class of books do the preceding remarks on reading chiefly relate? What should we do when reading works which were written to direct our practice? What,

Page.
when folly and vice are represented? What should we remember in all our pursuits of knowledge? What is said of history, poesy, &c.

47—What paragraphs and sentiments deserve remark? What histories, poems, &c. should be reviewed and closely studied? What is said of miscellaneous essays, the Spectator, &c.

48—What is said of dictionaries, &c.? What of permitting an unknown word to pass in reading? What is recommended when reading where we cannot consult books which would explain what we do not understand? Should we seek a knowledge of the best authors on a subject, or of the subject itself?

49—Mention the follies which those are apt to practice, who desire to increase their knowledge of books, but are content with the title pages? Who is said to be deplorably poor in understanding?

CHAPTER V.

49—What may assist us in judging of books we have not seen before?

50—What shall we ascertain by selecting and reading a few chapters? What is the substance of the second rule for judging of new books? How are we apt to judge of books which support our opinions? Of those which oppose them?

51—How should books be judged? What is said of several works called Characteristics?

52—What is said of the mistakes of those who read works on subjects with which they have but little acquaintance? How are we in danger of

Page.
judging of treatises on subjects with which we are familiar?

53—Are the prejudices which warp our judgment few or many? What is said of those who are fond of meddling with all appearances of knowledge? Of Divito and his companions?

54—What is said of those who form judgments from hearsay? What of Sonillus? Of Probus?

55—What feelings usually influence those who severely censure valuable books on account of trifling mistakes and errors? Mention the precept of Horace on this subject.

56—What is said of envy, and envious persons? How may an envious person correct his feelings? What is much more amiable than accusation?

57—Why is it easy to find mistakes in all human productions? What is said of authors who ridicule divine writings and sacred things, and exalt the writings of the ancient pagans? Whose writings are mentioned as differing from nature? What is said of the writings of Steele, St. Paul, Moses, and David? What course is recommended to little critics? What is the world said to love? What may teach us to judge more favorably of the performances of others?

58—Who may cavil at the noblest productions? Mention another fault in passing judgment upon books? What effect does this fault produce on the minds of others? Did Florus judge correctly of the writings of Fenelon, Archbishop of

Page.
Cambray? What is said of the writings of Fenelon?

59—Are there many such authors as the Archbishop of Cambray? What is said of the judgment of Altisono, and the writings of Casimire?

60—What is said of Milton? Of Paradise Lost? How must the reader be influenced who admires every line of that poem? What should we consider when we hear others pronounce judgment upon a book? Can every man of good sense judge correctly of the merits of a particular book?

CHAPTER VI.

61—Do most persons need the assistance of living teachers? Why is it advisable to have more than one instructor?

62—What should instructors possess in addition to competency in the sciences they teach? What pupils grow lean in their understanding? Why are some very learned men incompetent instructors? What is the character of a good tutor?

63—What is said of the example and spirit of a tutor? What of the duty of the learner to his teacher? Why should the student review lectures and note important results? Should we be satisfied with a bare attendance on lectures? What opinion should the learner maintain of his instructor?

64—When may the learner differ from his tutor? What is said of young persons who fancy themselves wiser than their teachers? Are teachers infallible? Mention the two

Page.
extremes to which youth are exposed? Should the pupil receive opinions on the authority of his tutor, without examining them for himself? When should we receive an opinion?

CHAPTER VII.

65—What is of first importance in reading and hearing lectures? How are living languages most easily learned? Dead languages?

66—What advice is given in rule third to those who have just commenced learning a language?

67—What is said to be the living language of the learned world?

68—What inference may be drawn from the fact that small children learn by conversation to speak their mother tongue?

69—What should always be carefully observed in committing rules and lessons to memory? What is said of requiring children to memorize lessons which contain unknown words and phrases, and convey no ideas to their minds?

72—How may we retain a language? Should we content ourselves with a doubtful translation?

73—What are languages said to be? What is their chief design? What is said of learning the words and phrases of a language, without obtaining corresponding ideas? What is in danger of puffing up the mind with vanity?

CHAPTER VIII.

Page.
73—Of what does this chapter treat? Is it sometimes difficult fully to understand a writer or speaker?

74—What is the substance of the first rule for determining the sense? Second rule? With what should we compare the words and phrases of an author? Why should we make such comparisons? Who is the best interpreter of any writer? Why are concordances valuable in the interpretation of scripture? Substance of fourth rule?

75—Of fifth rule? Of sixth rule? What is necessary to enable us to interpret scripture well? Substance of eighth rule?

76—How may we judge of obscure passages which occur in controversies? Substance of tenth rule? Of eleventh rule? How should we treat every author, writer, and speaker?

CHAPTER IX.

77—Of what does this chapter treat? With whom is it well to be acquainted? What advice is here given? Substance of second rule? Of third rule?

78—In what sense is a mechanic wiser than a philosopher? Why should we not always confine ourselves to one sort of company? Why did the king of Siam disbelieve the European merchants? What is said of conversation with foreigners?

79—How should we hear? Of what should we be cautious? What divine rule is here given? Whence does it come? Substance of the sixth rule? Should we imagine there is

Page.
no certain truth but in the sciences we study?

80—Why do we frequently fail to form correct conclusions? What is here said of corres pondents? What method is recommended for reviving conversation in company?

81—How may social visits be prevented from running to waste? What is here said of young ladies? What general rule should we observe, when it is in our power to lead in conversation? How should we hear the arguments of others? What is said to be an unhappy temper and practice?

82—What is the substance of the eleventh rule? Repeat the quotation from Horace. What is recommended in cases of obscurity in the language of those with whom we are conversing?

83—When we cannot assent to the expressed opinions of others, how should we present our objections? What should we impress upon the mind of the speaker? Mention Solomon's rule. What is said of confessing our ignorance, and asking for information?

84—What counsels are given to the young in the fifteenth rule?

85—Of what are weak minds ready to persuade themselves? How may a wise and modest person act when confronting a bold pretender, and innocent villifier? What is here said to be a pity? What advice is given in the seventeenth rule?

86—Should we introduce a warm party spirit into conversations designed for mutual improvement? What is said to bar the doors of the understanding against the admission of new sentiments? What of new discoveries, &c.? What is the substance of the nineteenth rule? Of the twentieth? Of the twenty-first?

87—Whose ignorance and prejudices should we be most ready to suspect? How should we bear contradiction? What might induce others to conclude that our opinions are not based upon the evidences of truth? What should be banished from conversation? What are the enemies of friendship, and tend to ruin free conversation? What does the impartial search for truth require?

88—What is the substance of the twenty-fourth rule? Of the twenty-fifth? What rule is given for selecting companions? Should we always regard their moral character?

88-89—Mention the several infirmities which are said to make some moral, intellectual, and scientific persons undesirable associates in our inquiries after truth.

90—Against what should we constantly watch? What should we do after retiring from company? What instruction should we draw from the thirtieth rule?

91—How may we learn to avoid the follies which injure or destroy good conversation? What may we acquire by pursuing such course? Where may we make the highest intellectual acquisitions which can be gained by conversing with mortals? With whom may we hope to converse hereafter?

CHAPTER X.

Page.

92—Of what does this chapter treat? What is here considered disputes? Do all disputants believe in the propositions they support? Do all disputes result in discovering or maintaining truth? What should be observed in commencing a debate?

93—How may disputants avoid running into remote propositions and axioms? How should every question be expressed? What advice is here given to a certain class of persons?

94—What should be distinctly settled between disputants? What prevents their running from the precise point of inquiry? What is the chief cause of the dishonest artifice which is said to give endless length to disputes?

95—What frequently prevents us from yielding our assent to the convictions of truth? What is said to be the bane of all real improvement, and to work with a secret influence in all disputes? To what does the mind often resort to ward off the convictions of truth? How should we enter upon every debate?

96—What is a more valuable acquisition than a victory over an opponent? What should we narrowly watch in every dispute? How did Cautio extricate himself from the difficulty in which he was involved by too readily yielding his assent to the proposition of Polonides?

97—What was the argument of Fatalio to induce Fidens to leave off prayer? What argument is used to induce Fidens to continue daily prayer?

Page.

98—What inquiry is made relative to Sodom and Gomorrah, the Deluge, &c.? What caution is given in relation to the subtle errors of men? What course should we pursue when an opponent makes a concession which may be serviceable to us in maintaining the truth?

99—Mention the entire argument of Rhapsodus in attempting to detract from the honor of Christianity? What concessions does he subsequently make? Can Christianity be supported by this concession? Repeat the argument given.

100—Mention the three questions here put to Rhapsodus? What good may have been accomplished from preaching the doctrines held by Rhapsodus? Is it probable that envy, revenge, and the secret vices of the mind have been subdued, and men been induced to forsake their sins and love God with hearts devoted to true piety, from the preachings of such doctrines? What has the gospel accomplished?

101—Who understands human nature better than Rhapsodus? What further concession does Rhapsodus make? What does he term a liberal education, and a liberal service? Mention the argument in favor of christianity which is drawn from this concession? What course may we sometimes pursue when engaged with a disputant of very different principles from our own?

102—What is said of holding an argument with a stoic, philosopher, or a Jew? Mention what is said of some of the arguments of St. Paul? What

Page.
should we guard against with great care? What frequently causes personal brawls? What is usually the result of such brawls?
103—What is said of those who guard themselves as to prevent evil influences from disturbing the superior operations of their minds? In what debates are the preceding directions useful?

CHAPTER XI.

103—Whence does the Socratic method of disputation derive its name?
104—How is it managed?
105—What is the first class of advantages mentioned of the Socratic method? Second class? Third class? Fourth class? What is said of a method nearly akin to this?
106—What advantage would be derived from framing Christian catechisms in the manner of a Socratical dispute? What inconvenience would arise from such catechisms?

CHAPTER XII.

106—Of what does this chapter treat? What was the former? From what do Forensic disputes derive their name? What may be properly classed under this head?
107—Where are these disputes practised? Do persons in a forensic dispute usually succeed each other on the same, or opposite sides of a question? After all have spoken, what course is frequently pursued by the speakers? How is the controversy decided? When the matter in debate

Page.
consists of several parts, what is frequently done?
108—What is usually practised before the final decision is given? Would it be advisable to introduce forensic debates into academies and other schools?

CHAPTER XIII.

109—Mention the substance of the several steps in scholastic disputation given on this page? Of what should the first part of the writer's discourse consist? What should be given in the second part?
110—Why should not respondents indulge in reproaches, &c.? How are scholastic disputations conducted?
111—What is the most useful and best sort of disputation?
113—What advantages are here mentioned as arising from academical disputations? What inconveniences may overbalance these advantages?
114—What inconveniences are here mentioned as being liable to arise from scholastic disputations?
115—Is it advisable to dispute about mere trifles? Why should we not dispute about infinite and unsearchable things? Why should we not dispute about obvious and known truths? What would be the consequence, if every dispute could be made the means of searching out truth? What should be the aim and design of every disputant?
116—Of what should every opponent be solicitous? How should all disputants clothe their thoughts? What is here said of indulging in ridicule, jest, and merriment? What

Page.

of sarcasm, insolent language, personal scandal, &c.?

117—What is here recommended to both vanquished and victorious disputants?

118—Why does it seem necessary that these methods of disputation should be learned in schools?

CHAPTER XIV.

118—What has been established in some of the foregoing chapters?

119—What will do much of themselves toward the cultivation of the mind? Who has all human aids concurring to raise him to a superior degree of wisdom and knowledge? What direction is here given to the young? With what would scholastic divinity furnish us?

120—Mention the substance of the third rule? What effect is liable to be produced on the mind, by its attempting to search out and comprehend matters far above its power? What is the substance of the fourth rule? What should be observed in learning any thing new?

121—How may the mind cope with great difficulties? What is said of Mathon? What of engaging the mind in too many things at once? What of a variety of studies? Mention some studies which are esteemed entertaining?

122—In the pursuit of knowledge what should we always keep in view? In what manner should we exert our skill and diligence? Why are the fundamental truths of philosophy and religion of the

Page.

highest importance? Mention some of these principles?

123—Why should we be very careful in examining all propositions which claim to be general principles? Which are most important in the pursuit of knowledge, practical points, or mere speculations? Of what should we be most careful in matters of practice? What will advance us apace toward real misery?

124—In what comparison are the interests of this world of small importance? Mention what is here stated relative to our religious inquiries? What is the substance of the eighth rule? Of the ninth rule?

125—How must things be considered? To what must we bring our understanding? What is here said of becoming strongly prejudiced in favor of one study, and despising others?

126—What science should always be regarded as of first importance? What will be secured by order and method? Mention the substance of the twelfth rule. Of the thirteenth.

127—Should we expect to arrive at certainty in every subject we pursue? How should we balance our arguments? What would prevent our ever forming a wise resolution? To what are we bound to assent and act? How should we apply every study, however speculative?

128—To what should researches in Natural Philosophy lead us? What advantage may be secured by pursuing mathematical speculations? What should guard us against re-

Page.

jecting any revealed doctrine, though we cannot fully understand it? When should we change our sentiments? Is there equal necessity of our changing methods of study and practice? How is this illustrated?

CHAPTER XV.

129—What is highly necessary in order to the improvement of the mind?

130—Why do we judge falsely of many things? For what should we obtain a liking? What is said of the study of mathematics? Of history?

131—Mention the substance of the second rule. What is the objection to representing moral subjects by pictures? What authors should we read? What is the substance of the fourth rule?

132—What counsel is given in the fifth rule? In the sixth? What considerations should serve to engage and fix the mind in the pursuit of knowledge?

CHAPTER XVI.

133—Of What does this chapter treat? Mention the three things which go to make up that amplitude of mind which constitutes the noblest character of the understanding? What is said of the mind which can readily take in vast and sublime ideas? What is said of those whose minds have been confined to the common affairs of life?

134—How do persons who have acquired such contracted habits of thought regard the most glorious and sublime truths?

Page.

What is the first step recommended to be taken for the relief of such minds?

135—What might lead them to believe there are bodies amazingly great or small? How may such minds be taught to take in some of the vast dimensions, spaces, and motions of the heavenly bodies?

136—What writings are mentioned as having a natural tendency to enlarge the capacity of the mind, and familiarize it with sublime ideas?

137—Where may some of the most exalted ideas, elevated language, and glorious descriptions be found? Of whom does this enlargement of mind lead us to form exalted conceptions? When will it entertain our thoughts with holy wonder and amazement? Of whom beside God does this enlargement of mind enable us to form more just conceptions?

138—What ideas are here advanced of the various ranks of beings? Of whom shall we thus obtain more just ideas? What is a second evidence of the amplitude of the mind?

139—Who are justly charged with a narrowness of soul? What is here said of those who have never travelled? How may this narrowness of mind be cured? What causes the religious prejudices of many people?

140—Who think it just to censure all those severely whose religious opinions are different from their own? How is this defect to be relieved? To what test should we bring all doctrines? What will enlarge our charity toward others?

Page.

142—Mention a third qualification of the amplitude of mind? How does the ample mind survey subjects? What is a great impediment to wisdom and happiness? What is a sign of a large and capacious mind?

143—When are we in danger of passing a false judgment? What things must necessarily be taken in view in order to determine whether an action is wise or foolish, good or evil?

144—Do incompetent persons frequently pass judgments upon private and public affairs?

145—Why is it needful to possess a capacious mind? What is here said of the natural capacity of mind? Who should apply themselves to arts and professions which are easily learned? What of those whose minds are a little more capacious?

146—What makes a great man? What should we labor to gain? To what should we accustom ourselves? Mention what is said of one obscure idea? What should we further consider?

147—For what should we use all diligence? How may we furnish ourselves with useful truths, axioms, and observations to assist and direct our judgment? To what should we continually inure our minds?

148—What is here said of the science of ontology? How should we commence, and in what manner should we advance in the acquisition of knowledge?

149—By what process does the geometrician obtain that knowledge and skill which enables him to judge at one glance of the most complicated diagram? Is the advantage of this progressive method confined to mathematical learning? What is here said of Plato, Locke, and others? Mention another means of acquiring amplitude of mind. Where may such difficult questions be found?

CHAPTER XVII.

150—When are we said to remember a thing? Can we remember that of which we never had any knowledge? What must be done in order to make our learning really useful? What is here said of the excellency of the memory?

151—How does the memory enrich the mind? What would the soul of man be without memory? What is here said of the memory of hearers? Of speakers? What is said to give life and spirit to everything spoken?

152—Is a good memory always united with a good judgment? Upon what does a good judgment in some measure depend? How do we learn to judge of the future?

153—What is said of Penseroso? What advice relative to hasty judgment is here given to all? How are some persons of moderate abilities enabled to excel those of the brightest genius? Why is it that persons of a bright genius are often found to have but a feeble memory?

154—What is here said of crowding the memory and thus abusing other faculties of the mind? When may the mind be said to have large possessions but no true riches? Mention Milton's simile of the

Page.

books of the Fathers. What are said to compose the intellectual possessions of the greatest part of mankind?

155—What constitute a wealthy and happy mind? What joys are mentioned as not belonging to mortality?

156—What does the mind employ in all its operations? How does it obtain a knowledge of external objects? What is here said of the memory? Of the brain in early life? What does the improvement of the memory require? What is said of impressions made upon the mind? What of persons of advanced age? How is the memory affected?

157—What three cases are here mentioned of the influence of disease upon the mind? What of impressions which are deeply engraven on the mind? What prevents lasting impressions from being made on the minds of aged persons? What may help to preserve the memory? What excesses may impair it? Mention the four qualifications of a good memory?

158—What general direction is here given for the improvement of the mental faculties? How will the memory be improved or injured? Why should words be remembered as well as things? What caution is here given?

159—Should the memory be crowded with many ideas at one time? Why do those things which are read or heard make but a slight impression upon many minds? Will sloth and indolence bless the mind with intellectual riches? Why does Vario treasure up but little knowledge?

Page.

160—Why is it necessary to have distinct ideas of things? How should everything we learn be conveyed to the understanding? Why do many forget what has been taught them?

161—What is essential in teaching the principles of religion to children? What is the happiest way to furnish the mind with a variety of knowledge?

162—Does the mutual dependence of things aid the memory? Why are some writings more easily learned than others? What is said to be a fault in some preachers? What is here said of reviews and abridgments?

163—Mention the practice of Mnemon. In what particular is the art of short-hand useful?

164—What are we here counselled to avoid? What is a most useful manner of review? Mention the practice of Hermetas. What is said greatly to assist the memory? What of the natural inclination of the learner?

165–How was Spectorius taught? What is said of teaching children in rhyme and in way of play?

166—Why have moral rules and precepts been written in rhyme?

167—What is of great importance in aiding the memory? Mention the practice of Maronides. Of Animato. What is said of associating a new idea with time and place?

168—What is said of associating kindred or similar ideas? What of contraries? Wha of local memory? What meant by local memory?

169—What sense conveys the most perfect ideas to the mind?

Page.
Mention what Horace affirms of the sight. What is here said of the use of tables, diagrams, maps, charts, &c.?
170—What is here said of writing, map drawing, &c.?

CHAPTER XVIII.

171—Of what does this chapter treat? What should we consider when a question is proposed?
172—What should constitute a second subject to be considered? A third? A fourth?
173—A fifth? How may some questions be rendered less obscure? What caution is given relative to new statements? What frequently goes a great way toward answering a question? In what does the greatest part of true knowledge lie? What often shows the mind where the truth lies?
174—What caution is here given relative to questions which relate to axioms, or first principles? What is insufficient to determine the truth of a proposition? When may a proposition be considered an axiom? What should we observe in searching after truth in questions of a doubtful nature? What is here said of inheriting opinions?
175—What is the effect of inheriting local truths, and becoming positive on propositions whose evidence we have never examined? What is said of determining questions of difficulty and importance? In examining objects of sense, when is the examination partial? When, in the examination of those which are to be determined by reason?
176—When are examinations partial in questions depending

Page.
on human testimony? What is said of determining questions by natural reason, where we might be assisted by revelation? What of determining questions by doubtful revelations? What is the substance of the thirteenth rule? Of the fourteenth?
177—Of what should we take heed, and be watchful? What is here related of the ancient Romans? What is said of the belief in good and evil omens, unlucky days, &c.? What will tend to establish our minds in doubtful doctrines, and close the avenues of future light?
178—Of what should we be zealous? To what should our zeal be subject? What is here said of jest and ridicule? What of raillery and wit? What of a silly practice?
179—How may the strongest reasoning, the best sense, and the most obvious axioms be made to appear foolish and absurd? Does this deprive them of their real character? What is said of Euclid? Of the moral and religious duties?
180—To what is banter and ridicule here compared? What is here said to be a piece of contempt and profane insolence?
181—What should alone influence our opinions in controversies? What is oftentimes found to be true? Who are usually most positive? What has sometimes tempted men of learning to adopt these practices of the haughty and ignorant? When may writers of good sense be allowed to use a degree of assurance and confidence?
182—Should we decide all questions with one answer? What

Page.

is here said of Cicero? What is the substance of the twenty-first rule?

183—Substance of the twenty-second rule? What general rule should be observed?

184—What direction cannot be too often repeated? Should we be required to give our assent where we have not sufficient evidence?

186—What duties should exert most influence over our minds? What is here said of prayer and other Christian duties?

187—What is the substance of the first rule for judging of probabilities? Of the second? Of the third?

188—What is here said of standing firm in well established principles? Should we determine, positively, things wherein we may possibly mistake? Why are we liable to err in our interpretations of passages of scripture?

CHAPTER XIX.

189—Of what does this chapter treat? What should first be considered in tracing effects to their causes? What should be the second point of inquiry?

190—The third? The fourth? What should be the first point of inquiry in tracing causes to their effects?

191—The second? The third? The fourth? The fifth? The sixth? What is here said of the practice of physicians?

192—What is said of causes and effects which are necessarily connected?

CHAPTER XX.

192—What is the best way to learn any science?

Page.

193—To what should students apply themselves? Are we capable of judging correctly of a science until we have taken a survey of the whole? Mention the illustration?

194—Why do some persons cast contempt on systematic learning? What should be done after learning a short compendium of a science? When should we take a judicious review of the whole? Why do some persons waste their time in reading scientific treatises which are of little value?

195—When are languages most easily learned? What is here said of abstract sciences? Mention some of the sciences which are considered suitable for young children? Mention the first reason for considering that these sciences may be pursued by those of tender age with ease and advantage. What is the second reason? The third? How is it best to train up children? What is here said of the use of diagrams, &c.?

196—How may knowledge thus obtained be retained in the memory?

198—Who should gain some idea of most of the sciences? What parts of science should be chiefly studied at first? Of whom should the young ask advice? Name the three learned professions. Who should have some knowledge of each of these?

199—What is said to be an angelic pleasure? Mention some of the advantages of mathematical studies. What are often made of admirable service in human life?

200—What are the remarks of

Page.

Dr. Cheyne in relation to the abstruse depths and difficulties of mathematics? What may be made agreeable amusements to all young persons?

201—How have many young persons secured their time from running to waste, prevented foolish scenes and actions, and laid a foundation for the esteem and love of mankind? What is said of "the study of history? What are called the eyes of history? What is said of biography? Mention some of the benefits to be derived from reading biography.

202—What is here said of christian biographies? Of what sciences should all persons have some knowledge?

203—What does true logic teach us? Metaphysics? What is here said of the benefits to be derived from the study of natural philosophy, and natural history?

204—From what may much pleasure and profit be derived? What science eminently belongs to physicians? What is here said of lawyers? Of divines?

205—What science is here represented as worthy the study of a divine? Of what may we be informed by this science?

206—What is the first part of natural religion? Second part? What is contained and necessarily implied in all revealed religions? Whom should we know, and what are we bound to practice under whatever dispensation we live?

207—What is said to be needful to prove the truth of divine revelation most effectually? What science is of most importance?

208—Strictly speaking, what does the civil law signify? Whence did the Romans obtain their laws? What was called the body of the civil law? With what law is it most important we should be acquainted? Who defined the law of nature to be "the knowledge of right and wrong among men"?

210—Who is said to be the great master of physicians? With what book should theologians be most conversant?

213—How are all mankind taught to speak their common tongue? What is grammar? Rhetoric? Mention the first part of rhetoric. The second. The third.

214—What rules may be perused and learned with great advantage? What will do more to make an orator than all the rules of art?

215—What is the business of divines? How should the understanding be convinced? When that is done what motives should be used? How may the world be restored to virtue and happiness?

216—Mention the first reason for reading poetry. The second. What is said of the lyric ode?

217—Mention a third reason for reading poetry?

218—What is here said of Pope? Mention a fourth reason for reading poetry.

219—What is here said of writing poetry? What is the meaning of *muse*? What is necessary to enable us to read history to advantage?

220—What is criticism? What should all critics remember?

PART II

INTRODUCTION.

Page.

221—What has been the chief design of the first part of this book? What is to be considered in the second part? Do those who hoard up their intellectual treasures enjoy the greatest advantage their possession is capable of yielding? How may intellectual treasures be made to glitter? Mention the two chief ways of conveying knowledge to others.

CHAPTER I.

223—Who is generally best prepared to teach? Are all good scholars successful instructors? Why must a competent teacher have a good command of language? What is said of the disposition of the teacher?

225—What is here said of historical remarks, and of joining profit and pleasure?

226—What should be the style of instructors? What is here said of questioning learners?

227—To what should teachers accommodate themselves? What is here said of curiosity? Of commendatory words?

Page.

228—What course should be pursued with positive and presuming pupils? What should the teacher watch? How should he strive to instil knowledge into the minds of his pupils? What faculties of the mind should the teacher endeavor to call into exercise? What of uncommon occurrences?

229—How may the affections and attention of pupils be secured?

CHAPTER II.

229—Of what does this chapter treat? What style is most fit and useful for instruction?

230—What is the first error of style to be avoided? The second? What is said of learned terms? What of the lovers of geometry and astronomy?

231—Mention a third error to be avoided. A fourth. Fifth.

232—A sixth. What is the first method mentioned for acquiring a perspicuity of style suitable for instruction? The second?

CHAPTER III.

Page.

233—The third?

234—The fourth? Fifth? Sixth?

235—Of what should we divest ourselves in order to promote truth? What should we seek to acquire? What is the first thing to be observed?

236—The second? The third? What must be flattered? Why?

237—What should we always remember? Why should we set a constant watch over ourselves? To what is human nature likened? What does a wrathful spirit beget in others? How should we treat opponents? Why is there so little success in convincing disputants?

238—May we reasonably hope to convince others of their mistakes or errors by persecution or severe usage? Can men believe what they will? Mention the sixth direction to be observed in convincing others of any truth. The seventh. The eighth.

239—The ninth.

240—The tenth. What is the substance of the first concluding remark?

241—Of the second?

CHAPTER IV.

242—Of what does this chapter treat? From what sources do we derive our sentiments and belief? To what head may these influences be reduced?

243—What is frequently a hindrance to learners? Why? Has human authority any certain and undoubted claim to truth? What ancient and long established doctrine was refuted by Sir Isaac Newton?

Page.

What is here said of the poems of Homer and Virgil?

244—What would furnish a poem of just and glorious scenes? What must we do in many cases in order to find out the truth? What is here said of three eminent cases of authority? What is the case first mentioned?

245 Are children bound to adopt all the opinions of their parents?

246—Is any individual or society commissioned with authority to dictate opinions to others of mature years? In what cases may we be justly charged with criminal sloth? Mention a second case of authority which must govern our assent?

247—What is this usually called? When should testimony operate most forcibly on our minds? Should we readily yield our assent to the most forcible testimony without fairly examining its claims to credibility?

248—Mention a third case wherein authority must govern us. Of whom is this properly the authority? When are all mankind bound to receive the doctrines of divine revelation? Has God ever given any revelations which are contrary to the dictates of reason?

249—Mention, again, the three cases wherein authority must determine our sentiments.

250—What is the first case in which we should pay great deference to the authority and sentiments of others? The second? Third? Fourth? Fifth?

251—Under what circumstances should we follow probabilities?

CHAPTER V.

Page.

251—Why is it so difficult to convince others of common mistakes, or to persuade them to assent to plain and obvious truths ?

252—What is the first method to be practised in order to convince those whose prejudices are strong ?

253—The second ?

254—What were the principles of the Peripatetics ? What was the belief of the Platonists ? How may these believers in substantial forms and a universal soul, be led to give up their notions ? How may a person be convinced of his error, who is fully persuaded there is nothing but what has length, breadth, and thickness ?

256—Why may we ever dispense with the rule which requires different ideas to be expressed by different words ? What is the third method to be practised ?

CHAPTER VI.

260—Mention the principal ideas advanced in the first section of this chapter.

265—What are the chief ideas advanced in the second section ?

267—What ideas are advanced in section third ?

CHAPTER VII.

272—Of what should every writer observe a just medium ?

Page.

What will teach us when to explain, define, &c. ?

273—What rule of Horace is here given ?

274—On what should the study, time, and labor of every writer be chiefly employed ? What is here said of consulting the opinions of others, and reviewing our own productions ?

276—How may we obtain hints for improving our own writings ?

CHAPTER VIII.

276—What should be the first thing done by a good writer on any controverted subject ? The second ? The third ? What will be the course of an able opponent ?

277—If the first writer answers his opponent in an able manner, what may the reader generally presume ? What is usually the effect of greatly prolonged controversies ?

278—What exception is here given ? Substance of note ?

279—How should the sincere searcher for truth survey every argument ? What is the best way to try the force of arguments which are brought against our opinions ? What if we find arguments which we are not able to answer ?

280—What is here said of Volatilis ?

It affords [illegible] for explana-
-tion for professing objections -
for selecting a subject [illegible]
-ly eliminates the faculties allows
[illegible] without publick exposure
[illegible] human nature
exercises the mind improves
[illegible] improves manners
rendered more intelligible
and much more interesting
when we desire [illegible]
[illegible]

[illegible] and
Communicating [illegible]
when we desire [illegible]
[illegible]
[illegible]

"Universal ignorance or
all Temporal spiritual and eternal
Reformation from popery in 157_

It warps the mind aside strangely
from that steadiness honesty and
integrity that necessarily belong
to the pursuit of truth —

by observation we learn it
from ourselves and only what comes
within our own cognizance :

Locke 1674 religion
meditation of a day
is worth

better times than ever
lived

in the study of _ _____
from _____ by our
_ _ fections
in true _____

conversation

an assertion in which one thing is
declared respecting another

observation

very feeble

study without prayer is

[illegible]

(good reasoning)

a composition of [illegible] words

[illegible]

each of these five [illegible]

It forms our judgment [illegible]

makes the [illegible]

[illegible]

[illegible]

[illegible]

[illegible]

[illegible]

[illegible]

[illegible]

[illegible]

[illegible]

[illegible]

[illegible]

[illegible]

[illegible]

[illegible]

[illegible]

[illegible] according to [illegible]

[illegible]

[illegible]

[illegible]

[illegible]

[illegible]

[illegible]

[illegible]

[illegible] ignorance [illegible]

[illegible]

[illegible]

[illegible]

[illegible]

[illegible]

We shall be in danger of perverting
even or diminishing a love for truth
Too also any of disfeeling
Most important truths have been maintaind
and spread far and wide Tyrannies
Tel they understood the terms better
[illegible]

Lightning Source UK Ltd.
Milton Keynes UK
UKHW03f2206300518
323483UK00003B/152/P

9 781146 781572